TOPICS ON CREATING INNOVATIONS FOR GRADUATE STUDENTS

Edited by Eunyoung Kim

Written by
Thao Thanh Luong, Qianang Sun,
Nilima Haque Ruma, and Eunyoung Kim

博英社

Preface

Eunyoung Kim

As many educators in higher education are facing several challenges due to diverse changes in the social systems that support the institutions, when I first became a faculty member I was also not very clear on what and how to teach graduate students.

4 years have passed since I took over the half of the course entitled "Theories in Knowledge Management" without any guidance or teaching materials from the previous professor, who retired immediately before my appointment at the School of Knowledge Science, Japan Advanced Institute of Science and Technology. Since the establishment of the School of Knowledge Science by the world-famous guru of knowledge management, Prof. Dr. Nonaka in 1996, it has provided courses related to knowledge management, and continues to do so. Indeed, there was no textbook for the course, and even if there had been a textbook from the preceding lecturer, it would have been useless for teaching the students who will lead the upcoming society as knowledge professionals. Indeed, this is due to the fact that our circumstances have been changed dramatically by the rapid socio-technological evolution since the information revolution in early 2000.

Moreover, knowledge management itself was not my professional research area, and our institute changed the department system from a parochial, independent discipline, to an integrated, interdisciplinary convergence system. In line with such a change, there was no reason to continue teaching the traditional theories of knowledge management. This can be applied to any of us, regardless of which specific area we major in. Of course, I do not mean to belittle the importance of domain-specific knowledge. However, after graduating from university or graduate school with a certain degree, almost all of us cannot but encounter the moment that we should learn a whole new area, regardless of how much expertise we have in a specific field. Personally, I am somewhat of an expert in changing my area of specialisation, having changed major three times, from political science to international business, information study, and engineering education. In the meantime, I studied at five leading higher education institutes (HEIs) in four different countries, namely Korea, the USA, Germany, and Japan, as well as participating in various research projects in diverse fields.

In this regard, I set the course content based on the topics, so that it can be changed easily based on the rapid changes of our socio-technical environments. My main concern was how we can develop fundamental understanding of learning, creativity, and innovation to motivate students to learn and initiate or facilitate innovative idea generation, so that the students can utilise those process or methods they learn through this course in their future career. This course accounts for two credits and is divided into two parts, with my teaching part constituting half of it, specifically 100 minutes across seven classes.

In addition, learning styles have changed drastically from generation to generation, and there is thus the need to innovate pedagogical approaches. I tried various teaching tools for student-led learning, such as discussion, demonstration, case reading, and presentation, in addition to theory-based learning such as fundamental theory teaching, conducting various types of quizzes, and research paper reviews. In the first year of teaching, I tried to rely on student-centred learning. I adopted the case-based learning method which is widely used at many of the MBA (Master of Business Administration) schools. I introduced a number of cases of innovations and creative projects in business, regional communities, technology, and academia, then let the students find out how (in which process and circumstances) those innovations could be generated, be implemented, and lead to success, as well as how we can create new innovative ideas and implement them in the fields we study, or the communities in which we live. Unfortunately, I had to conclude that this trial teaching was not successful. Even though I explained the theoretical background of innovation and creativity study during the course, when it came to the final presentation, which constituted the final exam of the course, the students were easily repeating shallow knowledge based on their frequently-used web resources or personal experiences, without contemplation or fundamental understanding of the theories.

Following a trial and error process over the first two years of teaching, and given that our institute is a research-centred graduate school, I set up the outline of the course content based on six topics – learning, flow, creativity, innovation, disruptive innovation, thinking – and used the pedagogical approach, which includes peer discussion, classroom tasks, review of academic research, providing reading materials, and assignment. Surprisingly, with this teaching approach, students could recall their own experiences of individual flow and have aspiration for social flow (see Chap.3); they were also motivated to apply the acquired fundamental knowledge of creativity and innovation to their research area. Moreover, after setting up the new teaching content and tools, students who had already taken this course before attended again to learn from my new style of teaching, even on the severely cold winter mornings.

Of note here is a recently-introduced policy which states that university faculty members are evaluated, in terms of their performances, based on a quantitative index, such as how much in funding or grants they have attracted from outside campus, and how many indexed scientific journal papers they have published. In light of this, many of the professors are not able to spend enough time refining or re-organising their teaching content or teaching methods. However, regardless of personal performances for a teacher's tenure or annual incentive, it is still valuable to publish a textbook to share my ideas as an educator for students as well as lecturers and researchers. I would be extremely happy if any of the readers were influenced by this book, and I welcome them to create or add their own ideas for enhancing their learning experiences. In addition, I hope this book will give us an opportunity to start an open discussion on the educators or future educators community, so that we can share our constructive feedback on learning at HEIs, which will in turn hopefully foster the innovation leaders.

Last, but not least, I would like to thank my brilliant doctoral students, Ms. Thanh-Thao Luong, Ms. Qianang Sun, and Ms. Nilima Haque Ruma, who exhibited excellent performances throughout this course, contributed to the redesign of the course content, and readily decided to become the co-authors of chapters and sub-chapters of this book. Without their support, it would not be possible to publish this book. In addition, I would like to thank all the students who enrolled on this course; I took considerable inspiration from them which allowed me to grow both as an instructor and as a learner. I cannot forget to thank the publisher, PYbooks Japan, for offering me an opportunity to publish a book. Indeed, as a somewhat minor faculty member from Korea who works in Japan and teaches a course in English to non-native speakers from foreign countries, finding a publisher for my book has not been easy.

July, 15, 2021
Eunyoung Kim

Preface

Thao Thanh LUONG

For many adult learners who have spent a long time working in various business industries, returning to the academic path is undoubtedly exciting, yet it is not an easy task. One of the unique challenges that adult learners face is that their personal mindsets are somehow fixed in the context of their working experience, regardless of how senior their professional positions have been. In my own case, although I had not held a top corporate position, more than 10 years of working in business industries had lured me into a belief that wisdom would come with job experience, and that theories were less important than practice – that is, until I was lucky enough to realize the limitations of workplace learning in the context of today's knowledge society. At the same time, I also recognized that I had developed an obsession for seeking the true definition of knowledge and wisdom.

Although I had obtained a master's degree in Human Resources Management in Australia years ago, I now sought to pursue my doctoral study at an HE where I could change my perceptions regarding the significance of theories, and where an interdisciplinary approach to knowledge is adopted, rather than institutions that offer separate professional domains of knowledge, such as business management, education, or natural sciences. Therefore, in 2019, I quit my flourishing job in the hospitality and tourism industry, and decided to return to academic life by pursuing a Ph.D. degree in the School of Knowledge Science at the Japan Advanced Institute of Science and Technology (JAIST). I recognize that despite being frightened of the decision to change my long-established career path, I was driven by the desire to leave my comfort zone and reinvigorate my complacent mindset by seeking more knowledge in other disciplines.

What excited me about becoming a member of the KIM lab at JAIST, and being able to work under Professor Kim Eunyoung's guidance, was the fact that in my view, my supervisor has gained her academic and professional knowledge across many different fields. Her ongoing efforts and perpetual courage to cross disciplinary borders have genuinely inspired me in my search for the true meaning of knowledge and life. With my newly inspired passion, when I entered JAIST as a first-year doctoral student, I attended an intriguing course entitled "Theories of Knowledge Management" by Professor Kim in 2019. This course has changed me in various ways, including my approaches to the current societal development, and the paths for seeking happiness and positive psychology in lifelong learning. Above all, the course informed me that I had made the right decision in going back to school. I felt less anxious and more confident in the new road I had chosen. Perhaps pursuing a doctorate was not an exhausting journey, full of anxiety and loss of the student–life balance, as someone had told me before. It could be adventurous and challenging, yet worth the effort, because of the psychological rewards that it offers along the way.

What is offered in the course "Theories of Knowledge Management" by Professor Kim is a set of unique approaches to one's learning and developmental processes. It is not merely a comprehensive, systematic and up-to-date literature review on knowledge management theories, but also a dedicated educator's instructions on how to strive and thrive in the knowledge era, where the power of theories in guiding individual and societal advancement has become more vital than ever. Professor Kim's instructions in this course do not follow any particular textbook in this discipline. Instead, she uses different academic and practical sources to fulfil her aim of helping students identify the right ways to gain and manage knowledge. In fact, the whole course is very different from a traditional class where students have to read textbooks, listen to lectures, and complete their writing assignments. Here, we are required to make our best efforts to activate our prior knowledge and experience, in order to obtain new knowledge or perspectives accordingly.

Numerous discussions with thought-provoking questions during the course help us to continually reflect on ourselves and learn from the latest theories and frameworks. As I learn more about the importance and methods of innovations in today's life from this course, I realize that this course itself is an innovation, in both curricular and pedagogical terms. As a student, I authentically enjoy learning about the strategic views regarding our current society, introduced by this course. As an adult learner searching for the truth about knowledge and wisdom, I am fascinated by the fresh and advanced approaches to the role of higher education and lifelong learning discussed across all the lectures. As a KIM lab member, I truly wish to share what I have learned during this course with other researchers and graduate students, hoping that faithful joy in the pursuit of the academic path will be attained, just as I have found it for myself.

Therefore, when asked to become a co-author of the textbook for this particular course, I was overjoyed. Although I have always enjoyed thinking and writing, I am aware that writing a textbook for the first time is challenging. However, I am thrilled by the opportunity to offer my contribution to making the course even more successful, in terms of improving students' strategies and motivations towards lifelong learning. Perhaps someone with a less favourable view of academic education, or practitioners with a biased opinion of the importance of theories (as I had previously been), may be encouraged to change their perceptions when participating in the course or reading this book. For anyone who has realized their desire to step out of their comfort zone and seek new approaches to learning and developing, I hope that the course and its textbook will greatly benefit them, just as the course has benefited me in many ways.

As a final point, I am sincerely grateful to Professor Kim Eunyoung for letting me be the co-author of this book from a reputable publisher, PYbooks Japan. It is a privilege to be her student and co-worker simultaneously in this meaningful project. Without her trust, I would not have gained this precious opportunity to find confidence and joy in writing these book chapters, where I can share what I have learned, and my reflections on such unique knowledge. I also wish to thank my family members, who always have faith in every piece of work that I do, and my lab mates, who have never hesitated to share with me their know-how in various fields. Thanks to these great people, I always feel positive and energetic about pursuing my journey of seeking knowledge, wisdom and happiness in life.

July, 15, 2021
Thao Thanh LUONG

Preface

Nilima Haque Ruma

It is a great opportunity to be a part of this book writing project. I would like to thank my mentor, Professor Eunyoung Kim, who moulds all of her ideas and insights into this book. It is designed and presented from the reader's perspective, so that everyone can access the content easily. By taking the course, I have been able to flourish my core understanding of the concepts of learning, creativity and innovation. Consequently, this learning has motivated me to generate innovative ideas, not only in my research, but also in daily life. The way the instructor designed the course content was hugely helpful for finding the flow in individual life and reaching the highest level of happiness. For example, I love to do gardening and cooking. However, until I took this course, I was not very aware of how those activities can help to maintain the individual flow of life. In this regard, I would like to mention that the content of this book is not just something to read, memorize, give a presentation on, or study for exams, but lifelong learning that helps us to shape our lives positively and find happiness in every stage of life.

I especially appreciate the offer to be a co-author, and am sincerely grateful to Professor Eunyoung Kim for trusting me to choose to write any chapter I was interested in. I chose the topic named "Types of Innovation" because "innovation" is one of the key concepts of my major research. We are all innovators, in the sense that all of us deliberately innovate in our daily life and the way we do things. I became familiar with "innovation" during my undergraduate study, while taking several courses in social sciences. Many emergent theories on social and cultural change were born at the end of the 19th century. During that period, the term "innovation" was studied in terms of changes in cultural traits, whereas "invention" referred to novelties, inspirations, and works of genius in agriculture, trade, technology, social and political institutions. Hence, my perception of innovation had developed as "changes in social and cultural traits", through the lens of the social sciences.

After my graduating in Sociology, I worked for one year in a non-governmental organization (NGO) on a project named "Let Her Decide and Participate" (LHDP). As a project manager, I was responsible for facilitating the "Women's Empowerment and Leadership Programme". Throughout the project, I had to participate several times in training that focused on creativity and innovative thinking, to design the assigned project. This managerial position led me to design the leadership training module, tools to facilitate the group discussion, and to implement programme objectives for empowering marginalized women in the western part of Bangladesh. However, I did not have an in-depth understanding of the concept of innovation and its application until I entered the School of Knowledge Science at the Japan Advanced Institute of Science and Technology (JAIST). During my master's course at JAIST, I gathered profound knowledge about innovation through coursework and practical projects. Several courses, like "Innovation Theory and Methodology for Social Competencies", "Introduction to Knowledge Science", "Theories of Knowledge Management" and "Innovation Design" shaped my fundamental knowledge of the concepts of innovation and knowledge management in a wider aspect. The most essential part of these courses was to conduct innovation projects that were based on contemporary social and environmental problems. JAIST taught students to challenge their complacency by fostering creativity and intellectual toughness. Later in my doctoral studies, I took another advanced course titled "Innovation Theory and Methodology for Total Capability Development", which nurtured my inquisitiveness about innovation management. I also took the course "Theory of Knowledge Management", again under the instructor Professor Eunyoung Kim, with her new teaching style and updated contents. I found that the new version of this course helped me to recognize the flow I was experiencing in my daily life; this made me ambitious to achieve social flow, and I became highly motivated to apply the acquired knowledge on creativity and innovation to my research.

Engagement with "innovative thinking" is not merely crafted by learning; thus, I also worked as a teaching assistant (TA) during the above-mentioned courses. Nowadays, I act as a TA for the second time, for "Theories of Knowledge Management". Half of this course fully concentrates on the contents of innovation learning, and the rest concerns creating and managing the knowledge within organizations. Managing and sharing knowledge within an organization duly links to creative thinking, which propels the firm towards "innovation intent". The more I attend this course, either as a student or a TA, the more I learn from the latest theories and frameworks, and gather new knowledge from the different perspectives of the new students. Apart from the classroom work, I was influenced by several best-selling books: I must particularly mention *The Innovator's Dilemma, The Innovator's Solution, The Innovator's DNA and The Innovative Leader: How to inspire your team and drive creativity*. These texts offered me important insights into the characteristics of disruptive technologies, business models, innovative companies, and disruptive innovators. Moreover, my continuous involvement and deeper fascination with innovation studies motivated me to contribute a chapter to this book.

It was a very tough decision for me to be a co-author of this book, as a full-time doctoral fellow and a full-time mother of a new-born. However, my supervisor's confidence in me, along with my enthusiasm, accelerated my contribution to the knowledge society by providing a chapter of this book. This multidimensional adventure to maintain doctoral study, TA duty, RA duty, writing the chapter of this book, and maintaining a family with a new-born, gave me intense excitement while thinking about my future output. I also found that those novel duties together helped me to manage my time in a very creative and innovative way, and I learned how to utilize every moment of the day purposively. Throughout this journey, I would like to extend my gratitude to my beloved family members, who always encouraged me to be optimistic about reaching my goals. Their unconditional support helped me to stay focused on my work. Also, I am deeply thankful to my lab mates, who shared their knowledge and helped me to think out of the box. Last but not least, I am delighted to see that two of my favourite lab mates and friends are co-authors of this project. When I look at both of them, I feel inspired and motivated. I am lucky to have such friendly colleagues in the lab, as we grow together by sharing and exchanging knowledge and ideas.

July, 15, 2021
Nilima Haque Ruma

Preface

Qianang SUN

Over the past 20 years, Knowledge Management (KM) has become a key discipline (Hislop, 2010) that explains how "knowledge" has been created, developed, retained and applied in the workplace, and how it promotes learning and innovation (Martín-de Castro et al., 2011; Soto-Acosta, Colomo-Palacios & Popa, 2014). Moreover, the interest in KM has persisted (Ragab & Arisha, 2013; Serenko & Bontis, 2013), rather than being merely a fashion in academic research. Generally, the previous studies treat knowledge management as a set of practices related to the use of knowledge, which is a key factor in adding or producing value (Syed, Murray, Hislop & Mouzughi, 2018). Furthermore, the significant changes in the economy and the growing value of organizations have caused this century to be known as "the knowledge economy age" (Cooke & Leydesdorff, 2006). Given such rapid globalization, migration and communication, the knowledge economy is reflected in the dissemination and usage of knowledge, which is thus a source of competitiveness for organizations and countries.

With widespread data-mining technology, knowledge management's epistemology has abstracted the types of knowledge as either explicit or implicit. Alternatively, knowledge can be the quasi-physical and spiritual material of memory, experience and belief, and needs to be formally expressed for public consumption (McInerney & Day, 2007). A large portion of knowledge is implicit or implied, and it should be made explicit by "sharing" information that might improve productivity and retain the useful content.

Therefore, in many knowledge management discourses, the concept of "tacit" knowledge is equivalent to the concept of private or "unconscious" knowledge, while the word "explicit" refers to "sharing" or "expressing" private or unconscious knowledge. This not only means that we need to pay attention to the process of knowledge formation and dissemination; it also implies that the creative practice process and experience retrospection by organizations or individuals should be given sufficient attention, as this will give us a space to talk about interdisciplinary research and cooperation across domains (Robinson, 2009). We focus on the theory of creativity and thinking skills in topic 3 and topic 6; these are less-discussed but unignorable topics in knowledge management.

Generally, studying creativity theories and thinking skills may provide a fast channel for entering a complex area like knowledge management. When we talk about creativity, genius and invention, it usually means excellent performance, even a part of what makes us human. It can be delicate craftwork, a successful makeover, or a witty poem. Moreover, it could also be a great invention in technology, or changes in lifestyle. Our devotion to creating and thinking makes us different from any other creature, and therefore deeply satisfies us. It is necessary to consider where creativity comes from, before investigating its mechanism. However, creativity, such as integrating novel ideas and original practices, is complex and difficult to measure.

In this book, we will start the creativity research by illustrating three waves of approaches. One certainty is that creative practice plays a connective role between individuals and society, and enhances interaction. Therefore, it is natural to study creativity from both individual and societal perspectives. Many professionals have earned great accolades for their creativity, yet are sometimes associated with expertise or reputation. Part of the dilemma is that there are different ways to recognize creative expression, but it is hard to measure it on a common scale. How, then, do professionals in different fields acquire knowledge and develop their creativity? How can we assess creativity, or does creativity equate to intelligence? Accordingly, by defining creativity through various measurements, we illustrate the creative stages. Each of the stages will be discussed by combining remarkable studies in the domain. We then move to a broader view, to address creativity across domains such as culture, science and education. The aim above is to sketch creativity through individual and social approaches, in order to avoid the general perspective and consider creativity in different areas.

Thus, when creativity is examined, this paves the way for the creative process and thinking skills. With the ongoing development of cognitive science, the interest in brain activity continues to surge. Much attention is paid to how people think, and how they make decisions in different conditions. In topic 6, we introduce three thinking skills, namely "design thinking", "analogical thinking" and "reflective thinking". From a macro view, understanding the thinking skills will construct a foundation for further creative thinking, and even practice; it will also provide an opportunity to explore how the thinking skills affect creativity, which is embedded by ideation, incubation to reflection.

Design thinking has developed as a formal discipline with a shorter history than the other modes, especially in psychology. The core of design thinking is to define the problem and seek a good solution. This challenge is growing with industry development and product standardization, which is being further extended to business, the market, and human resources. The primary target to introduce design thinking here is inspired by its increasingly crucial role in several fields; it is even overused as a popular conception. Therefore, we clarify the essence of design thinking as distinct from other cognition styles, in order to rigorously examine where the problem is, and why we need to address it with design thinking or not. We focus on design cognition by presenting some cases to illustrate how professional designers frame their work, in order to learn from them, and even understand what design means. Compared to design thinking, analogical thinking is much more widespread, particularly in the learning process. Analogical thinking has been suggested as a basic mechanism for inspiring creative tasks, in which people transfer information from well-known, existing categories, and utilize it in constructing new ideas. This book will teach the basic components of analogical thinking through analogical reasoning, and how to generate new ideas. As the final part of the topic, reflective thinking has been less discussed, even though it is a higher-level cognitive ability. We can learn through experience as we practise and bring consciousness to our current state of thinking and feeling. Thus, thoughtfully focusing our attention enhances our ability to break out of our habitual thought patterns. In other words, it is an active search, with thoughtful consideration within the scope of the subject, and an attitude of logical inquiry. The different dimensions of reflection will be shown in this chapter, combined with a problem solution. It should be noted that each thinking skill introduced here is not independently inset in the creative process; they are normally interactive and have been flexibly applied when required.

Based on the starting point of this book, by introducing "Theories of Creativity" and "Thinking Skills", we attempt to provide a comprehensive landscape of these topics by illustrating the research progress, approaches in evolution, and applications to synthesize knowledge, to contribute to a better society. Simultaneously, we should realize that knowledge management does not mean that mixed perspectives and skills from various disciplines could generate new knowledge or enhance innovation capability. We're still not free to analyse and evaluate knowledge. Artificial intelligence may provide richer data sets in the near future, but we should ask why we need it, and how do we use it to build a deep connection with each other? Even with today's advanced technology, cognition, thinking and creation are still a mysterious area and cannot directly be observed. If knowledge is a relatively rational and reliable explanation, then we are always on the way. Therefore, in this textbook, the goal is never limited to expanding the field content; it aims provide multiple lenses for researchers, practitioners and students to achieve effective reference, in order to more systematically progress in integrating knowledge from different fields, and to apply it to construct new experiences. Similarly, knowledge management does not mean organizing existing resources, but integrating useful considerations in order to upgrade resources.

July, 15, 2021

Qianang SUN

Table of contents

List of figures

List of tables

CHAPTER

01

Introduction

Introduction

Eunyoung Kim

Although many of the higher education institutes (HEIs) face difficulties in recruiting students due to low birth rate and over-supply, within global society there are continually-increasing needs for higher education (Roser & Ortiz-Ospina, 2018). As we move into a super-smart society caused by "the fourth industrial revolution" (Schwab, 2016), tech-driven changes are influencing our socio-economical system extensively and it is more important than ever to create novel ideas, knowledge, and innovations. In this regard, almost all of the HEIs have built a consensus on reforming their curriculum to cope with future challenges (Johnson et al., 2016).

A number of educators have established educational programmes at HEIs proposing the value of creativity and innovation by adopting various instructional methods that used to be found only rarely in conventional academia. Those programmes provide a specified curriculum focusing on social entrepreneurship (e.g. Kaospilot in Denmark; Singularity University in the USA; Knowmads in the Netherlands), the multidisciplinary approach (e.g. STEAM education in CERN, Switzerland, D.school in HPI, Germany and the USA) and so on (see Table 1-1). As we can see from the trends in newly-established educational programmes, educators have been paying increasing attention to fostering leaders who can generate creative ideas and initiate innovative projects which harness the technology that can contribute to creating social value.

TABLE 1-1 Examples of innovative educational programmes

HEIs	Country	Type	Programme content
Singularity University	USA	Non-degree	Global Solution Program, Exponential Regional Partnership, Global Impact Competition, Innovation Hub.
Kaospilot	Denmark, Switzerland	Degree & Non-degree	Creative Business Design, Creative Leadership Design, Creative Project Design, and Creative Process Design. 10-week Global Solution Program partnership with Singularity University.
Olin College	USA	Degree & Non-degree	Hands-on engineering and design project-based teaching. I2E2 (Initiative for Innovation in Engineering Education) for global educators.
42(school)	France, USA, Armenia	Non-degree	Peer-to-peer pedagogy and project-based learning for software development through the realisation of an arcade game, artificial intelligence or a computer virus.
HumTec, RWTH Aachen University	Germany	Degree	Center for Human-Technology, promoting interdisciplinary research projects: Living Lab Incubator, Ethics & Responsibility in energy use, language behaviours in context, etc.
D.school	EU, USA	Non-degree	Established by Hasso Plattner Institute. And partnership with world-class universities such as Stanford university and global companies based on design thinking.
CDIO Initiative	USA, EU, etc.	Degree	Conceived by MIT in collaboration with KTH, Sweden and other engineering universities; it is an educational framework that stresses engineering fundamentals set in the context of conceiving, designing, implementing and operating through active learning and problem-based learning.

The main target readers for this book and the course are graduate students, educators and researchers at HEIs. As such, we need to raise a fundamental question on why we learn and how and what to teach. In line with this, we must understand the skillsets that have to be achieved at HEIs as we reform curricula and practices. To conduct a systemic literature review, all related academic papers were searched for in the Web of Science Core Collection database, with the keywords "higher education" and "skills" and "learning" used to scan the topic of the research; the criteria specified that the papers had to have been published during the period spanning 2010-2020, in the category of education. As a result of the search, 4,135 papers were found, and 1,000 papers were selected for analysis based on the relevance of the topic (see Figure 1-1). To conduct a qualitative analysis and thus extract the key conceptual words for the skills from the existing research, all of the selected references were imported into a qualitative analysis software tool to explore the key concept and ascertain the highlighted skillset from the recent studies (see Figure 1-2).

FIGURE 1-1

Search results of HEI, Skill, and Learning in WoS database

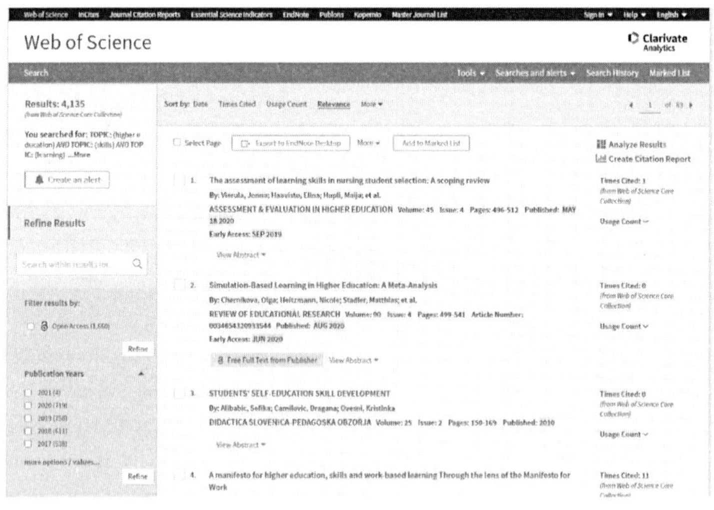

FIGURE 1-2

Importing the reference data into qualitative analysis software (Nvivo11)

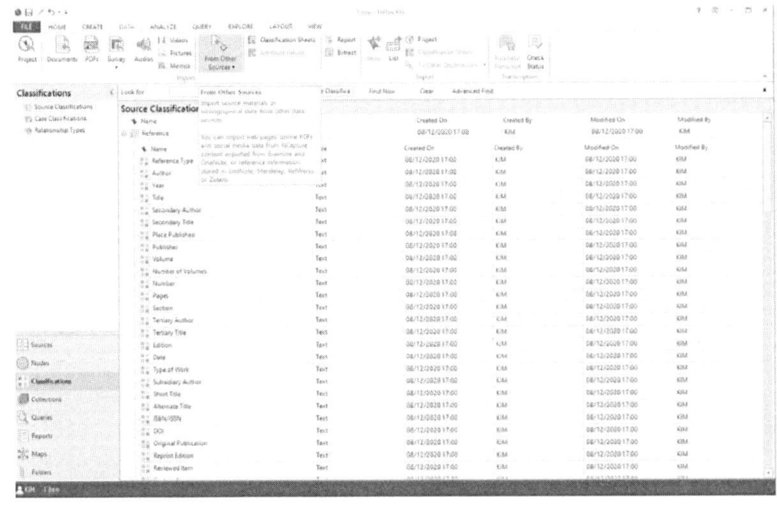

Through the "Text search" query, which finds the occurrence of the concept, a lot of words which occurred alongside "skill" were identified on the left side of the word-tree (see Figure 1-3).

Due to too many corelated words appearing in length based on the alphabetical order in the word-tree analysis, Figure 1-3 shows only a small part of the word-tree in the centre, and the skills that were researched in the recent studies are listed as: academic skill, analytical skill, artistic expression skill, cognitive skill, collaborative skill, communication skill, critical thinking skill, creative skill, cross-curricular skill, emotional skill, employability, entrepreneurial skill, ethics and responsibility, generic skill, global competency skill, human innovation skill, leadership skill, learning skill, life-long skill, linguistic skill, ICT skill, intellectual skill, interpersonal skill, management/managerial skill, mathematical skill, market skill, metacognitive skill, practical skill, procedural skill, professional skill, quantitative skill, reasoning skill, reflective skill, research skill, self-regulatory skill, soft skill, problem-solving skill, industry-specific skill, self-study skill, technical skill, verbal skill, and writing skill.

FIGURE 1-3

Word-tree of "skills" and its related words which appeared in the relevant papers (1,000 records)

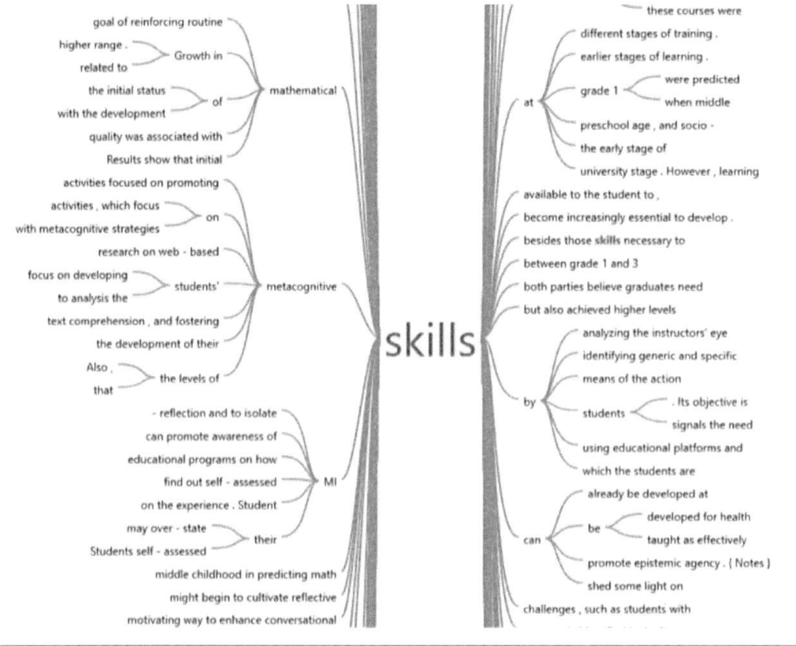

In the existing research, 41 skills were stressed for fostering future leaders through the educational programmes provided by HEIs. Here, we need to refine that number of skills according to their meanings and relation with each other. In a broad view, all the skills can be divided into two dimensions: generic and specific. The majority of the listed skills include both generic and specific attributes; however, based on their definitions and relationship with other skills, they can be structurised and categorised as Fig. 1-4. In this course, we are mainly focusing on the five highlighted skills as the topics we are going to discuss: 1) knowledge and learning; 2) learning and creativity; 3) creativity and cognitive process; 4) creativity and innovation; 5) disruptive innovation; 6) cognitive skills for innovation. All of those six topics will be discussed based on the findings from academic research.

FIGURE 1-4

Relationship between skills

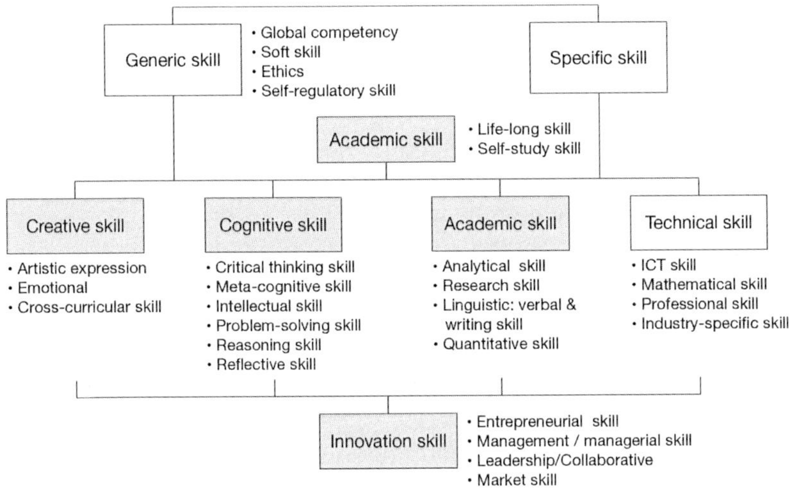

The main objective of this course is to provide answers to the question of "What do we need to learn, and how should we learn, in order to become a leader in the upcoming society as a knowledge professional?". Here, knowledge professional means *"a person who contributes to humanity by employing their mental capabilities to create new value, through discovering, inventing, making or creating"*[1], and this explains what we expect from the graduate degree holders.

To answer the main question, the following sub-questions will be asked through the course as follows:

- Topic 1: What is learning?
  - How are our learning environments?
  - How can we enjoy our learning experience?
  - What are the most required skills for graduate students in order for them to become leaders in future society?

1 Speech by the President of the University of Tokyo, at the graduation ceremony in 2016 (accessed through http://www.u-tokyo.ac.jp/gen01/b_message28_07_j.html)

- Topic 2: How can you create a new value from learning?
  - How is the balance between your learning environments and skill level?
  - How can you describe your mental mode regarding learning and conducting research?
  - How can your learning create valuable outcomes?
- Topic 3: What is creativity?
  - How is creativity defined?
  - What is different from innovation?
  - How has creativity been researched?
  - What is the cognitive process for creativity?
- Topic 4: What is innovation?
  - How are creativity and innovation different?
  - How can we classify different types of innovation?
  - What are the cases of innovation?
- Topic 5: How can we find an opportunity for creating innovations?
  - Why is innovation difficult?
  - What is disruptive innovation?
  - How can we initiate disruptive innovation?
- Topic 6: How can you facilitate idea generation for creating innovative ideas?
  - How can we create a new idea from familiar ideas?
  - How can we train our thinking skill for creating new ideas?
  - What is analogical thinking?
  - How can we recognise the structural similarities among superficially different ideas?

This book consists of eight chapters:

Chapter 1 presents an introduction to the whole book. It briefly explains the importance of the topics we are going to discuss throughout the book, which meets the demands of the times and current academic trends. It also explains the purpose of this course and how the topics were selected according to the said purpose; it then presents an outline of each chapter.

Chapter 2, entitled 'Topic 1: knowledge and learning', introduces social backgrounds of rethinking on learning at HIEs and reviews the theoretical studies and empirical investigations on facilitating learning.

Chapter 3, namely 'Topic 2: learning and creativity', introduces the flow theory put forth by Csikszentmihalyi (1990) to reflect on personal learning activities and to discuss how to enhance our quality of experiences, which can make it possible for us to create or accomplish something difficult and worthwhile.

Chapter 4, 'Topic 3: creativity and cognitive process', reviews the past and current trends in creativity studies since their establishment, and introduces the creative cognitive process as well as its related research.

Chapter 5, 'Topic 4: creativity and innovation', defines the concept of innovation and its related terms, following which it categorises types of innovation in a couple of different ways, and introduces related cases.

Chapter 6, 'Topic 5: disruptive innovation', explains the difficulties of creating innovation and how to find an opportunity to initiate innovation by introducing the concept of disruptive innovation (Christensen, 2013).

Chapter 7, entitled 'Topic 6: cognitive skills for innovation', introduces tools for thought and suggests a method with which to generate new ideas based on analogical thinking.

Key conceptual words

knowledge and learning, learning and creativity, creativity and cognitive process, creativity and innovation, disruptive innovation, cognitive skills for innovation

REFERENCE

✦ ✦ ✦

Christensen, C. M. (2013). *The innovator's dilemma: when new technologies cause great firms to fail: Harvard Business Review Press.*

Csikszentmihalyi, M. (1990). Flow: The psychology of optimal experience.

Johnson, L., Adams Becker, S., Cummins, M., Estrada, V., Freeman, A., & Hall, C. (2016). NMC Horizon Report: 2016 Higher Education Edition. Retrieved from Austin, Texas:

Roser, M., & Ortiz-Ospina, E. (2018). Tertiary Education. from Published online at OurWorldInData.org https://ourworldindata.org/tertiary-education

Schwab, K. (2016). *The 4th industrial revolution. Paper presented at the World Economic Forum. New York: Crown Business.*

CHAPTER 02

Topic 1 Knowledge and learning

Topic 1

Knowledge and learning

Thao Thanh Luong and Eunyoung Kim

This chapter describes ground for learning as a graduate student to become a leader in upcoming society, and reviews academic research on knowledge and learning to understand which factors facilitate learning of both individual and organization.

2.1. The society we live in

Numerous studies have characterized the significant changes that have occurred in economies and society in general. One of the most influential historical studies, entitled *The Coming of Post-Industrial Society*, was published in 1973 by Daniel Bell. This work has disseminated the notable concept of "post-industrial society", where the role of knowledge and information has become increasingly significant since the mid-1970s, when economies started generating values more from the provision of services than from manufacturing products. In other words, while the primary source of employment in the industrial society was from the production of goods, in today's post-industrial economy the service sector has generated more jobs. It has been argued that such work is based more on information and knowledge, which gives the learning, innovation and creativity processes more importance in social and economic life (Hislop et al., 2018). Furthermore, Bell (1973) stresses that as diverse forms of knowledge are given more attention in the post-industrial society, the role of theoretical knowledge – which is often referred to as abstract or conceptual ideas or frameworks, and is not limited to knowledge in academic research – will expand exponentially (see Figure 2-1 for the main characteristics of post-industrial society). Consequently, the development of a wide range of service industries will be founded on the growth and application of such knowledge, leading to the tremendous importance of white-collar workers such as scientists, information technology experts, or creative-industry professionals.

FIGURE 2-1

Characteristics of a Post-Industrial Society

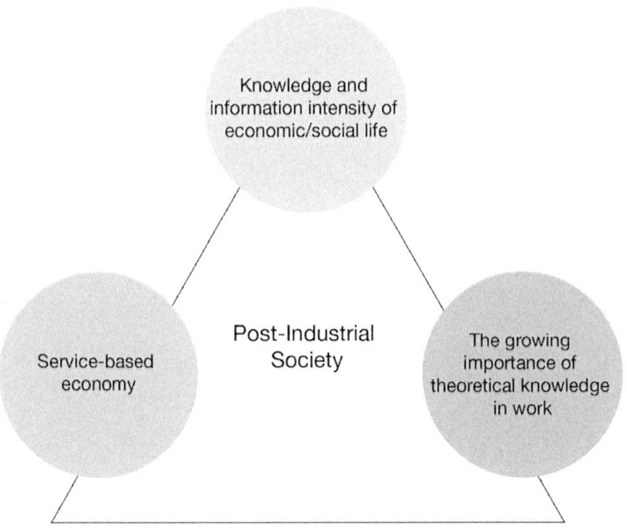

Note. This figure highlights characteristics of a *Post-Industrial Society*. Redrawn from *Knowledge Management in Organizations: A Critical Introduction* (4th Edition, p. 4), by Hislop et al., 2018, Oxford University Press.

While the concept of "post-industrial society" focuses mainly on the changes in modes of employment and the role of knowledge in economic development, its emphasis on the service sector has indeed brought attention to a bigger picture of the society we are living in, where countries ¬– especially those in the Third World – are urged to establish a more knowledge-based economy, accompanied by other sustainable development goals. The "triple helix model of innovation" framework was first theorized by Henry Etzkowitz and Loet Leydesdorff in the 1990s, to show the strategic interplay between universities, governments and industries (together termed "UGI"); this model has widely popularized the promotion of the critical relationship between social and economic development. The model characterizes how the UGI can influence each other and create different types of bilateral interactions – despite their diverse roles, where universities engage in academic research and education, governments take charge of regulating the economic development, and industries commercialize products and services. Nevertheless, the levels at which such strategic interactions take place vary according to the development of countries. For example, in developing countries, the UGI appear to function independently as silos in different industries and sectors (see Figure 2-2), and thus fail to benefit from each other's operations.

FIGURE 2-2

Triple Helix interaction in developing countries or Silo Confinement

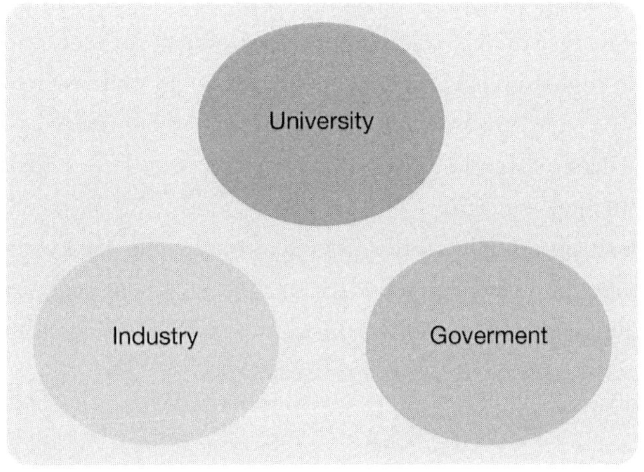

Note. This figure shows the Triple Helix interaction in developing countries. From "Evolution of Strategic Interactions from the Triple to Quad Helix Innovation Models for Sustainable Development in the Era of Globalization", by Kimatu, 2015, *Journal of Innovation and Entrepreneurship*, 5(1), p. 3 (http://dx.doi.org/10.1186/s13731-016-0044-x). CC BY 4.0.

In middle-income countries, more strategic interplays among UGI have been shown (see Figure 2-3). For instance, universities and industries in these countries have established their initial interactions to promote innovations and knowledge co-creation. By pursuing their two perennial missions – i.e. providing educational services, and conducting scholarly research – universities in these countries develop human resources for industries, and provide innovative ideas for designing new products or services. Concurrently, as a key actor in the national innovation system, industries also play a significant role in creating and transferring knowledge. Professional knowledge workers at firms, such as those in leadership or senior management positions, can participate in knowledge-sharing projects, where their professional expertise and experience can be used as a resource for identifying research needs and ensuring the production of relevant research.

Regarding the linkage between universities and governments, there have been strategic mutual demands. As universities are required to participate more in forming national sustainable goals, they also press governments for more funding and infrastructural support. Finally, under the need to enhance market-driven technological advancement for economic growth and maintain high employment rates, governments in middle-income countries need to provide direct support to industries, while preserving their control over the economy and industrial relations. As firms have sufficient legal and environmental conditions to operate efficiently and sustainably, they can contribute substantially to the national economy. In essence, given the need to form and implement strategic national development goals, the triple helix in middle-income countries is claimed to have been initiated, although scant evidence for such interplays is provided.

FIGURE 2-3

The beginning of Triple Helix Strategic Interactions in Middle-Income Countries

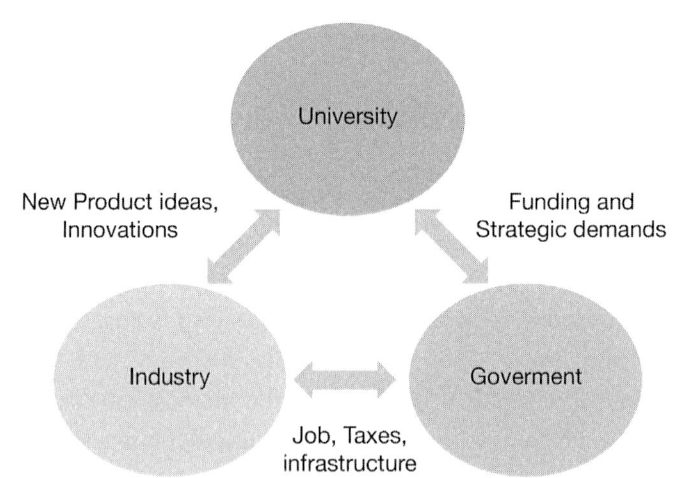

Note. This figure shows the beginning of Triple Helix Strategic Interactions in Middle-Income Countries. From "Evolution of Strategic Interactions from the Triple to Quad Helix Innovation Models for Sustainable Development in the Era of Globalization", by Kimatu, 2015, *Journal of Innovation and Entrepreneurship*, 5(1), p. 3 (http://dx.doi.org/10.1186/s13731-016-0044-x). CC BY 4.0.

In developed nations, however, such strategic interactions have evolved to a higher level. They have accordingly caused the UGI to become decidedly dependent on each other in tackling problematic national issues or creating innovations (see Figure 2-4). In numerous advanced countries, the triple helix model has also engendered the creation of different intermediaries, such as science parks, technology transfer offices, and most recently, technopolis and innopolis (Kimatu, 2015). These institutions play a crucial role in creating necessary conditions for knowledge sharing, innovation promotion, and sustainable economic development among the UGI. They also enhance the emergent properties of the UGI linkage system by obscuring the boundaries of the UGIs' conventional primary roles (Etzkowitz & Leydesdorff, 1995). For example, universities will expand beyond their fundamental roles in education and research, and will increasingly participate in commercializing products and services through patenting or licensing activities. Similarly, Etzkowitz (2008) highlights the evolution by introducing the model of the "entrepreneurial university", where knowledge becomes a source of human capital that helps advance strategic interactions among the UGI. The Massachusetts Institute of Technology (MIT) was mentioned by Etzkowitz (2008) as an illustration of this "entrepreneurial university" framework.

FIGURE 2-4

Triple Helix Strategic Interactions in Developed Countries

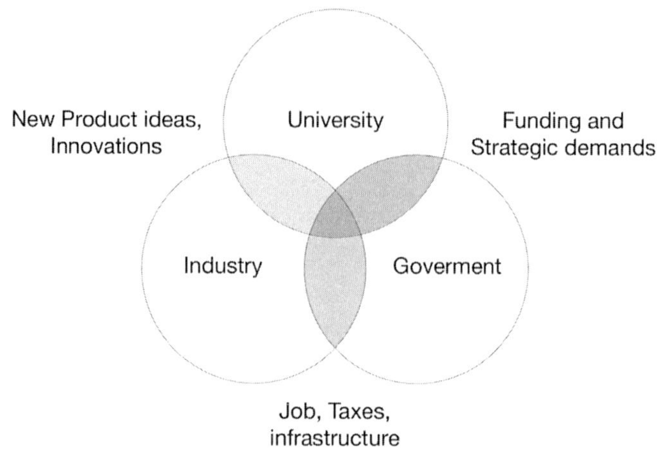

Note. This figure shows the Triple Helix Strategic Interactions in Developed Countries. From "Evolution of Strategic Interactions from the Triple to Quad Helix Innovation Models for Sustainable Development in the Era of Globalization", by Kimatu, 2015, *Journal of Innovation and Entrepreneurship*, 5(1), p. 4 (http://dx.doi.org/10.1186/s13731-016-0044-x). CC BY 4.0.

As the internet is increasingly conducive to advancing technological innovations for social and economic development, the evolution of the triple helix proceeds by a series of significant changes. Such transformation puts pressure on the "informed watchdogs for sustainable interactions" in the triple helix (Kimatu, 2015). As a consequence, a fourth component has been added to the framework by Carayannis and Campbell (2009): namely "the civil society" (see Figure 2-5), which develops the triple helix into the quadruple helix innovation model. This newly added element represents the voice of the society's citizens, whose demands are not always prioritized by the operations of the triple helix. Therefore, the new model has required the UGI to be more committed to their traditional essential missions to serve society. Numerous large-scale European Union-sponsored projects, such as the EU-MACS (European Market for Climate Services) project (Vaittinen, n.d.), have adopted this quad helix approach, to ensure that innovations genuinely serve the needs of the society, both globally and locally.

FIGURE 2-5

The Quad Helix innovation model, to raise the social responsibilities of UGI in creating and implementing innovations

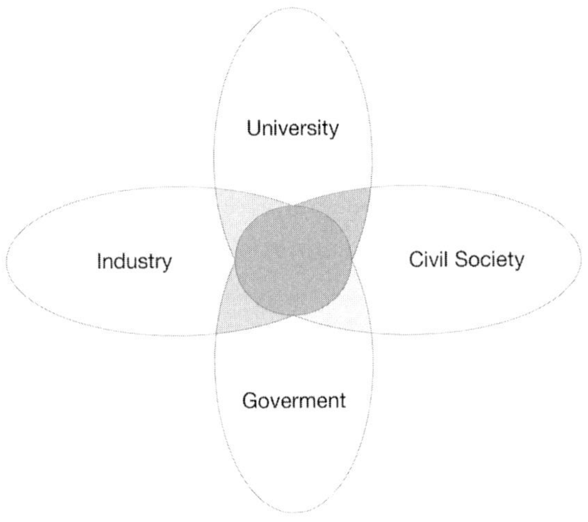

Note. This figure shows the Quad Helix innovation model, to raise the social responsibilities of UGI in creating and implementing innovations. From "Evolution of Strategic Interactions from the Triple to Quad Helix Innovation Models for Sustainable Development in the Era of Globalization", by Kimatu, 2015, *Journal of Innovation and Entrepreneurship*, 5(1), p. 5 (http://dx.doi.org/10.1186/s13731-016-0044-x). CC BY 4.0.

As the quadruple helix innovation model compels a knowledge-based society to align with human beings' various needs, it has placed more emphasis on creating a higher quality of life. In fact, even though social values in the current society are becoming progressively diverse and complex, achieving peace and prosperity for people has been a shared purpose of all nations for many years. The Japanese Council for Science, Technology and Innovation has recently termed this ultimate goal as "Society 5.0" in its 5th Science and Technology Basic Plan, approved by the Cabinet in January 2016 (Cabinet Office, 2015). The Japanese government coined this term to distinguish the future information society from earlier societies in human history. "Society 1.0", for instance, refers to the early community of people whose existence was in harmony with nature, and life in this foraging time depended on hunting and gathering activities. "Society 2.0" is defined as an "agrarian society", where societal development was based on agricultural advancement and organizational formation. The next civilization stage, termed "Society 3.0", characterizes a flourishing period of industrialization, with the expansion of mass production and consumption. Approaching the most current stage, "Society 4.0" is referred to as the information age, in which the invention of computers and their networks paved the way for a rapid historic shift from the traditional industry established by the Industrial Revolution, to an economy primarily based upon information technology.

Most recently in this evolution, "Society 5.0", also defined as "super-smart society", has emerged as "a human-centred society" that focuses on the balance between developing the economy and cultivating solutions for social problems, by utilizing the integration of cyberspace and physical space (Cabinet Office, n.d.). Accordingly, the rapid evolution of digital technologies in Society 5.0 – such as the internet of things (IoT), artificial intelligence (AI), big data, robotics, and the sharing economy – is expected to generate high-quality data for resolving current societal challenges, including the ageing population, inequality, or environmental pollution. Despite the fact that Society 5.0 is a strategy proposed by the Japanese government, these social issues are confronted by not only Japan but also other advanced countries, and eventually they will be faced by numerous developing and middle-income nations (Fukuyama, 2018). Therefore, from the perspective of Society 5.0, it is worth noting that the general well-being of people and societies nowadays is not independent of the digital transformation, the diverse emergent social values, and the worldwide efforts to resolve current social problems.

Just as importantly, several decades before the COVID-19 pandemic spread around the world, the global agenda had promoted the advancement of international trade, which is often regarded as being a result of globalization. The onset of the contagion, however, has seriously affected the process of globalization, and this worldwide interconnectedness has become a primary means of infection (Shrestha et al., 2020). In most nations, the pandemic has also brought a challenging dilemma for nations, between preserving efficiency and economic gain, or ensuring safety for their citizens (Lee et al., 2020). Nevertheless, despite its destructive effects on various aspects of economic and social life, the contagious disease has appeared to continue pushing society towards taking maximum advantage of digital technology (Sheth, 2020). Accordingly, digital technology is no longer merely an alternative for business, education and everyday life; rather, it will become practically a necessity, with its widespread use in various daily activities. In this context, the aforementioned concepts of the post-industrial economy, the quad helix innovation model, and Society 5.0 have become even more essential for speculating about a future society in the post-pandemic context. Striving and thriving in such a circumstance require individuals to foster continuous self-development by concentrating on perpetual learning. Also, the leading role that individuals play in the current society needs to be taken into account, as the chances of successfully coping with the pandemic depend on the leaders' abilities, knowledge, and perspectives towards the crisis (Lee et al., 2020). Thus, it is noteworthy that by pursuing an unceasing lifelong education, individuals can act as leaders who can add significant values to the advancement of a sustainable society, despite any chaos or disorientation taking place in the modern world.

The next part of this chapter will focus on the recognition of today's learning environments and speculation regarding post-pandemic life, in order to understand why formal lifelong education is vital for developing genuine leaders who never stop looking for happiness and wisdom.

2.2. Purpose of postgraduate education

In general, postgraduate education refers to higher degree programmes, defined by the Organisation for Economic Cooperation and Development (OECD) (2015) as master's degree or equivalent (ISCED 2011 Level 7), or doctoral degrees (ISCED 2011 Level 8). Acquiring these qualifications represents the possession of higher-order levels of professional and academic knowledge, which also increases people's accountability in conducting more complex tasks in the current modern world. Thus, whether they are self-funded or receive sponsorship for pursuing these higher programmes, individuals who complete postgraduate degrees are expected to create better outcomes for their quality of life and society – not only in the forms of sharing knowledge or paying higher taxes, but also through indirectly creating technological innovations that are conducive to sustainable economic development and human well-being (Erwee et al., 2018).

In various developmental stages of society, the question of "What is the purpose of postgraduate higher education in today's world?" has always been a primary theme of numerous studies and publications. For instance, in a recent volume entitled *Postgraduate Education in Higher Education*, while focusing on the administrators' perspective on how to develop universities in the new technological era, Erwee et al. (2018) discussed the value of master's and doctoral degrees by analysing how these higher degrees contribute to job creation, employability, or societal advancement. Other studies also take similar approaches, where various stakeholders' viewpoints on the pros and cons of higher education are taken into consideration. The focal point of this chapter, however, concerns realizing the benefits of postgraduate education, mainly from the learners' angle. Notably, instead of focusing on these higher degrees' financial or career advantages, this book section promotes lifelong learning for its own sake. The chapter also recognizes the power of postgraduate educational institutions, through their changing role from merely academic research centres towards becoming places where future leaders are nurtured and maturated to serve societal development.

When looking at how postgraduate education has changed over time, it is worth noting that despite being transformed throughout history, the value of these higher degrees has always endured. However, unlike traditional views on master's and doctoral degrees, which often refer to these credentials as a means to obtain full-time academic positions, the current approaches to higher education have altered in many different ways, given the decline in government funding and increasing operational costs (Erwee et al., 2018). One way to recognize the changing role of postgraduate education is through the declining amount of academic positions in universities (Erwee et al., 2018) and the growing number of professional jobs in various industries or social life areas. This situation was defined earlier by Burgess et al. (2000) as "the gross creation and destruction of jobs, reflecting the expansion and contraction of establishment". Similarly, yet more recently, Gallagher (2016) used examples of large American multinational enterprises that prioritized job applicants with higher educational degrees, and found that "degrees still matter", especially in hiring for senior leadership positions. Nowadays, the movement towards a knowledge-based society, as identified via the concepts of the post-industrial economy, the quad helix innovation model, or Society 5.0, has placed more emphasis on the advanced professional or academic knowledge provided through master's or doctoral programmes. In such a society, achievers of these higher degrees will not hold solely academic positions, but are to become future leaders, whose visions and competence are essential to deal with current social problems and unknown future challenges in the modern world.

At this point, the question now turns to "How have leaders shaped the societal development?". When we look back at when and how leaders have appeared throughout history, although most of such great human beings achieved fame during the history of wars, there have also been scientific and corporate leaders, whose efforts are ceaselessly devoted to improving themselves, their countries, and the world, through science and economic advancement. In the first stage of the post-war era, for instance, numerous admirable corporate leaders made efforts to revive economies. In Japan, between the post-World War II period to the end of the Cold War, while most large cities, industries and transportation networks had been critically damaged, the country's economy thrived; it experienced a "miracle recovery", owing to the appropriate policies for economic development and effective corporate strategies (Otsubo, 2007). Accordingly, in this economic boom, Japanese business leadership played a significant role in maintaining the well-organized interest groups, which contributed considerably to making the country the world's second-largest economy (Drucker, 1981). World-renowned Japanese corporate leaders such as Akio Morita[1] and Kazuo Inamori[2] were famous not only for their strategic visions and decision making, but also for their management philosophy, which concentrated

---

1 The founder of SONY

2 The founder of Kyocera and KDDI

primarily on prioritizing national interests and enhancing human well-being. In the later period, not long after the 1973 oil crisis, the world witnessed the appearance of great American innovators and leaders, such as Steve Jobs and Bill Gates, who founded two of the five most extensive and dominant companies in the United States information technology industry; these firms are often referred to as "tech giants", and include Amazon, Apple, Google, Facebook and Microsoft. Following the oil shock period was the era of transition and the "Bubble Economy", which lasted from the early 1970s to the late 1980s; this period involved tremendous crises and catastrophic consequences, which Mitsuhiko (2010) claimed that even "human wisdom could not avoid". Such economic instability has pushed numerous economists and leaders to make recommendations on reconstructing a more sustainable international financial architecture – for example, Eichengreen and Baldwin's (2008) report on advice from G20 countries' leaders, regarding on how to recover economies after the global financial crisis. Lastly and most recently, the current "Industry 4.0." period, which highlights the inevitable trends towards automation and data exchange in manufacturing industries (Oberer & Erkollar, 2018), is forcing national leaders to create and undertake strategic plans necessary for the systematic transformation of society in the digital era. As an illustration, the Korean government's initiatives for updating industries to the age of "Industry 4.0." explained and examined by Sung (2018), indicate that although a more concrete and actionable strategy is needed, national leaders have shown their serious consideration of global competition in the fourth industrial revolution, and are accordingly shaping the future world economy and society.

The new era of "Industry 4.0." has also seen the rise of digital leaders such as Elon Musk or Mark Zuckerberg, who possess various traits and bodies of new knowledge that are essential to effectively lead their organizations, and respectively frame the indiscernible future of the information age. Nevertheless, not all companies are tech giants in the current information technology industry. In Europe, low-performing firms appear to be more common than those operating effectively, regardless of which specific methods are used to measure firms' performance, such as turnover or added value per worker (Altomonte, Aquilante & Ottaviano, 2012). Figure 2-6 compares the standard assumed distribution of European firms' performance (normal, in blue) with the actual distribution (Pareto, in red); both generate a similar average performance. This chart reveals that the assumed distribution underrates the proportion of low-performing firms. Thus, the reality is that the percentages of bad and good firms are not balanced, with more bad firms in place than high-performing ones. Accordingly, this situation implies the insufficient number of effective leaders in European organizations, and thus requires workable strategic actions in human resources development.

FIGURE 2-6

Actual (Pareto) vs. assumed (normal) distribution of firms' performance

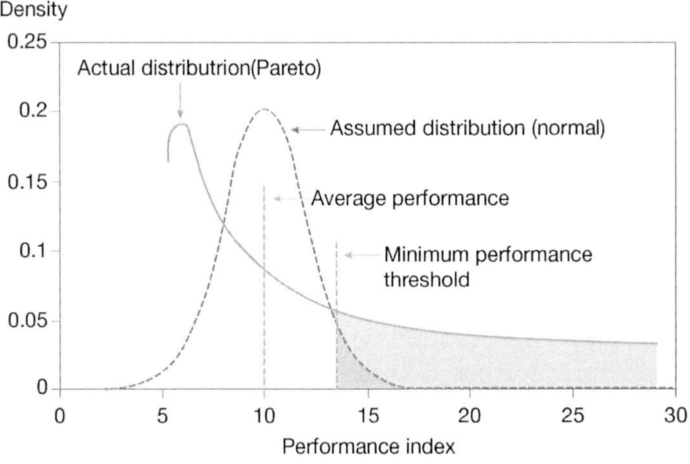

Note. This figure compares the actual (Pareto) vs. assumed (normal) distribution of European firms' performance . From *The Triggers of Competitiveness: The EFIGE Cross-Country Report. Bruegel Blueprint Series*, by Altomonte, Aquilante and Ottaviano, 2012 (https://www.bruegel.org/wp-content/uploads/imported/publications/Blueprint_XVII_web.pdf). In the public domain.

In a similar way, in one of the most recent studies on common traits of the best digital leaders, Gerald Kane (a professor of information systems at the Carroll School of Management at Boston College and the MIT Sloan Management Review) claims that all types of American companies are currently lacking qualified leaders; although more mature organizations are often known to have a talent development strategy, unlike developing- or early-stage companies. Kane (2018) urges companies to stop deploring the inadequacy of competent digital leaders and start forming actionable strategic plans to find and develop the right talents, who have the essential traits to face new challenges brought by the new uncertain digital environment. In addition, it is worth pointing out that although some leadership traits have remained necessary throughout history, such as providing directions or critical thinking, other emergent digital leadership traits – including digital knowledge and literacy (Promsri, 2019), or a people-centric mindset (Hensellek, 2020) – are becoming genuinely desired in today's organizations. In essence, there is no doubt that the digital age has changed the global competition and organizational environment. Hence, leaders need to develop new knowledge and skills, in order to proactively and productively navigate their companies through this increasingly complex and rapidly changing environment.

This chapter's brief discussion of when and how leaders appear in different historical contexts highlights the urgent need for postgraduate educational institutions to focus on innovation and collaboration in the current digitalization era. In his recent eminent book, named *Future Skills: Future Learning, Future Higher Education*, the educational scientist and professor Ulf-Daniel Ehlers (2020) stresses that digitalization will press universities towards having more didactic, curricular and administrative innovations. Ehlers (2020) also emphasizes the importance of close interactions among universities themselves, and with other interest groups. Such collaboration is vital to ensure that the shift from physical to virtual learning spaces aligns with the increasing quality of the educational environment. Last but not least, whereas the interplays among technology and education were obscure in the previous historical contexts, the rapid economic growth in recent eras has created a race between technological and educational development, where the former appears to continually beat the latter (see Figure 2-7); this causes a lack of qualified employees with the necessary skills to adapt to the emergent working environment (Goldin & Katz, 2009). Accordingly, as shown in Figure 2-7, today's society can achieve prosperity and lessen social pain, provided that educational institutions ensure that knowledge and skill development catch up with the speed of technological advancement. In other words, postgraduate programmes are expected to continuously innovate in their curricular and pedagogical strategies, in order to participate in the process of creating future leaders for organizations. As perpetual educational innovations include identifying the appropriate strategies and approaches to teaching and learning in the digital era, the next sub-chapters will introduce and discuss the most recent theories on learning and factors that influence the learning processes, given the importance of knowing how to learn in the right way, and how to enjoy the learning experience in today's world.

FIGURE 2-7

The race between technology and education

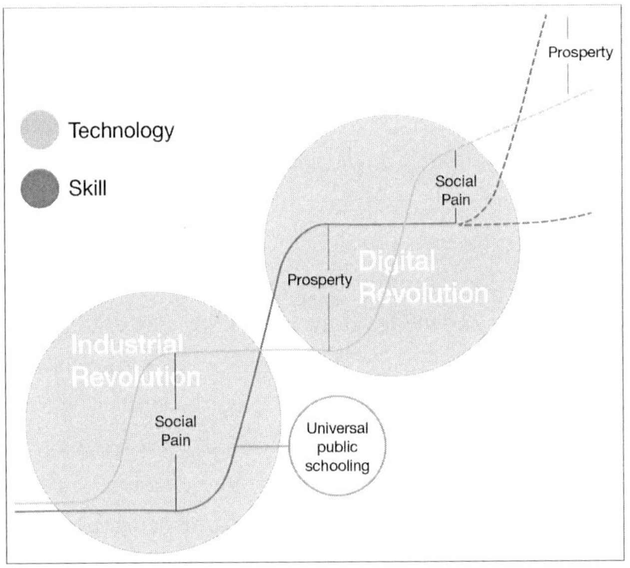

Note. This figure shows the race between technology and education. From *Future Skills: Future Learning, Future Higher Education* (p. 186), by Ehlers, 2020, Springer (https://nextskills.org/wp-content/uploads/2020/03/Future-Skills-The-Future-of-learning-and-higher-education.pdf). CC BY-NC-SA 4.0

2.3. Typologies of knowledge and learning

TThere have been various approaches to characterizing and defining knowledge. On the one hand, objectivism endorses the positivistic epistemology in defining knowledge as an objective entity that is independent from human beings who possess it (Scott, Cook & Seely, 2014). On the other hand, instead of focusing on the importance of objective knowledge, prominent studies such as that by Nonaka and Takeuchi (1995) promote the value of subjective knowledge, or knowledge that is personally possessed by every human being and is very difficult to transfer from one person to another. Although there are other different definitions and ways to characterize knowledge, when developing learning strategies, educators and researchers often refer to this prevalent typology of knowledge, which involves considering whether knowledge is tacit or explicit (see Table 2-1).

As knowledge plays a critical role in the information age, the distinction between tacit and explicit knowledge – and their interweaving presence – is critical, because of the continual needs to create, acquire, evaluate, share and apply knowledge (Smith, 2001). Accordingly, numerous researchers have attempted to build models of knowledge creation based on this differentiation between tacit and explicit knowledge, and their importance in today's society. The knowledge creation spiral, or the SECI model, by Nonaka and Takeuchi (1995) is a notable contribution in this discipline (see Figure 2-8). In this model, there are four knowledge conversion processes, each named after the SECI initials, where S stands for "Socialization" (the conversion from tacit to tacit knowledge though social interactions); E signifies "Externalization" (the conversion from tacit to explicit knowledge via language, visual aids, or concepts); C represents "Combination" (the creation of new systematic explicit knowledge by combining different preceding bodies of explicit knowledge); and finally, I indicates "Internalization" (the conversion from explicit to tacit knowledge through the application of such explicit knowledge to performing work tasks).

TABLE 2-1 The characteristics of Tacit and Explicit Knowledge

Tacit Knowledge	Explicit Knowledge
Not easily expressed or codified	Could be codified and expressed in words
Often in the forms of subjective opinions, approaches, viewpoints, personal competencies	Often in the forms of objective facts, rules, laws
Personal	Impersonal
Based on context	Independent from context
Not easily be shared	Could be shared from person to person

FIGURE 2-8

The SECI Model of Knowledge Creation by Nonaka & Takeuchi (1995)

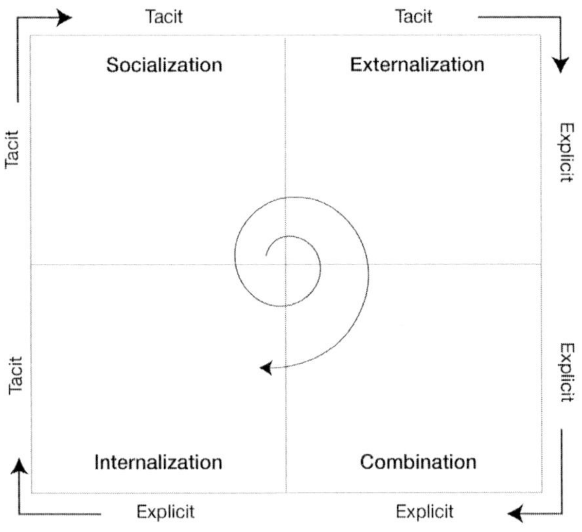

Note. This figure shows the SECI model. From *SECI model of knowledge dimensions*, 2012, (https://en.wikipedia.org/wiki/SECI_model_of_knowledge_dimensions). CC BY-SA 3.0

The SECI model of knowledge creation by Nonaka and Takeuchi (1995) is valuable not only because of its elaboration of the dichotomy between tacit and explicit knowledge, but also due to its specification that knowledge does not exist merely at the individual level. Without the process of human interaction – e.g. communication, sharing, or discussing – new knowledge, both in tacit and explicit form, will not be created accordingly. In other words, group knowledge also exists, often in the forms of shared knowledge, habits or values (Razmerita et al., 2014), and may be either tacit or explicit as well. In fact, Spender (1996) has introduced the concept of organizational knowledge, where knowledge can be viewed in two dimensions: the tacit-explicit form, and individual-group level. This combination has proposed four different concepts, comprising *Conscious* (Explicit-Individual knowledge, e.g. codified notes, laboratory notes), *Automatic* (Tacit-Individual knowledge, i.e. knowledge which individual accesses in a state of flow), *Objectified* (Explicit-Social knowledge, e.g. documented rules, standard operating procedures, official work practices, libraries), and *Collective* Knowledge (Tacit-Social knowledge, i.e. knowledge which comprises both meaning - cognitive, affective, symbolic, and cultural - and praxis - behaviours, rituals, organizational routines).

According to Spender (1996), each type of knowledge "must be defined in terms of each other, and are only meaningful in terms of particular practices" (p. 75). It is thus noteworthy that as there are different typologies of knowledge, diverse systematic classifications for learning have also been established. That is to say, by means of interactions among various types of knowledge, learning takes place differently between the individual and group or organizational level. The literature about learning, therefore, posits that, similar to the heterogeneity of knowledge, learning can be defined and characterized through a diverse range of mechanisms and processes (for a brief discription of typologies of learning, see Hislop et al. (2018)).

Although there are a wide range of approaches to learning, this chapter focuses only on the dynamic interaction between individual, group, and organizational learning levels, just as it has focused on how new knowledge is created by virtue of the interplay between individual and group knowledge. In addition, since there has been a vast literature on the complexity of how learning occurs at different levels, this chapter takes into account the concept of organizational learning, which is not simply "learning in an organization" (Vince, 2014), but rather learning, either at individual or group levels, that "impacts organizational structures and processes" (Hislop et al., 2018). Accordingly, for anyone who is working in an organization – either as a senior leader or a blue-collar employee, or groups from small teams to large departments in an organization – it is necessary to be aware of how the characteristics of the learning processes impact the organizational values, structures and operations, to ensure that proposed change initiatives can be genuinely effective.

Despite its long-standing existence in the literature, the term "organizational learning" has nevertheless generated little agreement on how it is defined and conceptualized. Table 2-2 outlines some of the most pre-eminent definitions for this term, according to publication years. As highlighted by numerous notable researchers, such as Tsang (1997), the concept appears in both descriptive and prescriptive studies. Although these two research streams are theoretically supposed to help refine the concept and create a consensus on its definitions, there remains a gap between academic researchers and practitioners in understanding this term. Consequently, when attempting to search for a definition of the term, it is necessary to examine the nature and perspectives of the studies, in order to establish whether such definitions have been based on rigorous research methodologies, regardless of their theoretical or practical approaches.

TABLE 2-2 Definitions of Organizational Learning

Authors	Year	Definitions of Organizational Learning
Fiol and Lyles	1985	"Organizational learning means the process of improving actions through better knowledge and understanding"
Levitt and March	1988	"...organizations are seen as learning by encoding inferences from history into routines that guide behavior"
Huber	1991	"An entity learns if, through its processing of information, the range of its potential behaviors is changed"
Swieringa and Wierdsma	1992	"By the term *organizational learning*, we mean the changing of organizational behavior"

Cook and Yanow	1993	"a definition of organizational learning as *the acquiring, sustaining, or changing of intersubjective meanings through the artifactual vehicles of their expression and transmission and [through] the collective actions of the group*"
Cummings and Worley	2009	A change process improving organizational capabilities to acquire and create new knowledge
Namada	2018	"a composition of individual learning, development of culture, continuous improvement, innovation, and applying systems which learn"
Hislop et al.	2018	"The embedding of individual- and group-level learning in organizational structures and processes, achieved through reflecting on and modifying the norms and values embodied in established organizational processes and structures."

To better characterize individual, group, and organizational learning processes, the next part of this chapter will discuss factors which have an impact on these mechanisms. In addition, it will explain how different levels of learning interact with each other, to form a complex interrelationship that is crucial to organizations' competitive advantage and innovation capabilities.

2.4. Factors affecting different types of learning

Let us start this section by looking at what factors motivate individual learning. The literature on this discipline is indeed so broad that, in order to develop hypothetical theories regarding such factors, the diversity of learner types, learning contexts, and research methodologies need to be taken into account. To illustrate this, the literature has emphasized the role of deliberate practice as an important factor that influences the effectiveness of learning (Ericsson et al., 1993); especially in the fields of online game playing (Stafford & Dewar, 2014), chess, and music (Hambrick et al., 2014). However, Macnamara et al.'s meta-analysis (2014) revealed that although deliberate practice – or "engagement in structured activities created specifically to improve performance in a domain" – is critical, it is not as critical as had been claimed. In addition, these authors point out that the age at which a person starts engaging officially in a professional field affects their learning outcomes. This means that the earlier a person starts becoming seriously involved in a domain, the greater the likelihood that he or she can succeed and become an expert. In other words, there is a higher possibility of older adults being experts in a specific domain, compared to younger ones. Nevertheless, this starting-age factor is also controversial. For instance, Baltes and Kliegl (1992) observed significant negative effects of ageing on cognitive performance level (their experiment results show that young learners considerably outperform the elderly in terms of developmental reserve capacity). By contrast, Chen et al (2019) recently revealed that higher education in early life has a positive facilitative impact on cognitive and brain reserve performance; they studied 659 participants from the Beijing Ageing Brain Rejuvenation Initiative (BABRI) database, using the Structuring Equation Modelling (SEM) technique to test the relationship between cognitive performance and the interaction between age and higher education. This result shows that higher-educated older individuals, by enjoyably participating in daily intellectual activities such as reading or taking academic courses, experience lower risks of Mild Cognitive Impairment (MCI) (Chen et al., 2019). It is thus underlined that when considering deliberate practice or age as factors that influence learning activities, researchers should take into account learners' characteristics, professional domains and cultural contexts.

Regarding methodologies for research on factors that have an impact on learning, SEM techniques such as AMOS, LISREL, or PLS are used in numerous studies. For example, when analysing the effect of negative emotions on individual learning due to errors in the workplace context, Zhao (2011) conducted a business simulation called the "Furniture Factory", where these authors tested their complex model of learning from errors by using PLS-Graph version 3.0. Their hypotheses are as follows:

> Hypothesis 1: Perceived managerial intolerance of errors is positively related to the negative emotionality that employees experience regarding self-made errors.
>
> Hypothesis 2: Emotional stability is negatively related to the

negative emotionality that employees experience regarding self-made errors.

Hypothesis 3: Negative emotionality is negatively related to motivation to learn.

Hypothesis 4: Motivation to learn is positively related to learning from errors.

Hypothesis 5: Motivation to learn mediates the effect of negative emotionality on learning from errors.

In this study, Zhao's study hypothesizes that the extent to which employees believe that workplace errors are not acceptable (or the "perceived managerial intolerance of errors") positively contributes to their negative emotionality regarding errors. These negative emotions, defined as fear, guilt and sadness, are speculated to reduce motivation to learn, which is an antecedent of learning from errors. This model also hypothesizes that negative emotions about making errors at work can be effectively regulated by emotionally stable people, who are often aware of their personal strengths and weaknesses, and thus can quickly bounce back from negative emotional experience. Accordingly, to test this model, the researchers designed a managerial task for 127 undergraduate participants to perform in a computer laboratory on campus. Surprisingly, despite the suggestion of general behaviour motivation theory (e.g. Seo et al., 2004) ¬– i.e. that negative emotions can demoralize people and discourage their learning – the study's PLS testing results indicate that employees' negative emotions about making workplace errors in fact increase their motivation to learn. However, it is worth noting that this laboratory simulation is claimed to have failed to establish whether a high level of negative emotions genuinely increases motivation to learn from errors, since participants were limited to undergraduate students. Therefore, conclusions could not be reached on whether extreme negative emotions have an impact on motivation to learn from errors at the workplace.

The study by Zhao (2011), on the impact of negative emotionality on learning from workplace errors, is illustrative of a sound approach to identifying factors that influence learning processes. The authors followed a meticulous procedure, where hypotheses were carefully designed based on measurement concepts by which hypothetical statements were tested. Necessary pre-hypothesis testing steps, including a manipulation check, and tests of the validity and reliability of measures in PLS, were conducted and reported thoroughly using one-way analysis of variance (ANOVA). Then, the data analysis process in PLS was described and discussed in detail, to help readers understand the testing results. The research also included the theoretical implications and the limitations of the study, in order to suggest directions for future research. It is thus important to note that, as in any other disciplines, research on learning factors requires rigorous research methodologies, to enable scholars to reach meaningful conclusions about what truly motivates individuals to learn.

In addition to deliberate practice, age, and emotional stability, researchers have also highlighted other factors that are critical to learning in specific domains or contexts. Talent and individual interests are among such variables. In a popular science book by the psychologist Gary Marcus (2012), called *Guitar Zero: the Science of Becoming Musical at Any Age*, the author acknowledges the role of talent, stating that "it would be a logical error to infer from the importance of practice that talent is somehow irrelevant, as if the two were in mutual opposition". This emphasis on the importance of talent in learning to acquire a musical ability is indeed advocated by numerous other researchers, and the book was in the New York Times Best Seller list for hardcover nonfiction in 2012. More specifically, general intelligence (Hunt, 2011) and working memory capacity (Engle, 2002) are illustrative of specific abilities and traits that can be used to predict learning outcomes and performance in various fields, such as chess (Grabner et al., 2007) and music (Meinz & Hambrick, 2010). Aligned with talent and abilities is the concept of individual interests – this is another important factor that has a close relationship with learning, according to the German philosopher Johann Friedrich Hebart. The term "interest", defined by Hidi (1990) as the "one energetic feature" of the living world, has gained an influence in the literature through many of the most-cited studies in history (e.g. Fransson, 1977; Hidi, 1990), and it still maintain its impact in the most recent research (e.g.

Renninger & Hidi, 2019; Fuseda & Katayama, 2021). Accordingly, despite the claim of insufficient empirical evidence, scholars continue to advocate the major role that interests play in human learning and cognitive functioning.

As mentioned in the previous section of this chapter, the complex interaction between learning at different levels (individual, group, organization) is essential in the literature, because organizational learning indeed cannot take place independently of individual and group learning in organizational operations (Hislop et al., 2018). Recognizing how organizational learning occurs, or which factors facilitate the organizational learning process, is thus crucial; especially when the need to build organizational competitive advantage is compelling. For this reason, the topic of learning in organizations is covered by an extensive literature, in which the "4I learning framework" developed by Crossan et al. (1999) is among the most influential studies. By emphasizing the interrelationship between different levels of learning in organizations, Crossan et al. (1999) filled the prior literature gaps regarding organizational learning. The core concept that was highlighted in this eminent study was the process of strategic renewal, which requires organizations to continually explore and create new knowledge while simultaneously exploiting knowledge that has been acquired. Although the tension between these exploration and exploitation processes in organizational learning had been recognized by March (1991), the study by Crossan et al. (1999) discusses this conflict further by additionally considering how different learning levels in an organization interact and affect each other. The 4I framework of organizational learning developed by these authors refers to four processes – Intuiting, Interpreting, Integrating, and Institutionalizing – that take place across three different levels of learning in organizations: individual, group, and organization.

According to Crossan et al. (1999), intuiting is a learning process that occurs uniquely at individual level, since it is "the pre-conscious recognition of the pattern and/or possibilities inherent in a personal stream of experience" (p. 525). People manage to find new ways of thinking and acting through this mechanism. As intuitions are explained and shared with others by means of conversation, individual or group interpretations are formed. During this interpreting process, people refine their existing cognitive maps and form new ones, as they interact with others and the context in which they function. Accordingly, collective interpretations will lead to a group integration process where shared understanding is formed, which thus encourages meaningful collective action among group members. Finally, at the organizational level, learning takes place via the institutionalizing process, whereby shared interpretations and newly formed actions are fixed into the organizational routines, rules, information systems, strategy, and structure.

Crossan et al. (1999) also propose a feedback–feedforward framework to characterize the dynamic nature of organizational learning. In this framework, whereas feedforward processes facilitate the creation of innovative solutions to help organizations adjust to emergent conditions, feedback stresses the exploitation of knowledge that has been formed through institutionalized learning. Zietsma et al. (2002) later refined the model by placing more emphasis on the importance of feedforward, rather than feedback, as these researchers assert that feedback, in some specific situations, could be harmful to all levels of organizational learning. Feedback can enhance the shared understanding in organizations, yet it might restrict individuals or groups in activating their intuitions if such intuiting does not conform to the collective cognition. In contexts where organizations are facing changes and need to quickly adapt for survival, too much feedback will abolish feedforward processes and accordingly limit organizational adaptability. The refined feedback–feedforward model (see Figure 2-9) has thus been improved with more active processes, namely Attending and Experimenting, added to clarify the feedforward mechanism (see Hislop et al. (2018) for the definition of each process).

FIGURE 2-9

An extended framework for feedforward learning processes

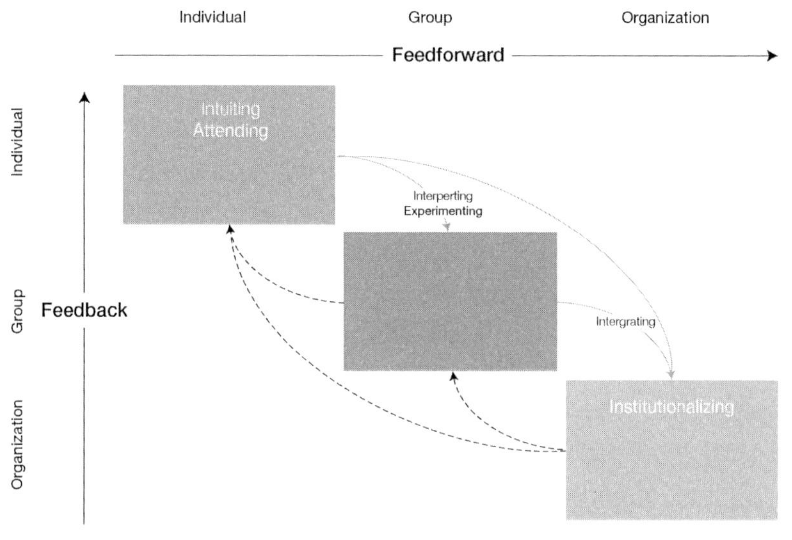

Note. This figure shows the extended framework for feedforward learning processes. Redrawn from "The War of the Woods : Facilitators and Impediments of Organizational Learning Processes", by Zietsma et al., 2002, *British Journal of Management*, 13(2), p. S63 (https://doi.org/10.1111/1467-8551.13.s2.6). Copyright 2002 by John Wiley & Sons, Inc.

In the in-depth longitudinal study by Zietsma et al. (2002), the improved model was examined through a wide range of data sources that related to MacMillan Bloedel (MB), the oldest and largest among forestry companies in British Columbia (Canada). The case study illustrates how a company which had constantly resisted changes for a long time due to its highly institutionalized system finally underwent adaptation and strategic renewal, in order to resolve conflicts with its stakeholders and continue developing sustainably. Accordingly, using the MB case study, the authors of the refined model also identified facilitative and counteractive factors that had an impact on the feedforward processes carried out by this company (see Zietsma et al. (2002) for descriptions of these factors).

In light of the refined theory, an organization can be more flexible in adjusting itself and learning from environmental changes, if feedforward processes such as intuiting and interpreting are informed by alternative perspectives – despite the fact that these viewpoints may appear to be illegitimate and have not been institutionalized. In addition, if new solutions formed through intuiting/attending and interpreting/experiment are officially endorsed by organizational leaders, the integrated learning from individual and group levels is more likely to be institutionalized at organizational level. Nevertheless, the MB case is not an unprecedented example of organizational learning; although the possibility to generalize this case to other fields is limited. There are indeed numerous organizations that undertake learning processes which are conducive to enhanced adaptability and strategic competitive advantage. Such organizations have stimulated research on what constitutes a "learning organization" – a concept that is different from, yet often confused with, organizational learning. Hence, the next section of this chapter will outline characteristics of a learning organization and distinguish this concept from its related term "organizational learning".

2.5. Learning Organization

Although "organizational learning" and "learning organization" are two different concepts, they are closely related to each other. Tsang (1997) simply notes that "a learning organization is one which is good at organizational learning", and that "once the definition of organizational learning is settled, that of the learning organization will follow". Nonetheless, despite being related and sometimes used interchangeably, each of the two concepts generates its own vast literature. This is often because researchers in the "organizational learning" discipline often attempt to answer the key question of how an organization learns, whereas studies focusing on the "learning organization" tend to instruct practitioners on how an organization should learn (Tsang, 1997). As a result, the literature on the "learning organization" appears to place more emphasis on improving organizational learning and its performance, rather than building and testing theories on how organizations learn.

Among the numerous studies on this discipline, the influential book by Peter Senge (1990), titled *The Fifth Discipline: the Art and Practice of the Learning Organization*, is praised by book reviewers as stimulating research that widely spread the "learning organization" concept. The book reveals why top-performing companies survive through difficult times by having transformed themselves into learning organizations, which the author defines as organizations "where people continually expand their capacity to create the results they truly desire, where new and expansive patterns of thinking are nurtured, where collective aspiration is set free, and where people are continually learning how to learn together". In order to create such an organization, the author proposes a framework of five disciplines: Shared Vision, Mental Models, Team Learning, Personal Mastery, and Systems Thinking. The characteristics of these disciplines are summarized in Table 2-3.

TABLE 2-3 Description of the Five Disciplines based on Senge (1990)

Discipline	Description
Shared vision	A vision shared across organizational levels (yet not in a top-down manner), creating employees' commitment and energy for organizational learning.
Mental models	Not only attempting to understand and interpret reality, but also to build the organizational values and the perception of what the organizational mission/business is all about, to be continually stable yet adaptive; how the organizations are aware of who they are, in order to seek ways to progress and develop.
Team learning	The discipline by which personal mastery and shared vision are connected; a discipline that requires dialogue, actual communication among employees who nurture collegiality and supportive relationships; team learning takes place only if individuals are courageous enough to risk adopting new and applicable values.
Personal mastery	"The discipline of continually clarifying and deepening our personal vision, of focusing our energies, of developing patience and of seeing reality objectively." In order to practise personal mastery, individuals need to build their knowledge and skills, so as to clearly understand the reality and make appropriate decisions to move forward confidently.

Systems thinking	The fifth discipline ensures the other four are integrated in a "big picture". Systems thinking is about having a vision that covers the whole system, rather than looking at complex individual issues separately; it also refers to the idea that actions and consequences are correlated over time.

Although they are discussed mostly in business contexts, these five disciplines defined by Senge (1990) have been investigated and applied in various fields. For example, in higher education, where learning does not take place as effectively as it could (Bauman, 2005), the framework has been developed and evaluated by numerous researchers. Specifically, Bui and Baruch (2010) adopted a systems approach, to propose a detailed framework for creating a five-discipline learning organization in the field of higher education. Later in 2011, these authors evaluated their refined model using a sample of 687 employees in the UK and Vietnam, by testing the relationship between the five disciplines and their proposed antecedents and outcomes (see Figure 2-10). Bui and Baruch's hypotheses in this study are as follows:

Hypothesis 1: Personal values, personal vision, motivation, individual learning, and development and training are positively associated with personal mastery.

Hypothesis 2: Organizational commitment, leadership, and organizational culture are positively associated with mental models.

Hypothesis 3: Team commitment, leadership, goal setting, development and training, organizational culture, and individual learning are positively associated with team learning.

Hypothesis 4: Personal vision, personal values, leadership, and organizational culture are positively associated with shared vision.

Hypothesis 5: Competence, leadership, and organizational culture are positively associated with systems thinking.

Hypothesis 6: The five disciplines are positively associated with individual performance, knowledge sharing, self-efficacy, work–life balance, and strategic planning.

Hypothesis 7: (tested via the combination of hypotheses 1 through 6): The five disciplines mediate the relationship between the antecedents and outcomes.

FIGURE 2-10

The Learning Organization model with antecedents and outcomes of the Five Disciplines

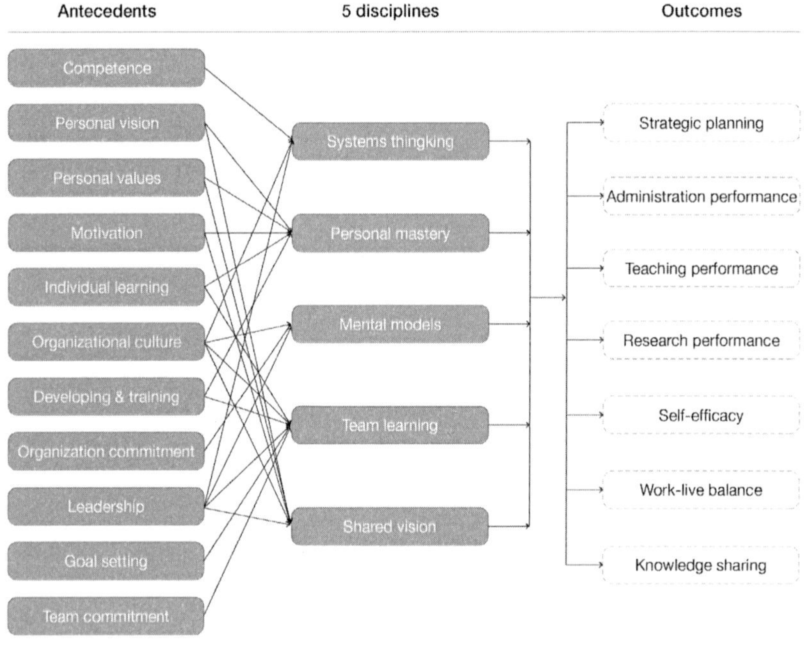

Note. This figure shows the Learning Organization model with antecedents and outcomes of the Five Disciplines. It is redrawn from "Learning Organizations in Higher Education: An Empirical Evaluation within an International Context", by Bui and Baruch, 2011, *Management Learning*, 43(5), p. 518 (https://doi.org/10.1177/1350507611431212). Copyright 2011 by SAGE Publications.

Bui and Baruch (2011) tested their hypothetical model in two universities in Vietnam and the UK, using a large sample with rigorous data analysis methods. The results of this study confirm the hypotheses, and accordingly identify the three antecedents for mental models and systems thinking, four for personal mastery and shared vision, and five for team learning. As most of these antecedents are found within the literature on Human Resource Management (HRM), the study thus points out that HRM practices indeed play a vital role in enabling the organization to become a learning one. Further, this prominent study also reveals that the five disciplines bring out different effects in terms of anticipated outcomes in higher education. Specifically, in the HE context, whereas mental models appear to have a negative influence on research performance, self-efficacy and knowledge sharing, they facilitate organizational strategic planning and the pursuit of work–life balance. It is also noteworthy that team learning can help academic staff to increase teaching quality, and a teamwork-oriented culture fostered by an HE organization will thus be vital to its aim of becoming a genuine learning organization. Finally, yet importantly, this study observes the difference between a collectivist culture (represented by the Vietnamese university) and an individualistic culture (illustrated by the UK university) in terms of the possibility of becoming a learning organization. Accordingly, "a dynamic, interactive, proactive, group-oriented, and accommodating culture" is more advantageous to becoming a learning organization, compared to "a stable, bureaucratic, reactive, individual oriented, and aggressive culture" (Bui & Baruch, 2011).

The study by Bui and Baruch (2011) is among contributions that use sound data collection and rigorous research methodologies to provide empirical evidence for a learning organization model in the HE field. However, not all studies on this concept receive similar recognition. In practical terms, the concept of the "learning organization" has generated various debates and critiques from scholars and practitioners. The nature of the employment relationship and the need to gain more power are often the first areas where a critique of the "learning organization" concept is applied. Hislop et al. (2018) note that while the literature on building a learning organization appears to suggest that an open and democratic work culture is necessary for fostering learning that is conducive to organizational survival and adaptability, scant research explains specifically and practically how managers should be more willing to share their control power with employees in decision making. Similarly, Caldwell (2012) urges that the lack of clearly defined social practices that can realistically form a learning organization based on its utopian theoretical background, is creating increasing doubts and criticism towards the concept. Grieves (2008) even suggests abandoning the concept because it is simply “naively apolitical” (p. 470), and an “impracticable and unobtainable myth” (p. 472). Nevertheless, despite such trenchant criticism, the five-discipline framework by Senge (1990) has been refined numerous times – not only by other researchers, but also by the author himself – and accordingly, it remains influential. Until there is a new theoretical model that can truly reconnect learning and practice, and recommend a new type of leadership that can resolve the political issues caused by the nature of the employment relationship, the five-discipline framework is still a powerful theoretical foundation on which other prominent concepts on organizational learning models can be built (Yeo, 2005).

2.6. Discussion and assignment

2.6.1. Group discussion in classroom

What do you need to prepare to become a leader in near future?

- What are the differences between generations in your country in terms of the economic and social background, learning style, expected roles from social norm, etc. while they were in their 20s and 30s?
- What are the issues or problems in an organization caused by the generation gap?
- How the different generation group harmonize each other in an organization?
- In the context of socio-economic and technological changes, who are the most successful global or nation-wide leaders 20 years ago, 10 years ago, and now?
- How do you expect our society will be like in the next 10 years considering technology, education, working environment, economy, etc?

- What type of person would remain in an obsolete organization? Conversely, what type of person would create a new organization as a leader?
- What and how do we need to learn as a leader during your graduate program as well as after the graduation?

Each group discuss the questions above. You can select the questions as many as possible.

Group Size: 3-5 (depending on the class size and its diversity)

Time: The group discussion is 25 minutes; preparation for the presentation: five minutes; presentation: five minutes; Q&A: five minutes.

Presentation: All group members should contribute to the presentation's group discussion and preparation. The presenter will be randomly selected by the instructor.

2.6.2. Assignment

Suggest influential factors which have been neglected in existing study or a process of learning for enhancing the individual or group learning in the organization you are belonging to. Reviewing the related academic papers on the topics below is required:

- Knowledge transfer
- Learning process
- Factors affecting learning
- The dynamics of organizational learning

Key conceptual words

Post-industrial society, society 5.0, quad helix innovation model, learning, organizational learning, factors affecting learning, learning organization

REFERENCES

Altomonte, C., Aquilante, T. & Ottaviano, G. I. P. (2012). *The Triggers of Competitiveness: The EFIGE Cross-Country Report. Bruegel Blueprint Series* (Issue July).

Baltes, P. B., & Kliegl, R. (1992). Further Testing of Limits of Cognitive Plasticity: Negative Age Differences in a Mnemonic Skill are Robust. *Developmental Psychology*, 28(1), 121–125. https://doi.org/10.1037/0012-1649.28.1.121

Bauman, G. L. (2005). Pronoting Organizational Learning in Higher Education to Achieve Equity in Educational Outcomes. In *New Directions for Higher Education* (Vol. 131, pp. 23–35). Wiley Periodicals. https://doi.org/10.1002/he.184

Bell, D. (1973). *The Coming of Post-Industrial Society*. Penguin.

Bui, H., & Baruch, Y. (2010). Creating Learning Organizations in Higher Education: Applying a Systems Perspective. *Learning Organization*, *17*(3), 228–242. https://doi.org/10.1108/09696471011034928

Bui, H., & Baruch, Y. (2011). Learning Organizations in Higher Education: An Empirical Evaluation within an International Context. *Management Learning*, *43*(5), 515–544. https://doi.org/10.1177/1350507611431212

Burgess, S., Lane, J., & Stevens, D. (2000). Job Flows, Worker Flows, and Churning. *Journal of Labor Economics*, *18*(3), 473–502. https://doi.org/https://doi.org/10.1086/209967

Cabinet Office. (n.d.). *Society 5.0*. Retrieved December 15, 2020, from https://www8.cao.go.jp/cstp/english/society5_0/index.html

Cabinet Office, G. of J. (2015). *Report on The 5th Science and Technology Basic Plan Council for Science , Technology and Innovation Cabinet Office, Government of Japan*. https://doi.org/https://www8.cao.go.jp/cstp/kihonkeikaku/5basicplan_en.pdf

Caldwell, R. (2012). Systems Thinking, Organizational Change and Agency: A Practice Theory Critique of Senge's Learning Organization. *Journal of Change*

Management, 12(2), 145–164. https://doi.org/10.1080/14697017.2011.647923

Carayannis, E. G., & Campbell, D. F. J. (2009). "Mode 3" and "Quadruple Helix": Toward a 21st century Fractal Innovation Ecosystem. I*nternational Journal of Technology Management*, 46(3–4), 201–234. https://doi.org/10.1504/ijtm.2009.023374

Chen, Y., Lv, C., Li, X., Zhang, J., Chen, K., Liu, Z., Li, H., Fan, J., Qin, T., Luo, L., & Zhang, Z. (2019). The Positive Impact of Early-life Education on Cognition, Leisure Activity, and Brain Structure in Healthy Aging. *Aging*, 11(14), 4923–4942.

Cook, S D Noam, & Yanow, D. (1993). Culture and Organizational Learning. *Journal of Management Inquiry*, 20(4), 355–372. https://doi.org/10.1177/105649269324010

Cook, Scott D N, & Seely, J. (2014). Bridging Epistemologies: The Generative Dance Between Organizational Knowledge and Organizational Knowing. *Organization Science*, 10(4), 381–400. https://doi.org/10.1287/orsc.10.4.381

Crossan, M., Lane, H. W., & White, R. E. (1999). An Organization Learning Framework : From Intuition to Institution. *The Academy of Management Review*, 24(3), 522–537. https://doi.org/10.2307/259140

Cummings, T. G., & Worley, C. G. (2009). *Organization Development and Change*. Cengage Learning.

Drucker, P. F. (1981). *Behind Japan's Success*. Harvard Business Review. https://hbr.org/1981/01/behind-japans-success

Ehlers, U.-D. (2020). *Future Skills: Future Learning, Future Higher Education*. Springer.

Engle, R. W. (2002). Working memory capacity as executive attention. *Current Directions in Psychological Science*, 11(1), 19–23. https://doi.org/10.1111/1467-8721.00160

Ericsson, K. A., Krampe, R. T., & Tesch-Römer, C. (1993). The Role of Deliberate Practice in the Acquisition of Expert Performance. *Psychological Review*, 100(3), 363–406. https://doi.org/10.1037/0033-295x.100.3.363

Erwee, R., Harmes, M. K., Harmes, M. A., Danaher, P. A., & Padro, F. F. (Eds.). (2018). *Postgraduate Education in Higher Education*. Springer Nature Singapore.

https://doi.org/https://doi.org/10.1007/978-981-10-5249-1

Etzkowitz, H. (2008). *The Triple Helix: University-Industry-Government Innovation in Action* (1st editio). Routledge.

Etzkowitz, H., & Leydesdorff, L. (1995). The Triple Helix---University-Industry-Government Relations: A Laboratory for Knowledge Based Economic Development. *EASST Review*, 14(1), 14–19.

Fiol, C. M., & Lyles, M. A. (1985). Organizational Learning. *Academy of Management, 10*(4), 803–813.

Fransson, A. (1977). On Qualitative Differences in Learning: IV-Effects of Intrinsic Motivation and Extrinsic Test Anxiety on Process and Outcome. *British Journal of Educational Psychology*, 47(3), 244–257. https://doi.org/https://doi.org/10.1111/j.2044-8279.1977.tb02353.x

Fukuyama, M. (2018). Society 5.0: Aiming for a New Human-centered Society. *Japan SPOTLIGHT, 27*(August), 47–50. http://www8.cao.go.jp/cstp/%0Ahttp://search.ebscohost.com/login.aspx?direct=true&db=bth&AN=108487927&site=ehost-live

Fuseda, K., & Katayama, J. (2021). A New Technique to Measure the Level of Interest Using Heartbeat-Evoked Brain Potential. *Journal of Psychophysiology, 35*(1), 15–22. https://doi.org/https://doi.org/10.1027/0269-8803/a000257

Gallagher, S. R. (2016). *The Future of University Credentials: New Developments at the Intersection of Higher Education and Hiring*. Harvard Education Press.

Goldin, C., & Katz, L. F. (2009). *The Race between Education and Technology*. Harvard University Press.

Grabner, R. H., Stern, E., & Neubauer, A. C. (2007). Individual Differences in Chess Expertise: A Psychometric Investigation. *Acta Psychologica*, 124(3), 398–420. https://doi.org/10.1016/j.actpsy.2006.07.008

Grieves, J. (2008). Why we Should Abandon the Idea of the Learning Organization. *The Learning Organization, 15*(6), 463–473. https://doi.org/10.1108/09696470810907374

Hambrick, D. Z., Oswald, F. L., Altmann, E. M., Meinz, E. J., Gobet, F., & Campitelli, G. (2014). Deliberate Practice: Is that all it takes to Become an Expert? *Intelligence, 45*(1), 34–45. https://doi.org/10.1016/j.intell.2013.04.001

Hensellek, S. (2020). Digital Leadership: A Framework for Successful Leadership in the Digital Age. *Journal of Media Management and Entreneurship*. https://doi.org/10.4018/JMME.2020010104

Hidi, S. (1990). Interest and Its Contribution as a Mental Resource for Learning. *Review of Educational Research, 60*(4), 549–571.

Hislop, D., Bosua, R., & Helms, R. (2018). *Knowledge Management in Organizations: A Critical Introduction* (Fourth Edi). Oxford University Press. https://learninglink.oup.com/access/knowledge-management-in-organizations-a-critical-introduction-4e-lecturer-resources#tag_classroom-activities

Huber, G. P. (1991). Organizational Learning : The Contributing Processes and the Literatures. *Organization Science, 2*(1), 88–115. https://doi.org/10.1287/orsc.2.1.88

Hunt, E. (2011). *Human Intelligence*. Cambridge University Press.

Kane, G. C. (2018). *Common Traits of the Best Digital Leaders*. MIT Sloan Management Review. https://sloanreview.mit.edu/article/common-traits-of-the-best-digital-leaders/

Kimatu, J. N. (2015). Evolution of Strategic Interactions from the Triple to Quad Helix Innovation Models for Sustainable Development in the Era of Globalization. *Journal of Innovation and Entrepreneurship*, 5(1), 0–6. https://doi.org/10.1186/s13731-016-0044-x

Lee, G. K., Lampel, J., & Shapira, Z. (2020). After the Storm Has Passed: Translating Crisis Experience into Useful Knowledge. *Organization Science*, 31(4), 1037–1051. https://doi.org/10.1287/orsc.2020.1366

Levitt, B., & March, J. G. (1988). Organizational Learning. *Annual Review of Sociology*, 14, 319–338. https://doi.org/https://www.annualreviews.org/doi/abs/10.1146/annurev.so.14.080188.001535

Macnamara, B. N., Hambrick, D. Z., & Oswald, F. L. (2014). Deliberate Practice and Performance in Music, Games, Sports, Education, and Professions: A Meta-Analysis. *Psychological Science*, 25(8), 1608–1618. https://doi.org/10.1177/0956797614535810

March, J. G. (1991). Exploration and Exploitation in Organizational Learning. *Organization Science*, 2(1), 71–87.

Marcus, G. (2012). *Guitar Zero: The Science of Becoming Musical at Any Age*. Penguin

Books.

Meinz, E. J., & Hambrick, D. Z. (2010). Deliberate Practice is Necessary but Not Sufficient to Explain Individual Differences in Piano Sight-Reading Skill: The Role of Working Memory Capacity. *Psychological Science, 21*(7), 914–919. https://doi.org/https://journals.sagepub.com/doi/10.1177/0956797610373933

Mitsuhiko, I. (2010). *Postwar Japanese Economy: Lessons of Economic Growth and the Bubble Economy*. Springer-Verlag New York. https://doi.org/10.1007/978-1-4419-6332-1

Namada, J. (2018). Organizational Learning and Competitive Advantage. In *Handbook of Research on Knowledge Management for Contemporary Business Environments* (pp. 86–104). IGI Global. https://doi.org/10.4018/978-1-5225-3725-0.ch006

Nonaka, I., & Takeuchi, H. (1995). *The Knowledge-Creating Company: How Japanese Companies Create the Dynamics of Innovation*. Oxford University Press.

Oberer, B., & Erkollar, A. (2018). Leadership 4.0: Digital Leaders in the Age of Industry 4.0. *International Journal of Organizational Leadership*, 7(4), 404–412. https://doi.org/10.33844/ijol.2018.60332

Organisation for Economic Cooperation and Development (OECD). (2015). ISCED 2011 Operational Manual: Guidelines for Classifying National Education Programmes and Related Qualifications. In *ISCED 2011 Operational Manual*. European Union. https://doi.org/10.1787/9789264228368-en

Otsubo, S. T. (2007). *Post - war Development of the Japanese Economy* (Issue April, pp. 1–73). Nagoya University. https://www.gsid.nagoya-u.ac.jp/sotsubo/Postwar_Development_of_the_Japanese Economy(Otsubo_NagoyaU).pdf

Promsri, C. (2019). Developing Model of Digital Leadership for a Successful Digital Transformation. *International Journal of Business Management, 2*(8), 1–8. http://gphjournal.org/index.php/bm/article/view/249

Razmerita, L., Kirchner, K., Nabeth, T., & Platforms, S. (2014). Social Media in Organizations : Leveraging Personal and Collective Knowledge Processes. *Journal of Organizational Computing and Electronic Commerce*, 24(1), 74–93. https://doi.org/10.1080/10919392.2014.866504

Renninger, K. A., & Hidi, S. E. (2019). Interest Development and Learning. In *The Cambridge Handbook of Motivation and Learning* (pp. 265–290). Cambridge

University Press. https://doi.org/10.1017/9781316823279.013

Senge, P. M. (1990). *The Fifth Discipline: The Art and Practice of the Learning Organization*. Currency Doubleday.

Seo, M., Barrett, L. F., & Bartunek, J. M. (2004). The Role of Affective Experience in Work Motivation. *The Academy of Management Review*, 29(3), 423–439. https://doi.org/10.2307/20159052

Sheth, J. (2020). Impact of Covid-19 on Consumer Behavior: Will the Old Habits Return or Die? *Journal of Business Research, 117*, 280–283. https://doi.org/10.1016/j.jbusres.2020.05.059

Shrestha, N., Shad, M. Y., Ulvi, O., Khan, M. H., Karamehic-Muratovic, A., Nguyen, U. S. D. T., Baghbanzadeh, M., Wardrup, R., Aghamohammadi, N., Cervantes, D., Nahiduzzaman, K. M., Zaki, R. A., & Haque, U. (2020). The Impact of COVID-19 on Globalization. *One Health*, xxxx, 100180. https://doi.org/10.1016/j.onehlt.2020.100180

Smith, E. A. (2001). The Role of Tacit and Explicit Knowledge in the Workplace. *Journal of Knowledge Management*, 5(4), 311–321.

Spender, J.-C. (1996). Organizational Knowledge, Learning and Memory: Three Concepts in Search of a Theory. *Journal of Organizational Change Management*, 9(1), 63–78. https://doi.org/10.1108/09534819610156813

Stafford, T., & Dewar, M. (2014). Tracing the Trajectory of Skill Learning with a very Large Sample of Online Game Players. *Psychological Science*, 25(2), 511–518. https://doi.org/10.1177/0956797613511466

Sung, T. K. (2018). Industry 4.0: Korea Perspective. *Technological Forecasting and Social Change*, 132, 40–45.

Swieringa, J., & Wierdsma, A. (1992). *Becoming a Learning Organization*. Addison-Wesley Longman Ltd.

Tsang, E. W. K. (1997). Organizational Learning and the Learning Organization: A Dichotomy Between Descriptive and Prescriptive Research. *Human Relations*, 50(1), 73–89.

Vaittinen, I. (n.d.). *Guidelines for Living Labs in Climate Services*. Retrieved December 14, 2020, from http://eu-macs.eu/outputs/livinglabs/

Vince, R. (2014). Power and Emotion in Organizational Learning. *Human Relations*,

54(10), 1325–1351. https://doi.org/10.1177/00187267015410004

Yeo, R. K. (2005). Revisiting the Roots of Learning Organization: a Synthesis of the Learning Organization Literature. *The Learning Organization*, 12(4), 368–382.

Zhao, B. (2011). Learning from Errors : The Role of Context , Emotion , and Personality. *Journal of Organizational Behavior, 32*(3), 435–463. https://doi.org/10.1002/job

Zietsma, C., Winn, M., Branzei, O., & Vertinsky, I. (2002). The War of the Woods : Facilitators and Impediments of Organizational Learning Processes. *British Journal of Management, 13*(2), S61–S74.

CHAPTER 03

Topic 2 Flow and creativity

Topic 2

Flow and creativity

Thao Thanh Luong and Eunyoung Kim

This chapter introduces flow theory by Csikszentmihalyi (1990). By presenting the conditions that foster flow status, it encourages personal reflection upon moments where the quality of daily-life experience could be enhanced to a greater level, leading to growth and discovery. The positive relationship between flow and creativity is also discussed, revealing how flow contributes to human beings' creative moments.

3.1. Flow theory

Of all positive psychology's major concepts, "happiness" is a term that throughout history has been revisited by countless scholars. The great philosopher, Aristotle, in his influential work titled, "Nicomachean Ethics," posited that happiness is "the end of human concerns" (Aristotle et al., 2012, p. 221); in other words, people have an everlasting aspiration for happiness.

This prominent perspective on the nature of happiness has stimulated ceaseless academic interest in defining this term. Nevertheless, although vast literature on the concept of happiness exists, people are still wondering why they are not equally happy at any time, not even when they are in similar contexts. Enthralled by this question, Dutch psychologist Ruut Veenhoven, "the godfather of happiness studies" (Weiner, 2008), in 1984 published the book *Data-Book of Happiness*, which summarizes hundreds of empirical studies on factors that promote happiness in various contextual conditions and during the period between 1911 and 1975. This work redefined the meaning of happiness as an ultimate goal for public policy. Accordingly, this renowned author argues that happiness can be used as a reliable measure for evaluating societal development.

Similarly, yet more recently, Michael Argyle, one of the best-known English social psychologists of the 20th century, provided a thorough and up-to-date account of research about the nature of happiness via his book *The Psychology of Happiness* (Argyle, 2001). This study, by employing research from various disciplines such as sociology, physiology, economics, and psychology, brought up remarkable conclusions about what genuinely constructs human beings' positive and negative emotions.

Another integrative and comprehensive collection of significant research on happiness is the volume *Subjective Well-being: An Interdisciplinary Perspective* by Strack et al. (1991), which aims to document all the disparate perspectives on the status of subjective well-being. Despite the divergent viewpoints about this common topic, this volume sought ways to foster interaction and communication between numerous disciplines that are involved in constructing the concept of happiness.

Given all the comprehensive definitions and sophisticated measurements for happiness, this term remains controversial among different people and nations. It is worth noting that in Aristotle's previously mentioned work, *Nicomachean Ethics*, this philosopher pointed out an incontrovertible view about happiness:

> ...honor, pleasure, intellect, and every virtue we choose on their own account – for even if nothing resulted from them, we would choose each of them – but we choose them also for the sake of happiness, because we suppose that, through them, we will be happy. But

> nobody chooses happiness for the sake of these things, or, more generally, on account of anything else. (Aristotle et al., 2012, p. 11)

People in the modern era, just like in Aristotle's time, continually search for ways that lead to happiness. Some believe that happiness means joy and satisfaction, occasionally caused by external and instinctual factors such as social contacts, sexual activity, and success (Argyle & Martin, 1991). In contrast, some seek happiness in inner moments where they are indulging in daily-life activities.

This book's chapter, however, does not attempt to present the inactive or lazing-around paths to happiness. Rather, it aims at introducing a theory on how human beings can proactively improve the quality of their experiences in almost every daily-life activity. This influential theory was recognized and named "the flow status" by Mihaly Csikszentmihalyi; he is one of the world's leading researchers in positive psychology and whose works on happiness and creativity have been intriguing to numerous modern psychologists. By focusing on the literature about flow theory, this chapter is expected to encourage individuals to strive for living up to their potential and reflect on such rewarding and enjoyable experiences.

According to Csikszentmihalyi (1990), happiness "is a condition that must be prepared for, cultivated, and defended privately by each person." (p. 2) In other words, happiness depends on whether a person can control his or her consciousness and thereby can determine the quality of life experiences. Specifically, Csikszentmihalyi (1990) refers to the *optimal experience*, when one intrinsically and enjoyably experiences total control over his or her life. The *optimal experience* might occur during exhilarating moments, which are illustrated by the author as:

> It is what the sailor holding a tight course feels when the wind whips through her hair, when the boat lunges through the waves like a colt – sails, hull, wind, and sea humming a harmony that vibrates in the sailor's vein. It is what a painter feels when the colors on the canvas begin to set up a magnetic tension with each other, and a new thing,

> a living form, takes shape in front of the astonished creator. Or it is the feeling of a father has when his child for the first time responds to his smiles. (p. 3)

Nevertheless, such experiences do not take place just in exquisite contexts. Csikszentmihalyi (1990) also noted that life moments of extreme hardship may also bring on "extraordinarily rich epiphanies;" although such revelations may take place in the form of the most modest actions, such as "hearing the song of a bird in the forest, completing a hard task, or sharing a crust of bread with a friend." (p. 3) Accordingly, in either advantageous or adverse situations, the *optimal experience* must be actively created through human beings' substantial efforts to achieve something genuinely challenging yet rewarding. It also brings people the status of being mentally efficient, highly inspired, or contented all at the same time (Engeser & Schiepe-Tiska, 2012).

To develop his theory on what causes the optimal experience, Csikszentmihalyi (1990) has based on the concept of flow. Initially, this psychologist was amazed by how artists had concentrated so persistently on creating their artworks that they had forgotten about their hunger or tiredness. Since then, Csikszentmihalyi has developed his research about *flow* to understand this phenomenon (Nakamura & Csikszentmihalyi, 2014). Later, in his best-seller book on the concept of flow and the psychology of optimal experience, the author defined flow as "the state in which people are so involved in an activity that nothing else seems to matter" (Csikszentmihalyi, 1990, p. 4).

From this perspective, *flow* can be achieved as one manages to control his or her inner life, specifically when one's *psychic energy*, or attention, is entirely devoted to a particular goal that he or she forgets anything else that is happening in the surrounding environment. When a person is in the *flow* status, his or her skills match the perceived challenges of a particular activity. As this activity becomes more challenging, it encourages the person to spare more effort to advance his or her skills to a higher level. For this reason, *flow* leads to human growth and discovery, just as how an artist, after moments of indulging himself in creating his or her artworks, has grown into a complex being and can produce masterpieces.

Although Mihaly Csikszentmihalyi is best known as the architect of the ideas on *flow*, the history of positive psychology demonstrates that this notion has numerous eminent theoretical precursors. Engeser and Schiepe-Tiska (2012) have listed these studies and their key terms associated with the concept of *flow*. A summary of each work is provided in Table 3-1 below.

TABLE 3-1 Theoretical precursors of flow theory, based on Engeser and Schiepe-Tiska (2012)

Studies	Key Terms	Description(s)
Piaget (1951) Caillois (1958)	*Play*	*Play* pleases people through processes of stretching, exploring limits, seeking new experiences or risks, and reshaping consciousness.
Groos (1899) Bühler (1922)	*Funktionslust*	Feelings of pleasure (or "*lust*") are intrinsically rewarding and can be achieved when an individual "functions" effectively.
Hebb (1955) Berlyne (1960)	*Optimal Stimulation*	An appropriate level of stimuli is vital for constructing intrinsically motivated behavior. An optimal degree of stimulation is sought by animals and human beings. Novel stimuli can lead to enjoyable sensations. However, too much novelty causes anxiety, whereas too little leads to searching for more stimulation.
White (1959)	*Competence*	The concept of "effectance" motivation in coping with environmental changes is introduced. Accordingly, as individuals enjoy creating effects on the environment, they also develop their learning and competencies. Such new developments lead to enjoyable and rewarding feelings of efficacy or competence.

DeCharms (1968)	*Personal Causation*	The state of being free ("Origin") and the state of being under someone else's control ("Pawn") were compared. An Origin is a person who perceived his/her behavior as determined by his/her choosing; a Pawn is a person who perceives his/her behavior as determined by external forces beyond his/her control. From this perspective, the feeling of being free, or being the origin of one's action, is essential to one's enjoyment.
Maslow (1968)	*Peak Experience*	*Peak experience* refers to the feeling of being one whole and harmonious self, free of dissociation or inner conflict. A *peak experience* takes place during a person's loss of awareness of time and space, as he or she is in total control of his or her perceptions and behaviors. No fear, doubt, hindrance, or self-criticism exists during moments of *peak experiences*. The result is a free, open, and creative mind.

Flow theory, despite being based on a large body of research about positive psychology and human intrinsic motivation, has numerous distinct characteristics. Csikszentmihalyi's (1975) early book to introduce flow theory listed six components of flow status. In later works, other researchers and Csikszentmihalyi revised and added more elements of flow, yet with only slight changes. The primary ones constructed by Csikszentmihalyi (1975) still maintain their influence on recent research and are explained as follows:

(1) *Merging of action and awareness* (p. 39): when experiencing an activity with a flow status, a person is aware of the activity but not of the awareness itself;

(2) *Centering of attention* (p. 40): an intense concentration on doing the activity that nothing else can cause a distraction;

(3) *Loss of self-consciousness* (p. 44): when in flow status, one seems

to forget him/herself and experience what is called "the loss of ego";
(4) *The feeling of control* (p. 44): a person in flow status feels that he or she has full control over his or her actions during the activity, with confidence in being able to deal with the situation or what will come next during the activity;
(5) *Coherent, noncontradictory of demands* (p. 46): there are clear and consistent goals to achieve, as well as unambiguous and logically arranged ways to reach these goals;
(6) *Autotelic nature* (p. 47): Without the need to have extrinsic rewards, there is an intrinsic motivation for experiencing the activity. In other words, joy and satisfaction come from doing the activity.

The last component, often referred to as "autotelic experience," is a noticeable feature of the flow status. The word "autotelic" consists of two Greek roots: auto (self) and telos (goal), which means that people do an autotelic activity for the sake of the activity itself. The reason is that the experience gained while doing such an activity is the primary goal, rather than the possible extrinsic rewards obtained from completing the activity (Csikszentmihalyi et al., 2014; Hallowell, 2002; Heutte et al., 2016; Nakamura & Csikszentmihalyi, 2002).

This description of the autotelic experience may lead to an assumption that only entertainment activities, such as play or games, with their intrinsic nature, could contribute to achieving the flow status. However, "such an assumption is not necessary for flow" (Csikszentmihalyi, 1975, p. 36). Essentially, autotelic moments, despite being relatively rare, can happen during any daily activity. Even jobs requiring special, advanced skills, such as surgery, which offer reputation and monetary rewards, can also lead to the flow status (Csikszentmihalyi, 1990).

This chapter's next section, by describing conditions that foster the mental state, presents why flow can be experienced in any activity. These include *a clear set of goals, a balance between perceived challenges and perceived skills, clear and immediate feedback, culture, and having an autotelic personality*. An overview of the primary methods that have been established in past research to measure flow will also be introduced.

3.2. Conditions for flow experience

For people to achieve flow status, three salient conditions are required (Csikszentmihalyi et al., 2014).

Having *a clear set of goals* during an activity is necessary. Although these goals provide guidance and purpose for completing the activity, attaining them is not central to achieving the flow status. Rather, such goals are more conducive to the process of directing the attention, or psychic energy, that is required for attaining flow while engaging in the activity.

The second condition for flow is *a balance between perceived challenges and perceived skills*. According to Csikszentmihalyi (1990), the challenges and skills involved in an activity are the two most critical dimensions of the flow experience. As necessary conditions for flow, the attained levels of these dimensions have to be subjectively perceived by the person who is immersing in the activity rather than being objectively evaluated, as was defined in the concept of "optimal arousal" (Berlyne, 1960).

While engaging in the activity, if one's perceived challenges and skills are evenly matched, his or her psychic energy can be captivated and flow status will be experienced accordingly. Nevertheless, according to Csikszentmihalyi et al. (2014), the balance between these two dimensions is "intrinsically fragile" (p. 232). As the balance is lost due to an excess of perceived challenges or skills, the status will then quickly become switched to either being anxious (when extreme challenges cause the lack of necessary skills to continue performing the activity) or being bored (as the activity becomes effortless and thus requires limited skills).

Specifically, as shown in Figure 3-1, various mental states that are incurred by an imbalance between perceived challenges (vertical axis) and perceived skills (horizontal axis) were depicted by Csikszentmihalyi (1997). It is noteworthy that while performing an activity, if one negatively perceives him or herself as being apathetic (low challenge – low skill level), bored (low challenge – medium skill level), worried (medium challenge – low skill level), or anxious (high challenge – low skill level), he or she is then not likely to achieve the flow status.

More positive psychological modes that could be experimented to reach toward flow status are arousal (high challenge – medium skill level), being in control (medium challenge – high skill level), or relaxation (low challenge – high skill level). It is also underscored in Figure 3-1 that the apathy status, which Goldberg et al. (2011) describe as "a neuropsychiatric syndrome of primary motivational loss" (p. 650), is in the opposite zone with the flow experience. Therefore, to avoid this adverse psychological state and be closer to the flow zone, it is essential to shift both the perceived challenges and skills in doing a particular activity to higher levels.

FIGURE 3-1

Mental states in accordance with the levels of perceived challenges and skills in an activity (Csikszentmihalyi, 1997)

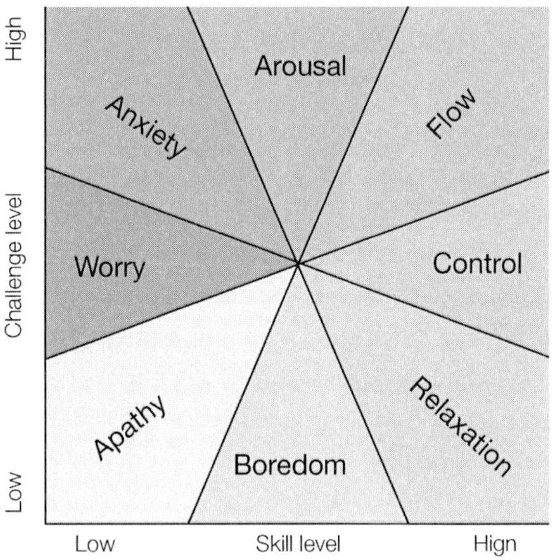

Note: This figure shows different mental states, in accordance with levels of perceived challenges and skills in an activity, as proposed by Csikszentmihalyi (1997). From *Challenge vs Skill* (2017) (https://en.wikipedia.org/wiki/File:Challenge_vs_skill.svg). In the public domain.

To effectively upgrade the level of one's perceived challenges and skills in doing an activity, the third fundamental condition is *clear and immediate feedback*. Being *clear* means that the feedback needs to be specific and constructive to support one in recognizing how effectively he or she is proceeding with the activity. Kiili (2005) stresses that the "reflective observation" of clear and appropriate feedback may help one to have a better understanding of how to perform an activity more creatively and productively (p. 19). Being *immediate* suggests that feedback needs to be continuously given to help the individual stay focused. If one has to repeatedly wait for feedback, he or she can have difficulty knowing what effect the action has created and thus would become distracted.

In a study about adopting flow theory for the design of game-based learning experiences, Kiili et al. (2012) warn that "the delayed feedback may create interpretation problems and in the worst-case even lead to misconceptions and negative learning transfer" (p. 82). Such unfavorable circumstances will hinder people in their efforts to experience the flow state. Therefore, *clear and immediate feedback* plays a crucial role in fostering flow's optimal conditions.

The enormous literature on flow theory suggests that all three conditions (*clear goals, a balance between perceived challenges and perceived skills, and clear and immediate feedback*) are essential for the formulation of various flow components that are mentioned in this chapter's previous section.

Landhäußer and Keller (2012) graphically summarize these flow conditions and components in Figure 3-2. In this diagram, several consequences of flow experience are also introduced. Csikszentmihalyi and Hunter (2014) have posited that such positive effects on emotions, cognition, physiological development, and performance quality will lead to more happiness in everyday life.

FIGURE 3-2

Preconditions, components, and consequences of the flow experience (Landhäußer & Keller, 2012)

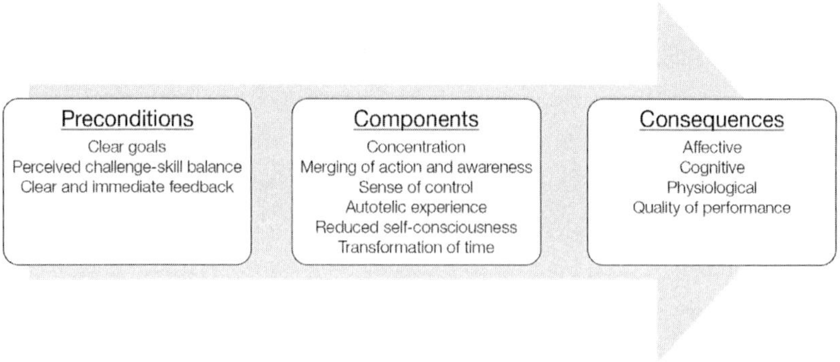

Preconditions
Clear goals
Perceived challenge-skill balance
Clear and immediate feedback

Components
Concentration
Merging of action and awareness
Sense of control
Autotelic experience
Reduced self-consciousness
Transformation of time

Consequences
Affective
Cognitive
Physiological
Quality of performance

Note. This figure is redrawn from "Flow and Its Affective, Cognitive, and Performance-Related Consequences," by Landhäußer and Keller (2012). *Advances in Flow Research*, p. 68 (https://doi.org/10.1007/978-1-4614-2359-1_4). Copyright 2012 by Springer Science + Business Media, LLC.

In addition to the three aforementioned conditions, past research suggests that several other factors influence the degree to which people achieve the flow status. Two conditions often mentioned by researchers are *culture* and the *autotelic personality*. In his best-seller book, Csikszentmihalyi (1990) places great emphasis on the importance of culture in creating an environment that is conducive to the flow experience.

To illustrate this perspective, he mentions the *Athenian polis*, the Roman law, or the "divinely-grounded bureaucracy of China," as examples of how a culture was thriving at establishing a forceful and persuasive set of goals and values that matched well with the skills of the people at that time. Respectively, the Athenian citizens and Romans who molded their lives into *virtus* principles, or the Chinese intellectuals who had acquired their wisdom and joy from attempting to persistently pursue the harmony of their actions, were people who had experienced the flow of psychology by virtue of the cultures that were formed during earlier times.

Nevertheless, it should be noted that in Csikszentmihalyi's (1990) original concept of flow, moral principles are not essentially a precondition for the flow experience. The rules of Sparta, the Tatar Hordes, the Turkish Janissaries, and the Nazi-fascists are illustrative of cultures that generated joy from the challenges of winning battles. In such "needlessly cruel" cultures (Csikszentmihalyi, 1990, p. 81), clear goals, obvious feedback, increasing demands, and skills development were involved for the flow states to be achieved.

Recent studies, such as Thatcher et al. (2008) and Schüler (2012) address the ethical issues associated with the flow experience. Accordingly, although flow is a hedonic mental state, in some circumstances, it goes against the ethical and moral values that humans embrace. Thus, it is necessary to determine which activities people should engage in to seek flow and enhance their quality of life experiences, while instilling moral values into human life. Without a doubt, the dark sides of flow should be further studied to provide sufficient theoretical, empirical, and practical attention (Schüler, 2012).

The last condition that fosters flow, introduced earlier in this chapter, is the *autotelic personality*, which, according to Csikszentmihalyi (1990), could be shaped by a combination of "biological inheritance," "early upbringing," and the efforts needed to acquire and sharpen skills (p. 93). In other words, although this kind of personality could be an innate quality, it could also be fostered by environmental conditions (Moneta, 2012b) or through diligent exertion required for building skills (Csikszentmihalyi, 1990). Autotelic people are those who are often inclined to enjoy life (Nakamura & Csikszentmihalyi, 2014), or "generally do things for their own sake, rather than to achieve some later external goal" (Csikszentmihalyi, 1997, p. 117). This personality type is characterized by the components of *meta-skills* or competencies that enable one to generate curiosity, affection for life, persistence, and low self-centeredness (Nakamura & Csikszentmihalyi, 2014). Autotelic people thus tend to be capable of managing and enjoying a balance between the pleasure of overcoming the challenge and the efforts put into skill development (Telążka, 2015).

On the contrary, people with a non-autotelic personality, referred to as *schizophrenics* or *anhedonia*, are often incompetent to achieve the flow experience due to their insufficient interest in pleasure. The *schizophrenic's* tragedy is generally incurred by the loss of concentration that is due to "attending indiscriminately to everything," and these patients thus fail to enjoy any life activity (Csikszentmihalyi, 1990, p. 84). In addition to the inability to concentrate, excessive self-consciousness also leads to failure to seek joy (Csikszentmihalyi, 1990). A person with a high degree of self-consciousness regularly pays much attention to how he or she is perceived or judged by other people. Accordingly, such concern leads to the inability to enjoy life activities, as the fear of taking risks outweighs the enjoyment of taking up a challenge. Another disadvantageous trait of a non-autotelic personality is self-centeredness. Although self-consciousness and self-centeredness are different, both hamper efforts to experience flow. Self-centered people think only about themselves and not about others' needs or feelings and tend to be more aggressive (Dean & Malamuth, 1997). Such aggression and illusion about oneself are significant barriers to forming new knowledge and skills and thereby experiencing flow.

In essence, to experience flow, people with an innate, autotelic personality have more advantages than those who struggle with mental disorders or character issues that significantly prevent them from achieving the flow status. Yet, without a diligent effort to control consciousness and self-centeredness, an inherent autotelic character does not guarantee that one will experience flow (Csikszentmihalyi, 1990).

The next section discusses how to measure flow. Although the flow's core concepts and conditions mentioned above have not changed since being first introduced by Csikszentmihalyi (1975), various measurement methods and their respective modified models of flow have been established in past research. Indeed, Moneta (2012a) stresses that different methods to measure flow have led to the "corroborations and disconfirmations" of the revised flow models (p. 23). Thus, this author suggests that future research should focus on integrating, standardizing, and developing the existing methods so that the definition for flow state and its model can be consistent.

There are three primary methods for measuring flow that were constructed in previous studies: the *Flow Questionnaire* (FQ), *Experience Sampling Method* (ESM), and the *standardized scales of the componential approach*.

The FQ was first built and used by Csikszentmihalyi and Csikszentmihalyi (1988). It was developed from the interviews conducted by Csikszentmihalyi (1975) when he constructed his original flow model (see Figure 3-3). This questionnaire is embedded with a richly written depiction of the flow status in numerous human-life areas. In the FQ, the flow experience is characterized in detail to help respondents recognize the level to which they achieve the status. The FQ can be combined with the Flow Scale (Mayers, 1978), which reveals the estimation of the frequency a person experiences flow dimensions.

FIGURE 3-3

The first model of flow state by Csikszentmihalyi (1975)

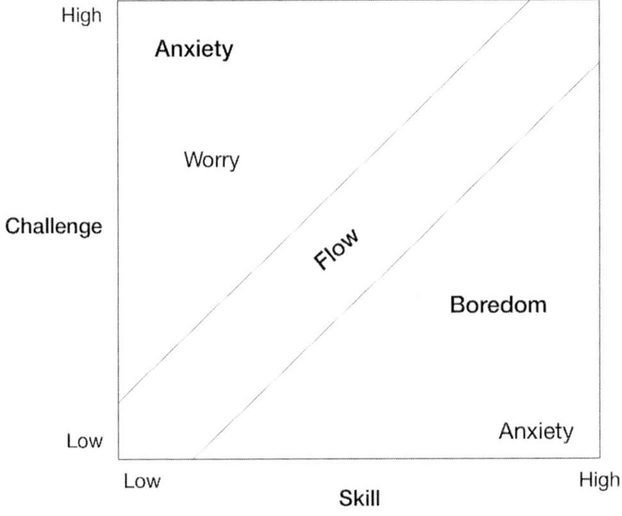

Note: This figure is redrawn from *Beyond Boredom and Anxiety: Experiencing Flow in Work and Play*, by Csikszentmihalyi, 1975, Jossey-Bass.

The second measurement method, ESM, was developed by researchers in the 1970s and is often used for capturing flow in daily experience. This method was conducted to construct three modified models of flow theory. These are the Quadrant Model (Csikszentmihalyi & LeFevre, 1989) (Figure 3-4), the Experience Fluctuation Model (Massimini et al., 1987) (Figure 3-1), and the Regression Modeling Approach (see. e.g., Moneta & Csikszentmihalyi, 1996). The description of each model, its strengths, and its weaknesses are thoroughly reviewed in the study by Moneta (2012a).

FIGURE 3-4

The Quadrant Model of the flow state (Csikszentmihalyi & LeFevre, 1989)

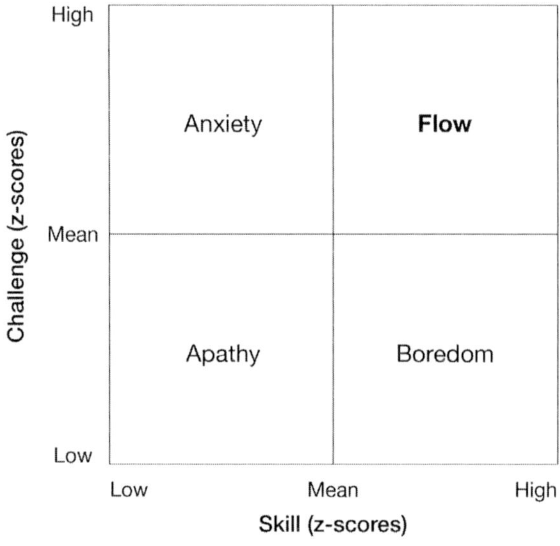

Note. Adapted from "Optimal Experience in Work and Leisure," by Csikszentmihalyi & LeFevre (1989). *Journal of Personality and Social Psychology, 56*(5) (https://doi.org/10.1037/0022-3514.56.5.815).

Nakamura and Csikszentmihalyi (2014) note that ESM's development has paved the path for significant progress in research about flow. According to this method, participants are equipped with a device such as a pager, programmed watch, or handheld computer. This equipment requires the subjects to, at the pre-programmed times, respond to a questionnaire and describe that moment.

Accordingly, the ESM can be conducted based on a random sampling of everyday life activities. Its original form collected eight self-reports per day, according to the random signals from the pagers worn by the participants.

After each signal, the subjects complete the Experience Sampling Form (ESF), which comprises 13 categorical items and 29 scaled items (Larson & Csikszentmihalyi, 2014). Categorical items are used to classify activities (e.g., main activities, concurrent activities, and content of thought) and contextual situations such as date, the pre-programmed time, a time filled out, location, and influential facts. The scaled items serve to measure the degree of feelings in a particular activity. All responses are continually gathered within a week.

While the first two methods, the FQ and the ESM, are essential because they prepared the ground for later measurements, they are "far from being psychometrically sound" (Moneta, 2012, p. 40).

A more advanced approach to flow measurement is the componential view of flow by Jackson and Marsh (1996). These authors built a flow scale that includes nine components that are consistent with the original concept of flow. This scale was later used by Jackson and Eklund (2004) to develop the Flow State Scale – 2 (FSS-2) and the Dispositional Flow Scale – 2 (DFS-2). Whereas the FSS-2 measures flow as a state, the DFS-2 views flow as either a common or a domain-specific personality trait. Noticeably, these two questionnaires have been appraised as having sound psychometric quality (Moneta, 2012a).

With these two highly advanced measurement methods, more advanced tools and technology, such as eye tracking, facial expression analysis, electroencephalogram (EEG), or Galvanic Skin Response (GSR), have been designed to provide more accurate measurement of human feelings and emotions.

3.3. Flow and creativity

Research about flow originated when Csikszentmihalyi was studying creativity as a graduate student. He observed and was curious about how artists can focus so heavily on their artwork that their hunger and fatigue become forgotten. This phenomenon, at that time, led him to wonder whether creative works were indeed motivated by a highly intrinsic subjective experience rather than the extrinsic rewards that are offered to the creator afterward. Such contemplation ultimately resulted in the vast literature on flow. Consequently, flow and creativity have always been closely associated in the fields of positive psychology and creativity (Cseh, 2016).

In this section, we do not intend to provide definitions or the broad literature on the topic of creativity. This book's Chapter 4 articulates the details of such content. Instead, this section presents studies that relate to the positive relationship between flow and creativity; this is to reveal how the flow experience has contributed to human beings' creative moments.

There are numerous conditions for creativity that have been identified throughout the enormous literature on creativity. Nevertheless, as this section focuses on flow within creativity, it aims to provide an overview of the related conditions that pertain to flow experiences that are accordingly responsible for creativity.

The first factor that directly influences one's degree of creativity is the degree to which he or she achieves the flow status. To illustrate, conducted a sample of 532 participants in the software houses of Rawalpindi and Islamabad (Pakistan), a study on creativity in the workplace by Zubair and Kamal (2015b) shows that work-related flow experience and psychological capital dimensions, which refer to self-efficacy, hope, resilience, and optimism, are substantial factors that positively influence employees' creativity. Similarly, in research with a narrower sample, Zubair and Kamal (2015a) discovered another factor, authentic leadership, which directly and indirectly impacts staff's creativity. Noticeably, in this study, psychological capital and employees' flow status played mediating roles in the relationship between authentic leadership and the degree of work-related creativity. The results of Zubair and Kamal's studies (2015a, 2015b) are demonstrated in Figure 3-5.

FIGURE 3-5

The positive effects of authentic leadership, psychological capital, and work-related flow on employees' creativity. Adapted from Zubair and Kamal (2015a, 2015b).

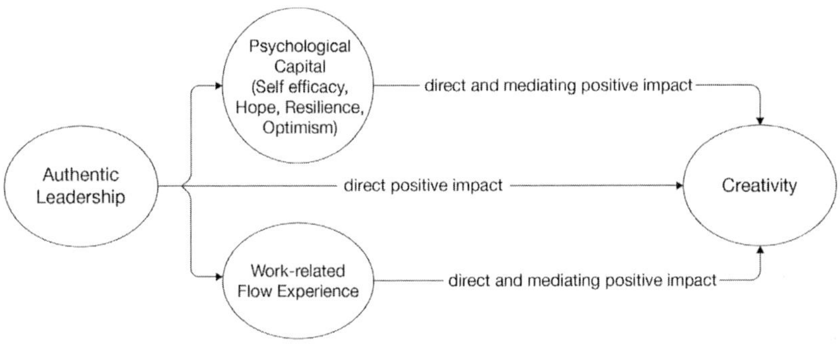

In the context of virtual work environments, Yan et al. (2013) conducted a study in China. This study proposes and evaluates a model that reveals the relationship between knowledge-sharing behavior, flow experience, and knowledge creation in the form of employee creativity. Specifically, the authors hypothesized that the action of using Web 2.0 to seek and share knowledge in the virtual workplace is *autotelic* (i.e., high levels of perceived challenges and skills) and positively connected with the two dimensions of work-related flow: employees' perceived enjoyment and attention focus. These two types of flow experience were also hypothesized to positively influence employees' creativity at work. The proposed research model is illustrated in Figure 3-6.

FIGURE 3-6

The hypothesized relationship between knowledge sharing, flow experience, and knowledge creation (Yan et al., 2013)

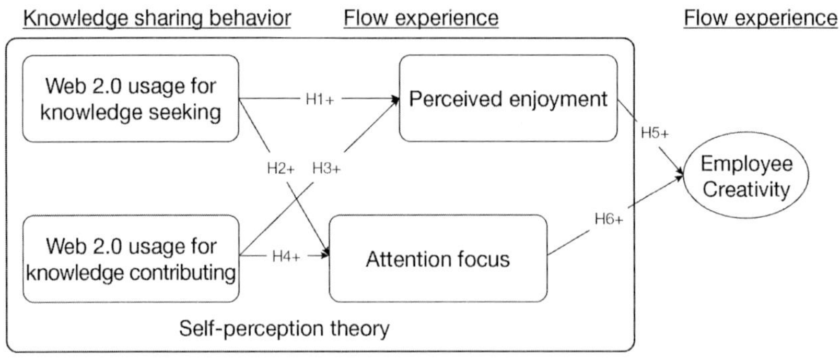

Note. This figure is redrawn from "Employee Creativity Formation: The Roles of Knowledge Seeking, Knowledge Contributing and Flow Experience in Web 2.0 Virtual Communities," by Yan et al. (2013). *Computers in Human Behavior*, 29(5), p. 1925. (http://dx.doi.org/10.1016/j.chb.2013.03.007). Copyright 2013 Elsevier.

These authors used the Structural Equation Modeling (SEM) technique to test the hypotheses and evaluate the theoretical model. The results confirmed all the hypotheses (see Figure 3-7). In other words, the use of Web 2.0 for knowledge seeking and contributing can result in the flow experience and can accordingly lead to work-related creativity.

Although this study ignores other flow components and focuses only on two dimensions of the optimal experience (i.e., perceived enjoyment and attention focus), its practical implications are vital to the knowledge management practices that are needed to nurture organizations' virtual workplace creativity. Specifically, according to this research, Chinese small and medium enterprises should consider utilizing the Web 2.0 environment for informal knowledge-sharing activities. Such free and comfortable behavior can lead to employees' enjoyment and attention at work and further result in knowledge creation.

FIGURE 3-7

Using SEM to test the hypothesized relationships between knowledge-sharing behavior, flow experience, and knowledge creation

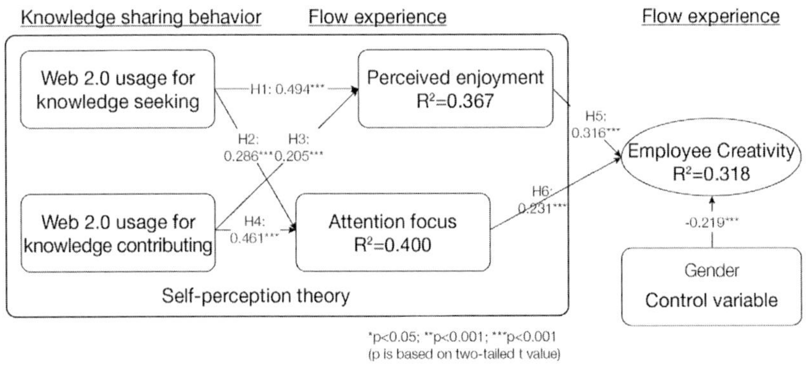

Note. This figure is redrawn from "Employee Creativity Formation: The Roles of Knowledge Seeking, Knowledge Contributing and Flow Experience in Web 2.0 Virtual Communities," by Yan et al., 2013. *Computers in Human Behavior*, 29(5), p. 1929. (http://dx.doi.org/10.1016/j.chb.2013.03.007). Copyright 2013 Elsevier

In an attempt to explore whether the psychology of flow leads to actual creative performance, Cseh et al. (2015)there is no empirical evidence about these links in visual creativity. Positive affect often—but inconsistently—facilitates creativity, and both may be linked to experiencing flow. This study aimed to determine relationships between these variables within visual creativity. Participants performed the creative mental synthesis task to simulate the creative process. Affect change (pre- vs. post-task designed an experiment in which participants were required to perform the *creative mental synthesis task* (Finke & Slayton, 1988) to stimulate their visual creative performance.

In this task, the study participants were given a set of basic alphanumeric and geometric patterns (see Figure 3-8); they were asked to, by drawing, combine these shapes into meaningful figures (see Figure 3-9). Participants were encouraged to be as creative as possible while being required to comply with the task's rules. During this task, participants' flow experience was measured.

This experiment, which used pre-and post-questionnaires, revealed that flow is positively associated with the affect-change that is caused by the task's stimulation. Nevertheless, while this improvement in the affect level was linked to self-rated creativity (indicated by the number of creative products generated during the task), its relationship with the quality of the creative performances was not found. In essence, despite not stressing the direct relationship between flow and objective, creative performance, this study places a significant emphasis on the role of self-perception and its power in motivating human beings toward achieving excellence. More empirical research is undoubtedly needed to examine flow's direct impact on creative performance, as has been claimed in numerous past studies.

FIGURE 3-8

The creative mental synthesis task by Finke and Slayton (1988): a set of basic alphanumeric and geometric patterns that were provided to participants

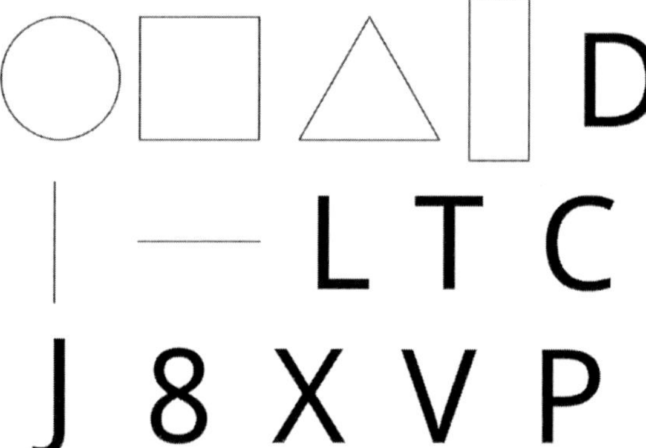

Note. This figure is redrawn from "Explorations of Creative Visual Synthesis in Mental Imagery," by Finke and Slayton (1988). Memory & Cognition, 16(3), p. 253. (https://doi.org/10.3758/BF03197758). Copyright 1988 Springer Nature.

FIGURE 3-9

Examples of sets of parts of noncreative pattern reported by participants in the creative mental synthesis task by Finke and Slayton (1988)

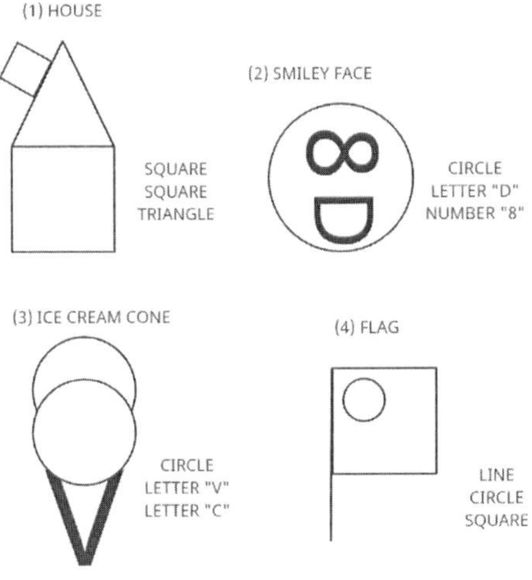

Note. This figure is redrawn from "Explorations of Creative Visual Synthesis in Mental Imagery," by Finke and Slayton (1988). *Memory & Cognition, 16*(3), p. 254. (https://doi.org/10.3758/BF03197758). Copyright 1988 Springer Nature.

3.4. Quality of experiences: types of flow

This section introduces Csikszentmihalyi's (1990) fundamental ideas about how flow can be experienced in various daily-life activities. Across his influential research on flow, the eminent author asserts that any life activities could become autotelic. Therefore, if human beings manage to have sufficient flow conditions, they can enjoyably develop their skills to the fullest potential and accomplish challenging yet rewarding tasks.

3.4.1 Flow experience in physical

"Everything the body can do is potentially enjoyable" (Csikszentmihalyi, 1990, p. 95). This is to say, almost any physical activity in which the human body engages every day can bring an optimal experience and joy. From merely walking to more complicated sports such as yoga or martial arts, which require both psychic and bodily energy, the body offers plentiful opportunities to experience flow.

A large body of empirical research on flow in sports has been established. The first studies about this topic, to help individuals flourish in sports and exercise, were published in 1992 (Swann, 2016). Markedly, flow states that are created from doing physical activities do not take place only among professional athletes. The simplest physical movement, if occurring in a context that embraces all the primary flow conditions (i.e., clear goals, a balance between high levels of perceived challenges and perceived skills, clear and immediate feedback), can be transformed into an autotelic activity. For instance, while walking, if one manages to set specific and measurable targets, such as the routes to take, landmarks to be seen, or the intended distance, to achieve health effects, s/he can track or improve the progress and accordingly experience the flow status.

In more complicated physical acts such as yoga or martial arts, the challenges posed by the need to control the mind, body, and experiences are advantageous for achieving flow. Although critics claim that yoga and flow produce opposite outcomes concerning the self, Csikszentmihalyi (1990) indeed refers to yoga as "one of the oldest and most systematic methods of producing the flow experience" due to its cheery, self-forgetful, and high psychic-energy nature (p. 106). A similar set of physical practices that is often compared to yoga is "martial arts," which refer to numerous forms of battling without using weapons. Despite the requirement to demonstrate physical performance, these combat techniques are genuinely directed toward controlling one's self-consciousness and improving mental strength. Thus, professional martial arts practitioners often refer to their daily practice as a transformation through which the mind and the body become harmonized. Martial arts, thereby, could be an illustrative form of flow created by body movements.

3.4.2 Experiencing flow through senses

Beyond the joyous physical movements, flow can also be experienced through the body's senses.

The visual sense, for example, is often said to be an aspect of an aesthetic flow experience. Although simply looking at daily-life sights may not lead to flow, improved visual skills to genuinely take pleasure in watching nature or a respected work of art can induce one's flow state. Nevertheless, it should be noted that training to upgrade one's visual skills is essential, and the attention that is needed for viewing a particular scenery is also necessary for one to experience flow.

Csikszentmihalyi (1990) quoted a man who was living in Chicago and commuted to work every morning via the elevated train.

On a day like this, or days when it's crystal clear, I just sit in the train and look over the roofs of the city, because it's so fascinating to see the city, to be above it, to be there but not be a part of it, to see these forms and these shapes, these marvelous of old buildings, some of which are totally ruined, and, I mean, just the fascination of the thing, the curiosity of it...I can come in and say, "Coming to work this morning was like coming through a Sheeler precisionist painting." Because he painted rooftops and things like that in a very crisp, clear style...It often happens that someone who's totally wrapped up in a means of visual expression sees the world in those terms. Like a photograph looks at a sky and says, 'This is a Kodachrome sky. Way to go, God. You're almost as good as Kodak.' (p. 108)

Created by the sense of hearing, listening to music is another rewarding experience. Nonetheless, listening does not mean hearing. It is not the hearing process that improves the quality of life experiences. It is through listening, which Csikszentmihalyi (1990) refers to as the process through which one's psychic energy, or attention, is massively invested in the organized auditory information that is embedded in music, that the pleasure brought by the ears can be experienced. Also, modern equipment that boosts music enjoyment is not necessary for achieving flow in music. Indeed, those who are attempting to devise strategies for listening to music have more opportunities to find flow. These people often schedule a specific time just to listen to the music they love. They may also adjust the lights and follow other invented procedures that can help them intensely concentrate on their songs list. In general, such people tend to have a painstaking plan to help themselves experience the flow of music and accordingly improve their quality of life.

According to Csikszentmihalyi (1990), the status of flow while listening to music can be reached through three distinct stages: *sensory experience, analogic mode, and analytic listening. A sensory experience* refers to the initial reaction to the quality of different sounds from various musical instruments. Such sounds activate the "pleasant physical reactions that are genetically wired into our nervous system" (p. 110). Notably, certain commonly-tempting melodies or rhythms created from the drums or the bass appear to attract attention during these beginning moments. In the second stage, the *analogic mode* of listening, one starts to enhance his or her skills to induce emotions and visualize the story that is being told through the music pattern. During this process, the sound of each musical instrument can result in one's mood(s) or imagined scenery and thus enhance his or her experience of the music. The last stage of listening, or the most sophisticated step that can lead to the flow status, is *analytic listening*. This process refers to the ability to analyze the music structure. *With their improved skills in understanding the underlying elements of music patterns*, analytic listeners can compare and evaluate the same piece of music that has been performed by various artists. During this analytic listening stage, advanced listening skills help one reach the flow status and truly enjoy the pleasant and harmonized musical sounds.

In addition to the senses of seeing and hearing, tasting can also be a source of the flow experience. In the ESM studies that involved electronic pagers, Csikszentmihalyi (1990) notes that despite lacking some flow components, such as high concentration or low self-consciousness, mealtime still offers people opportunities to experience pleasant moments. This is not to mention that the rapid development of global gastronomy has stimulated and upgraded the biological necessity of eating and drinking to a considerably higher level. Modern fine dining is characterized by the remarkable skills and expertise of professionals such as a *chef de cuisine* or *sommelier*, whose work contributes to the growth of a more sophisticated food culture that is conducive to a flow experience. Nevertheless, to enjoy the sophistication of tasting, one needs to intrinsically please his or her palate rather than consider the experience as an externally imposed challenge. In other words, one does not need to be a gourmet chef or a connoisseur to achieve a flow state while tasting food. Anyone can experience flow while dining if he or she "approaches eating – and cooking – in a spirit of adventure and curiosity, exploring the potentials of food for the sake of the experience rather than as a showcase for one's expertise" (Csikszentmihalyi, 1990, p. 115).

Finally, yet importantly, it is worth noting that the enormous pleasures caused by our bodily movements or senses can lead to one dark side of flow, which is the state of addiction. This mental issue depletes one's health conditions and psychic energy needed for other essential goals in life. Therefore, Csikszentmihalyi (1990) alerts that people must manage their instinctual cravings to experience flow states and without being dependent on such pleasure moments to experience happiness. Similarly, Schüler (2012) emphasizes that to avoid being addicted to a particular flow-producing and health-damaging activity, people should learn to invest their psychic energy in activities such as intellectual or physical exercises.

In the next section, a kind of flow that is necessary to enhance the quality of a large part of human existence will be discussed. Despite being considered difficult to acquire, work-related flow continues to occur in various world locations. Suggested strategies for transforming work into autotelic activities to improve the quality of life are also provided.

3.4.3 Work-related flow

There is no doubt that human beings spend a significant part of their existence earning a living. Therefore, seeking happiness via working has throughout history been an appealing topic for human society. It should be noted that although the nature of work appears to be ubiquitously identical, its various forms and levels indeed influence the degree to which people consider working as an enjoyable activity (Csikszentmihalyi, 1990). Therefore, to enhance one's quality of life through working, it is essential to explore conditions and methods where flow at work can be experienced.

Even in contexts where the work is hard and monotonous, to foster a flow status, one is compelled to develop an autotelic personality. Csikszentmihalyi (1990), to illustrate this perspective, lists numerous cases in his study about seeking flow at work. He uses a large part of a book chapter on this topic to discuss the case of Joe Kramer, a man who has been interviewed in a series of studies about flow. This welder, working in a South Chicago plant that assembles railroad cars, seems to be an exceptional example of a worker who has an autotelic personality. When distinguishing Joe Kramer's character from other welders who were employed to do tasks like that of Joe's yet have never managed to experience the flow psychology at work, Csikszentmihalyi (1990) highlights that:

> In the entire railroad plant, Joe appeared to be the only man who had the vision to perceive challenging opportunities for action. The rest of the welders we interviewed regarded their jobs as burdens to be escaped as promptly as possible, and each evening as soon as work stopped, they fanned out for the saloons that were strategically placed on every third corner of the grid of streets surrounding the factory, there to forget the dullness of the day with beer and camaraderie. Then home for more beer in front of the TV, a brief skirmish with the wife, and the day – in all respects like each previous one – was over." (p. 149)

Undoubtedly, the perspective that was adopted to interpret how Joe Kramer's experiences flow in his sterile working environment is essential to explore how work activities could make life more pleasurable. Viewing work as a way to transform experiential quality is a typical trait of the autotelic personality. Since such a viewpoint enables one to recognize the increasing complexity of the work one does rather than the external rewards offered by completing the job, one could develop himself or herself to the fullest potential and accordingly become a self-directed and skillful professional (Fraga & Moneta, 2016). Besides, having adopted such an autotelic mindset, individuals tend to invest their psychic energy in their performance. Such devotion helps with immersing themselves in even society's humblest jobs.

Compared with people who refuse to consider work as an opportunity to seek flow, those with an autotelic approach are assuredly able to develop their skills and quality of life experience to higher levels where intrinsic enjoyment and satisfaction can be achieved (Csikszentmihalyi, 1990).

Besides developing an autotelic personality, redesigning the job to make it more enjoyable is another strategy to improve the quality of life through work. The vast literature on the concept of flow suggests that any daily routines or tasks can be remodeled to have characteristics of a flow activity. These attributes refer to clear professional goals, continuous feedback, and opportunities to encounter challenges that require higher levels of skills (Csikszentmihalyi, 1990).

To further emphasize the importance of these components, Haworth (2004) notes that autotelic occupations tend to be more conducive to the human perception of well-being. Here, it is also worth stressing that such components of a flow activity are subjectively perceived rather than objectively evaluated. That is to say, jobs that are often considered highly autotelic due to their significant complexity still lead to discontent. Csikszentmihalyi (1990) illustrates this situation by referring to surgical operations, which have every characteristic of a flow activity, not to mention the significant extrinsic rewards that such work often offers in the forms of money and fame. Yet, according to Csikszentmihalyi, some surgeons still fail to experience the flow state. Thus, the structure of a job is crucial to experiencing flow at work, but it is not sufficient. People need to continually train themselves in their ability to strive and thrive even in allegedly barren work environments. In other words, cultivating an autotelic personality and redesigning job conditions are two complementary strategies one can adopt to reach the work-related flow experience and thereby enhance his or her quality of life (Csikszentmihalyi, 1990).

Nevertheless, due to the poor reputation that work has acquired throughout human history, developing an autotelic personality while at work is not easy. Csikszentmihalyi (1990) posits that there has been a "strongly rooted cultural stereotype of what work is supposed to be like," which makes people tend to refer to work as "an imposition, a constraint, an infringement of their freedom, and therefore something to be avoided as much as possible"

(p. 160). Therefore, although people tend to have more flow experiences when they are working than during their free time (Csikszentmihalyi & LeFevre, 1989; Haworth & Evans, 1995; Haworth & Hill, 1992), the psychological conflict in the way they regard their work endures. Csikszentmihalyi (1990) refers to this inner contradiction as the "paradox of work."

> On the job, people feel skillful and challenged, and therefore feel more happy, strong, creative, and satisfied. In their free time, people feel that there is generally not much to do and their skills are not being used, and therefore they tend to feel more sad, weak, dull, and dissatisfied. Yet they would like to work less and spend more time in leisure. (p. 159)

Researchers have attempted to identify the factors responsible for job dissatisfaction that may have led to this paradoxical situation. Accordingly, numerous determinants have been suggested. For example, feeling bored while at work due to the job's attributes and environmental conditions are often highlighted as reasons for job dissatisfaction. Fisher (1993) and van Hooff and van Hooft (2014) warn that the routine and inactive aspects of many jobs can induce boredom-related behaviors, which are positively connected with negative psychology at work. On the contrary, an influential study by Aiken et al. (2002) of the healthcare industry indicates that in hospitals with an immense patient-to-nurse ratio and a higher number of failure-to-rescue cases, nursing staff's dissatisfaction level escalated as the burnout caused by labor shortage became more significant. Although Csikszentmihalyi (1990) claims that feelings of boredom and stress are subjective perceptions toward a particular job and are thus most susceptible to the control of consciousness, these mental issues are often stimulated by environmental conditions that are not within one's command. Workplace bullying, for example, is another external factor that can create a toxic work atmosphere that diminishes people's spirit to enjoy work (Vega & Comer, 2005). In general, given the cultural stereotype about working, there is vast literature about why human beings are not happy while making their living.

Csikszentmihalyi (1990) points out the "paradox of work" not to discourage people's efforts to seek the flow experience while at work. Instead, through his meticulous research, he is convinced that people's favoritism of unstructured and passive leisure activities only leads to a loss of psychic energy and without receiving any strength in return. Investing time and effort in activities where one can develop knowledge and skills to the fullest potential will enable him or her to become stronger, healthier, and happier.

To complete his chapter on how to find work-related flow, Csikszentmihalyi (1990) fervently insisted that:

> Most jobs and many leisure activities – especially those involving the passive consumption of mass media – are not designed to make us happy and strong. Their purpose is to make money for someone else. If we allow them to, they can suck out the marrow of our lives, leaving only feeble husks. But like everything else, work and leisure can be appropriated for our needs. People who learn to enjoy their work, who do not waste their free time, end up feeling that their lives as a whole have become much more worthwhile." (p. 163)

3.4.4 Flow in mental activities

Flow can be experienced in any type of activity, ranging from those with muscle and senses to those that require intellectual efforts. Csikszentmihalyi (1990) asserts that the activities inside the mind can trigger some of the most invigorating experiences if one can control his or her thoughts. It is noteworthy that people tend to think they can effortlessly give order to their minds, as they often practice their daily habits with ease. Indeed, many young adults, despite not having to suffer from the aging effects, find it difficult to stop their minds from wandering and often commit "absentminded" errors (McVay et al., 2013). In a similar vein, the mental state of entropy also causes discontent. Adapted from thermodynamics and information theory, this concept, in the field of psychology, refers to the degree of confusion and disorder of human consciousness that leads to "uncertainly-related anxiety" (Hirsh et al., 2012, p. 304). When experiencing entropy, people have little control over their minds. They tend to invest their psychic energy in any passive leisure, which could jam minds with irrelevant information so that negative thoughts can be forgotten (Csikszentmihalyi, 1990). For this reason, the entropy conditions are not conducive to having enjoyable mental activities.

With a desire to experience flow in intellectual activities, one needs to learn how to control one's consciousness and establish an order for the mind. Based on the provocative suggestions by Csikszentmihalyi (1990), this section introduces the strategic roles of memory, language, and science in enabling one to pursue the pleasure of mental activities that support psychological and cognitive development. Renowned Academy Award filmmaker Luis Buñuel Portolés (1984), in his fascinating book, My Last Sigh, showed his ardent advocate for the importance of memory. "Life without memory is no life at all, just as an intelligence without the possibility of expression is not really an intelligence. Our memory is our coherence, our reason, our feeling, even our action. Without it, we are nothing."

Memory indeed plays a vital role in how one embellishes his or her life. A person with a highly cultivated memory can remember stories, events, poems, or scientific principles that are advantageous to establishing an order of thinking. This is because the accumulated knowledge inside the mind can enable one to self-explore meanings rather than depend on external information sources, such as TV or mass media, to prevent a chaotic mental world (Csikszentmihalyi, 1990). Also, the importance of memory in cognitive operations such as reasoning, language acquisition, and learning has been highlighted in extensive literature about neurology (Schacter et al., 2012) and psychology (Baddeley & Hitch, 1974). Without a retentive memory, it is challenging for individuals to comprehend and connect different pieces of information to think logically and sensibly. Therefore, to experience mental flow, one needs to cultivate his or her memory by selectively and intrinsically deciding what is necessary and enjoyable to memorize. Such decisions will help someone establish rules for the mind and accordingly gain control over his or her consciousness (Csikszentmihalyi, 1990).

Language is another realm of mental activity that offers opportunities for experiencing mental flow. According to Csikszentmihalyi (1990), using words in everyday conversations is not merely to convey words' literal meanings. Indeed, throughout history, language has contributed significantly to the development of human relationships.

Tannen (2007) extended her series of best-selling books about the role of language in relationship building through a perceptive analysis of dialoguing's auditory aspects. This influential study has been a reminder of "how complex conversational interactions are," appraised by the *Studies in Second Language Acquisition* journal. Without a doubt, at various complexity levels, the art of conversation can encourage people to organize their thinking so that they can choose the right words and arrange them appropriately. In such a conversation where the speaker pleases the listener through skillful word usage, both conversationalists can enhance their quality of communicative experience and consequently have more provocative and positive feelings.

Written language also offers opportunities to foster growth and happiness. Not only is it used as a learning tool (Arnold et al., 2017), the writing process was proven by Lewandowski (2009) to be effective in nurturing positive emotions and handling relationship dissolution. Nevertheless, the prevalence of mass media in the modern world has reduced the major roles of written text. Nowadays, instead of writing for the sake of creating, this process merely serves the purpose of passing along information (Csikszentmihalyi, 1990). This is not to mention the tremendous influence that, in today's society, extrinsic rewards have on writing; this is even though numerous studies, such as Amabile (1985) and Sabarun et al. (2020), have consistently emphasized the significance of intrinsic motivation in creative writing. Noting that people who are living in recent times tend to consider writing as a remunerative task and thus may not be able to genuinely experience flow in this mental activity, Csikszentmihalyi (1990) advocates the approach where one can be a writing amateur, yet he or she can intrinsically master the art of writing and achieve joy through such a recreational process. Csikszentmihalyi (1990) also insists that writing is like other activities that help someone to enter a flow state. It could be detrimentally addictive if one uses it to escape from an unpleasant reality and accordingly lets it control his or her mind. Therefore, one should attempt to use writing to establish order and discipline for the mind rather than have the process give order to one's experiences and thoughts. Such tight control over the consciousness is advantageous to entering the flow state while writing.

Last but not least, according to Csikszentmihalyi (1990), activities in the realms of history and science are conducive to all forms of mental flow. As a subject to be learned or memorized to make one become educated, history can hardly bring delight. Yet, when one intrinsically seeks knowledge about the past by trying to personally interpret the meaning of pivotal historical events, he or she will be able to, during this process, cultivate a love for history and accordingly experience flow.

Like history, science similarly offers the chance to enter various forms of mental flow. Jindal-Snape and Snape (2006) reveal fascinating insight into scientists' motivation at a government institute in the UK; Jindal-Snape and Snape state that extrinsic rewards have little influence as motivating factors for these research employees. Furthermore, these authors stress that "high quality, curiosity-driven research" (p. 1338), resources to implement research work, and management feedback are the conditions that motivate these scientists. Therefore, scientific work, if conducted in an environment where flow components are provided, can certainly become an autotelic activity. This is the reason why someone does not necessarily become a professional scientist to experience the mental flow in researching (Csikszentmihalyi, 1990). By observing and questioning the underlying laws of natural and social phenomena, an amateur scientist can learn to establish disciplined methods to explain such regularities. Also, it should be noted that multibillion-dollar scientific projects, despite being conducted by professional and reputable researchers, do not symbolize the entire spectrum of science. Through scientific research, anyone can find the pleasure of establishing rules for their mind. In other words, quality of life can be significantly improved as someone, in a controllable way, continually fosters mental growth.

Csikszentmihalyi (1990) notes that:

> The mental framework that makes science enjoyable is accessible to everyone. It involves curiosity, careful observation, a disciplined way of recording events, and finding ways to tease out the underlying regularities in what one learns. It also requires humility to be willing to learn from the results of past investigators, coupled with enough skepticism and openness of mind to reject beliefs that are not supported by facts. (p. 137)

3.5. The social psychology of flow

While there is vast literature about flow at the individual level, few studies have focused on achieving this optimal experience in group settings. According to Walker (2010), such social contexts are highly complex yet often fall in line with three types: "mere presence," "co-active," and "highly interdependent interactive" situations (p. 4). While distinguishing these three social groups, the author notes that individuals tend to be passive and less interactive among the *mere presence or co-active* groups. In contrast, *highly interdependent interactive* settings may indeed foster the social psychology of flow. In other words, in a *highly interdependent interactive* group, each individual can, for each other, become a promoter of flow. Rather than separately experiencing solitary flow, group members can mutually and reciprocally reach the peak experience. Triberti et al. (2016) refer to this social psychology of flow as an unusual type of optimal experience that creative groups can achieve. This peculiar, optimal experience is potentially even more enjoyable than solitary flow (Walker, 2010). Accordingly, in this section, the concept of social flow and its components will be introduced. More specifically, to outline factors fostering the preconditions for this shared experience, the notion of team flow in organizational contexts is discussed.

To explore the connection between flow and socio-cultural contexts, Boffi et al. (2016) conducted a series of studies and found that environmental conditions have a close relationship with positive psychology. This discovery refers to a mutual impact that flow and the social contexts exert on each other. In particular, the authors suggest that optimal psychology encourages social attachment and involvement in the pursuance of social values. In reverse, socio-cultural contexts (e.g., a classroom or heritage site) help young adults nurture a connection between themselves and their ever-changing environment. These surroundings also offer numerous factors that are enabling the young generations to select activities that promote flow. Therefore, although earlier studies about flow characterize the experience on an individual basis, researchers have started to look more closely at how social contexts advance this psychological status to a collective level.

When illustrating the potential of social flow, Walker (2010) states that "the individual act of instructors preparing for a challenging lecture was certainly associated with flow; however, the most joyful flow experiences recalled were vigorously engaging classroom discussions" (p. 3). Similarly, using the ESM, Csikszentmihalyi & Csikszentmihalyi (1988) reported that flow and its special, positive emotions were found in social more than individual circumstances. Such a viewpoint exists because shared tasks, to be completed, are often more challenging and require more advanced skills. These common goals often tend to be unattainable for someone to perform alone. Also, it is worth noting that group members may experience the significant effect of social contagion when individuals' positive emotions are freely shared while completing tasks together (Totterdell, 2000). In essence, as the existing literature on social flow suggests that this shared psychological state appears to take place more regularly among highly cohesive and interactive teams (Hackman et al., 2000; Sawyer, 2007), taking a closer look at how flow is experienced at the team level can facilitate the understanding of the characteristics and preconditions for the social psychology of flow.

There has been difficulty with applying flow research to a team level because the literature on solitary flow, group flow, and team dynamics has not congealed (van den Hout et al., 2016). Nevertheless, research on team flow has gained considerable advantages from such extensive work. Influential studies, such as those by Tuckman (1965), Tuckman and Jensen (1977), and Decuyper et al. (2010), have laid a concrete foundation for researchers to further explore ways in which a team, while its members work together, can perform, develop, and share positive feelings.

Based on an in-depth review of the literature about small group development, Tuckman (1965) proposed a group-development process that involves five stages: *forming*, *storming*, *norming*, *performing*, and *adjourning*, which was developed 12 years later by Tuckman and Jensen (1977); this is the final stage of the process, which renders the model a prominent framework through which organizations can build their team spirit and productivity. These five stages are described in Table 3-2 below.

TABLE 3-2 Stages of group development, based on Tuckman (1965) and Tuckman & Jensen (1977)

Stage	Characteristics
1. Forming	The first step is about bringing a group of individuals together. Experienced emotions tend to be high anxiety, uncertainty, and politeness. Group members are concerned with ensuring psychological safety, reducing uncertainty, and defining boundaries.
2. Storming	Group members need clarity about their activities, roles, and goals. Conflicts and power struggles can emerge. The group's internal structure is developing. Various members or coalitions may have different ideas about how to proceed.
3. Norming	The group consensually settles on a goal, structure, roles, and division of labor. Communication shifts from internal negotiation to the shared task.
4. Performing	A high-performing group in which members are comfortable and share information openly is formed. Each person knows others' strengths and expertise, and tasks are distributed optimally.
5. Adjourning	Tasks are complete, and the group dissipates.

The group-development model that was constructed by Tuckman (1965) and Tuckman & Jensen (1977) has been experimentally evaluated by numerous studies, among which Sweet and Michaelsen (2007) note that the aforementioned stages do not necessarily occur in the proposed order. The authors expressly point out that "Like individuals, groups may get stuck in a stage of development for some time, may regress when under stress, and may not always develop to full maturity" (p. 35). From this discovery comes why research on team flow is essential to search for methods that enable individuals to overcome destructive conflicts and achieve a shared optimal experience.

According to van den Hout et al. (2016), team flow refers to the shared psychological status experienced by all team members who "are completely involved in their common activities as part of a collaboration toward the common purpose" (p. 244). Based on the original conditions of flow provided by Csikszentmihalyi (1996) and the current literature on individual flow and team dynamics, these authors propose a list of precursors for team flow. Characteristics of these preconditions are characterized in Table 3-3.

TABLE 3-3 Precursors for team flow, based on van den Hout et al. (2016)

Precursor	Characteristics
1. Common goal	This is a shared goal of all the team members. This common goal should be clear, meaningful, compatible with members' individual goals, internalized by all members, and growth-promoting.
2. Aligned personal goals	Personal goals should be aligned and contribute to the achievement of the shared goal. These goals are like the common goal (i.e., clear, meaningful, specific, growth-promoting) despite being at the individual level.
3. High-skill integration	Complementary, high-level skills of the team members are integrated. Each member is assigned a challenging task or role that suits his or her preferences and competency. Individual forces are optimally utilized and combined to create synergy (win-win) through collaboration.
4. Open communication	Open and transparent communication ensures that all members know exactly how they contribute to the team's performance. Each member has his or her perspectives that are broadened by the other team members. Clear, constructive, and encouraging feedback is necessary for collaboration as well as individual and team performance. Active listening is also essential for this open communication process, as this helps members achieve familiarity with each other.
5. Safety	A psychologically safe environment amid which performing personal tasks to serve the team's interests. Unnecessary and unacceptable risks need to be eliminated, although possible failures exist. Failures are considered growth opportunities, and challenges are for releasing high skills. Such failures push the team toward a flow experience rather than being intimidated. This precursor is vital for a team-flow component, namely a *sense of shared trust*.
6. Mutual commitment	The responsibility to engage with each other to achieve the desired common goal with devotion and dedication. All members are aware of how tasks are distributed, the process of completing them, and the project's current state. Members, when mutually committed, are intensely involved in a shared, meaningful activity and can remain concentrated on this activity as long as necessary to achieve the common goals.

In addition to the precursors for team flow, van den Hout et al. (2016) also outline the components of this social psychology. These are summarized in Table 3-4.

TABLE 3-4 Components of team flow, based on van den Hout et al. (2016)

Precursor	Characteristics
1. Shared identity	The team's collective ambition, constituting the reason for its existence and also known as the shared sense of intrinsic motivation to operate and perform as a team, is based on shared values and recognition of complementary skills.
2. A sense of unity	A shared feeling that the team, together, forms a unity by expressing a collective ambition. This feeling of unity is partly the result of establishing aligned personal goals that contribute to the common goals that result from the collective ambition. This unity may be considered a blending of egos.
3. Trust	A feeling of trust results from the fact that people feel safe to act (i.e., no worry of failure), and they, through open communication and feedback, know exactly how they are doing. Trust reflects a willingness to accept a limited degree of control over the outcome and the readiness to depend on each other. Trust leads to the achievement of team flow by feeling reciprocally related.
4. Sense of joint progress	The shared feeling of cooperatively making progress together toward achieving goals. This component is the result of open communication and high-skill integration.
5. Holistic focus	This is the realization that there is a collective consciousness among team members that promotes collective ambitions, resulting in a shared focus on their cooperation and achievement of the established goals.

The existing literature on team flow, despite being fairly limited, demonstrates that this type of social psychology leads to numerous positive consequences. Not only is a higher level of satisfaction and better performance reached (Csikszentmihalyi, 1990, 1996; Landhäußer & Keller, 2012), team flow also fosters development at both individual and group levels (Asakawa, 2004). The positive emotions and psychology that are nurtured during the process of working together enhance all team members' experiential quality. Considering the substantial benefits of this social flow, more rigorous studies need to be conducted to explore how social flow contributes to the achievements of groups, organizations, and communities. At further levels, research on team flow can increasingly enhance humans' quality of life experiences and accordingly bring happiness and joy, which would take into account what Csikszentmihalyi (1990) emphasized:

> Whether we are in the company of other people or not makes a great difference to the quality of experience. We are biologically programmed to find other human beings the most important objects in the world. Because they can make life either fascinating and fulfilling or utterly miserable, how we manage relationships with them makes an enormous difference to our happiness. If we learn to make our relations with others more like flow experiences, our quality of life as a whole is going to be much improved." (p. 164)

3.6. Discussion and assignment

3.6.1. Group discussion in the classroom

Using the Quadrant Model (Figure 3-4, share your personal experiences of flow status.

- How did you reach the state of flow?
- Have you felt the state of flow in your graduate school life? When?
- Do you feel anxiety about your graduate school studies? When and in what ways?
- Do you feel bored in your graduate school life? When and in what ways?
- How do you evaluate your current skillsets compared to the skill level that is required for a graduate student?

- Do you experience enough challenges that require you to advance your skillsets??
- What are the obstacles that hinder you from reaching the state of flow?

Each group discuss the questions above. You can select the questions as many as possible.

Group Size: 3-5 (depending on the class size and its diversity)

Time: The group discussion is 25 minutes; preparation for the presentation: five minutes; presentation: five minutes; Q&A: five minutes.

Presentation: All group members should contribute to the presentation's group discussion and preparation. The presenter will be randomly selected by the instructor.

3.6.2. Assignment

Design a series of tasks in your area of interest to encourage us to reach the flow status. Reviewing the academic literature on the topic of flow is required (see this chapter's References section, or you can do a keyword search that is based on your topic of interest).

REFERENCES

✦ ✦ ✦

Aiken, L. H., Clarke, S. P., Sloane, D. M., Sochalski, J., & Silber, J. H. (2002). Hospital Nurse Staffing and Patient Mortality, Nurse Burnout, and Job Dissatisfaction. *Journal of the American Medical Association, 288*(16), 1987–1993. https://doi.org/10.1001/jama.288.16.1987

Amabile, T. M. (1985). Motivation and Creativity: Effects of Motivational Orientation on Creative Writers. *Journal of Personality and Social Psychology*, 48(2), 393–399.

Argyle, M. (2001). *The Psychology of Happiness*. Routledge.

Argyle, M., & Martin, M. (1991). The Psychological Causes of Happiness. In F. Strack, M. Argyle, & N. Schwarz (Eds.), *International series in experimental social psychology, Vol. 21. Subjective well-being: An interdisciplinary perspective* (pp. 77–100). Pergamon Press.

Aristotle, Bartlett, R. C., & Collins, S. D. (2012). *Aristotle's Nicomachean Ethics* (reprint). University of Chicago Press.

Arnold, K. M., Umanath, S., Thio, K., Reilly, W. B., McDaniel, M. A., & Marsh, E. J. (2017). Understanding the Cognitive Processes Involved in Writing to Learn. *Journal of Experimental Psychology*, 23(2), 115–127.

Asakawa, K. (2004). Flow Experience and Autotelic Personality in Japanese College Students: How do they Experience Challenges in Daily Life? *Journal of Happiness Studies*, 5(2), 123–154.

Baddeley, A. D., & Hitch, G. (1974). Working Memory. *Psychology of Learning and Motivation - Advances in Research and Theory*, 8(C), 47–89.

Berlyne, D. (1960). *Conflict, Arousal, and Curiosity*. McGraw-Hill.

Boffi, M., Riva, E., Rainisio, N., & Inghilleri, P. (2016). Social Psychology of Flow: A Situated Framework for Optimal Experience. In L. Harmat, F. Ø. Andersen, F. Ullén, J. Wright, & G. Sadlo (Eds.), *Flow Experience: Empirical Research and Applications* (pp. 215–231). Springer International Publishing Switzerland.

Bühler, K. (1922). *Die Geistige Entwicklung Des Kindes*. Fischer.

Caillois, R. (1958). *Les Jeux et les Hommes*. Gallimard.

Cseh, G. M. (2016). Flow in Creativity: A Review of Potential Theoretical Conflict. In L. Harmat, F. Ø. Andersen, F. Ullén, J. Wright, & G. Sadlo (Eds.), *Flow Experience: Empirical Research and Applications* (pp. 79–94). Springer International Publishing Switzerland.

Cseh, G. M., Phillips, L. H., & Pearson, D. G. (2015). Flow, Affect and Visual creativity. *Cognition & Emotion*, 29(2), 281–291. https://doi.org/10.1080/02699931.2014.913553

Csikszentmihalyi, M. (1975). *Beyond Boredom and Anxiety: Experiencing Flow in Work and Play*. Jossey-Bass.

Csikszentmihalyi, M. (1990). *Flow: The Psychology of Optimal Experience*. Harper Perennial.

Csikszentmihalyi, M. (1996). Creativity: *Flow and the Psychology of Discovery and Invention*. Harper Perennial.

Csikszentmihalyi, M. (1997). *Finding Flow: The Psychology of Engagement with Everyday Life*. BasicBooks.

Csikszentmihalyi, M., Abuhamdeh, S., & Nakamura, J. (2014). Flow. In M. Csikszentmihalyi (Ed.), *Flow and the Foundations of Positive Psychology": The Collective Works of Mihaly Csikszentmihalyi* (pp. 227–238). Springer Science+Business Media.

Csikszentmihalyi, M., & Csikszentmihalyi, I. S. (1988). *Optimal Experience: Psychological Studies of Flow in Consciousness*. Cambridge University Press.

Csikszentmihalyi, M., & Hunter, J. (2014). Happiness in Everyday Life: The Uses of Experience Sampling. In *Flow and the Foundations of Positive Psychology": The Collective Works of Mihaly Csikszentmihalyi* (pp. 89–101). Springer Science+Business Media.

Csikszentmihalyi, M., & LeFevre, L. (1989). Optimal Experience in Work and Leisure. *Journal of Personality and Social Psychology*, 56(5), 815–822. https://doi.org/10.1037/0022-3514.56.5.815

Dean, K. E., & Malamuth, N. M. (1997). Characteristics of Men Who Aggress Sexually and of Men Who Imagine Aggressing: Risk and Moderating Variables. *Journal of Personality and Social Psychology*, 72(2), 449–455.

DeCharms, R. (1968). *Personal Causation*. Academic.

Decuyper, S., Dochy, F., & Van den Bossche, P. (2010). Grasping the dynamic complexity of team learning: An integrative model for effective team learning in organisations. *Educational Research Review*, 5(2), 111–133. https://doi.org/10.1016/j.edurev.2010.02.002

Engeser, S., & Schiepe-Tiska, A. (2012). Historical Lines and an Overview of Current Research on Flow. In *Advances in Flow Research* (pp. 1–22). Springer Science+Business Media.

Finke, R. A., & Slayton, K. (1988). Explorations of Creative Visual Synthesis in Mental Imagery. *Memory & Cognition, 16*(3), 252–257. https://doi.org/https://doi.org/10.3758/BF03197758

Fisher, C. D. (1993). Boredom at Work: A Neglected Concept. *Human Relations*, 46(3), 395–417. https://doi.org/10.1177/001872679304600305

Fraga, D. De, & Moneta, G. B. (2016). Flow at Work as a Moderator of the Self-Determination Model of Work Engagement. In L. Harmat, F. Ø. Andersen, F. Ullén, J. Wright, & G. Sadlo (Eds.), *Flow Experience: Empirical Research and Applications* (pp. 105–123). Springer International Publishing Switzerland.

Goldberg, Y. K., Eastwood, J. D., Laguardia, J., & Danckert, J. (2011). Boredom: An Emotional Experience Distinct from Apathy, Anhedonia, or Depression. *Journal of Social and Clinical Psychology, 30*(6), 647–666. https://doi.org/10.1521/jscp.2011.30.6.647

Groos, K. (1899). *Die Spiele Der Menschen*. Fischer.

Hackman, J. R., Wageman, R., Ruddy, T. M., & Ray, C. R. (2000). Team Effectiveness in Theory and Practice. In C. L. Cooper & E. A. Locke (Eds.), *Industrial and Organizational Psychology: Linking Theory with Practice* (pp. 109–129). Blackwell.

Hallowell, E. M. (2002). *The Childhood Roots of Adult Happiness: Five Steps to Help Kids Create and Sustain Lifelong Joy*. Ballantine Books.

Haworth, J. T. (2004). Work, Leisure and Well-being. In J. Haworth & A. J. Veal (Eds.), Work and Leisure (pp. 168–183). Routledge. https://doi.org/10.1080/03069880412331335902

Haworth, J. T., & Evans, S. (1995). Challenge, Skill and Positive Subjective States in the Daily Life of a Sample of YTS Students. *Journal of Occupational and*

Organizational Psychology, 68(2), 109–121. https://doi.org/https://doi.org/10.1111/j.2044-8325.1995.tb00576.x

Haworth, J. T., & Hill, S. (1992). Work, Leisure, and Psychological Well-being in a Sample of Young Adults. *Journal of Community & Applied Social Psychology*, 2(2), 147–160. https://doi.org/https://doi.org/10.1002/casp.2450020210

Hebb, D. O. (1955). Drives and the CNS. *Psychological Review, 62*(4), 243–254.

Heutte, J., Fenouillet, F., Kaplan, J., Martin-Krumm, C., & Bachelet, R. (2016). The EduFlow Model: A Contribution Toward the Study of Optimal Learning Environments. In *Flow Experience: Empirical Research and Applications* (pp. 127–143). Springer International Publishing Switzerland.

Hirsh, J. B., Mar, R. A., & Peterson, J. B. (2012). Psychological Entropy: A Framework for Understanding Uncertainty-related Anxiety. *Psychological Review*, 119(2), 304–320. https://doi.org/https://doi.org/10.1037/a0026767

Jackson, S. A., & Eklund, R. (2004). Relationships between Quality of Experience and Participation in Diverse Performance Settings. *Australian Journal of Psychology*, 56(Supplement), 193.

Jackson, S. A., & Marsh, H. W. (1996). Development and Validation of a Scale to Measure Optimal Experience: The Flow State Scale. *Journal of Sport and Exercise Psychology*, 18(1), 17–35.

Jindal-Snape, D., & Snape, J. B. (2006). Motivation of Scientists in a Government Research Institute: Scientists' Perceptions and the Role of Management. *Management Decision*, 44(10), 1325–1343. https://doi.org/10.1108/00251740610715678

Kiili, K. (2005). Digital Game-based Learning : Towards an Experiential Gaming Model. *The Internet and Higher Education, 8*(1), 13–24. https://doi.org/10.1016/j.iheduc.2004.12.001

Kiili, K., Freitas, S. De, Arnab, S., & Lainema, T. (2012). The Design Principles for Flow Experience in Educational. *Procedia Computer Science*, 15, 78–91. https://doi.org/10.1016/j.procs.2012.10.060

Landhäußer, A., & Keller, J. (2012). Flow and Its Affective, Cognitive, and Performance-Related Consequences. In *Advances in Flow Research* (pp. 65–85). Springer Science+Business Media.

Larson, R., & Csikszentmihalyi, M. (2014). The Experience Sampling Method. In

M. Csikszentmihalyi (Ed.), *Flow and the Foundations of Positive Psychology": The Collective Works of Mihaly Csikszentmihalyi* (pp. 21–34). Springer Science+Business Media.

Lewandowski, J. G. W. (2009). Promoting Positive Emotions following Relationship Dissolution through Writing. *Journal of Positive Psychology*, 4(1), 21–31. https://doi.org/https://doi.org/10.1080/17439760802068480

Maslow, A. H. (1968). *Toward a Psychology of Being*. Van Nostrand Reinhold.

Massimini, F., Csikszentmihalyi, M., & Carli, M. (1987). The Monitoring of Optimal Experience A Tool for Psychiatric Rehabilitation. *The Journal of Nervous and Mental Disease*, 175(9), 545–549.

Mayers, P. L. (1978). *Flow in Adolescence and its Relation to School Experience*. University of Chicago.

McVay, J. C., Meier, M. E., Touron, D. R., & Kane, M. J. (2013). Aging Ebbs the Flow of Thought: Adult Age Differences in Mind Wandering, Executive Control, and Self-evaluation. *Acta Psychologica*, 142(1), 136–147. https://doi.org/10.1016/j.actpsy.2012.11.006

Moneta, G. B. (2012a). On the Measurement and Conceptualization of Flow. In *Advances in Flow Research* (pp. 23–50). Springer Science+Business Media.

Moneta, G. B. (2012b). Opportunity for Creativity in the Job as a Moderator of the Relation between Trait Intrinsic Motivation and Flow in Work. *Motivation and Emotion, 36*(4), 491–503. https://doi.org/10.1007/s11031-012-9278-5

Moneta, G. B., & Csikszentmihalyi, M. (1996). The Effect of Perceived Challenges and Skills on the Quality of Subjective Experience. *Journal of Personality, 64*(2), 275–310.

Nakamura, J., & Csikszentmihalyi, M. (2002). The Concept of Flow. In C. R. Snyder & S. J. Lopez (Eds.), *Handbook of Positive Psychology* (pp. 89–105). Oxford University Press.

Nakamura, J., & Csikszentmihalyi, M. (2014). The Concept of Flow. In M. Csikszentmihalyi (Ed.), *Flow and the Foundations of Positive Psychology: The Collective Works of Mihaly Csikszentmihalyi* (pp. 239–263). Springer Science+Business Media.

Piaget, J. (1951). *Play, Dreams And Imitation In Childhood*. Routledge.

Portolés, L. B. (1984). *My Last Sigh*. Jonathan Cape Ltd.

Sabarun, Nurbatra, L. H., Wiidiastuty, H., & El-Muslimah, A. H. S. (2020). The Relationship among Intrinsic/Extrinsic Motivation and Interest Toward L2 Writing Performance at Higher Education. *Elementary Education Online*, 19(2), 60–68. https://doi.org/10.17051/ilkonline.2020.02.107

Sawyer, R. K. (2007). *Group Genius: The Creative Power of Collaboration*. BasicBooks.

Schacter, D. L., Addis, D. R., Hassabis, D., Martin, V. C., Spreng, R. N., & Szpunar, K. K. (2012). Review The Future of Memory : Remembering, Imagining, and the Brain. *Neuron*, 76(4), 677–694. https://doi.org/10.1016/j.neuron.2012.11.001

Schüler, J. (2012). The Dark Side of the Moon. In S. Engeser (Ed.), *Advances in Flow Research* (pp. 123–137). Springer Science+Business Media.

Swann, C. (2016). Flow in Sport. In L. Harmat, F. Ø. Andersen, F. Ullén, J. Wright, & G. Sadlo (Eds.), *Flow Experience: Empirical Research and Applications* (pp. 51–64). Springer International Publishing Switzerland.

Sweet, M., & Michaelsen, L. K. (2007). How Group Dynamics Research can Inform the Theory and Practice of Postsecondary Small Group Learning. *Educational Psychology Review, 19*(1), 31–47. https://doi.org/10.1007/s10648-006-9035-y

Tannen, D. (2007). *Talking Voices: Repetition, Dialogue, and Imagery in Conversational Discourse*. Cambridge University Press.

Telążka, B. (2015). A Qualitative Study on Subjective Attitudes and Objective Achievement of Autotelic and Non-autotelic Students of English as a Foreign Language. In E. Piechurska-Kuciel & M. Szyszka (Eds.), *The Ecosystem of the Foreign Language Learner* (pp. 59–70). Springer. https://doi.org/https://doi.org/10.1007/978-3-319-14334-7_4

Thatcher, A., Wretschko, G., & Fridjhon, P. (2008). Online Flow experiences, Problematic Internet Use and Internet Procrastination. *Computers in Human Behavior*, 24(5), 2236–2254. https://doi.org/10.1016/j.chb.2007.10.008

Totterdell, P. (2000). Catching Moods and Hitting Runs: Mood Linkage and Subjective Performance in Professional Sport Teams. *Journal of Applied Psychology*, 85(6), 848–859. https://doi.org/10.1037/0021-9010.85.6.848

Triberti, S., Chirico, A., & Riva, G. (2016). New Technologies as Opportunities for Flow Experience: A Framework for the Analysis. In L. Harmat, F. Ø. Andersen,

F. Ullén, J. Wright, & G. Sadlo (Eds.), *Flow Experience: Empirical Research and Applications* (pp. 249–263). Springer International Publishing Switzerland.

Tuckman, B. W. (1965). Developmental Sequence in Small Groups. *Psychological Bulletin*, 63(6), 384–399.

Tuckman, B. W., & Jensen, M. A. C. (1977). Stages of Small-Group Development Revisited. *Group & Organization Studies, 2*(4), 419–427.

van den Hout, J. J. J., Davis, O. C., & Walrave, B. (2016). The Application of Team Flow Theory. In L. Harmat, F. Ø. Andersen, F. Ullén, J. Wright, & G. Sadlo (Eds.), *Flow Experience: Empirical Research and Applications* (pp. 233–247). Springer International Publishing Switzerland.

van Hooff, M. L. M., & van Hooft, E. A. J. (2014). Boredom at Work: Proximal and Distal Consequences of Affective Work-related Boredom. *Journal of Occupational Health Psychology*, 19(3), 348–359. https://doi.org/https://doi.org/10.1037/a0036821

Veenhoven, R. (1984). *Data-Book of Happiness*. Springer Netherlands.

Vega, G., & Comer, D. R. (2005). Sticks and Stones may Break your Bones, but Words can Break your Spirit: Bullying in the Workplace. *Journal of Business Ethics*, 58(1), 101–109. https://doi.org/10.1007/s10551-005-1422-7

Walker, C. J. (2010). Experiencing Flow: Is Doing It Together Better than Doing It Alone? *Journal of Positive Psychology*, 5(1), 3–11. https://doi.org/10.1080/17439760903271116

Weiner, E. (2008). *The Geography of Bliss: One Grump's Search for the Happiest Places in the World*. Twelve Books.

White, R. W. (1959). Motivation Reconsidered: the Concept of Competence. *Psychological Review*, 66(5), 297–333. https://doi.org/https://doi.org/10.1037/h0040934

Yan, Y., Davison, R. M., & Mo, C. (2013). Employee Creativity Formation: The Roles of Knowledge Seeking, Knowledge Contributing and Flow Experience in Web 2.0 Virtual Communities. *Computers in Human Behavior*, 29(5), 1923–1932. https://doi.org/10.1016/j.chb.2013.03.007

Zubair, A., & Kamal, A. (2015a). Authentic Leadership and Creativity: Mediating Role of Work-Related Flow and Psychological Capital. *Journal of Behavioural Sciences*, 25(1), 150–171.

Zubair, A., & Kamal, A. (2015b). Work Related Flow, Psychological Capital, and Creativity Among Employees of Software Houses. *Psychological Studies, 60*(3), 321–331. https://doi.org/10.1007/s12646-015-0330-x

CHAPTER

04

Topic 3 Theories of Creativity

Topic 3

Theories of Creativity

Sun Qianang and Eunyoung Kim

In this chapter, we first review the development of creativity research, after which we apply an individual approach to understanding the creative process. This approach will serve to anchor our subsequent discussion. By exploring the relationship between creativity and problem-solving abilities we will have the opportunity to introduce the theory of creativity from multiple perspectives and with reference to creative structures, components, processes, and evaluations. A series of rigorously designed tests from the field of cognitive science will also be presented and discussed with regard to their results and implications for current trends in creativity research. Additionally, we will cover some traditional topics to extend the study of individuals to more diverse social environments. Our reasoning for doing so is that we believe it is essential to understand the cognitive processes underlying individual ideas if innovations capable of changing the world are to be equally understood. Needless to say, there are a great many other topics worthy of discussion here. But doing so would be beyond the scope of this chapter. However, it is hoped that the present discussion of creativity and its manifestations in several fields will serve to motivate further research in these and other areas.

4.1. History of Creativity Research

Creativity, as a crucial capability that rises and falls throughout the lives of individuals, groups, and social environments. From a developmental perspective, creativity has a variety of connotations.

The discussions about the essence of creativity has a long history, however, it was not until the 1950s (Guilford, 1950) that creativity became a field of psychological research. There was a reasonable consensus on the definition of creativity, creativity, which, in the simplest terms, means the formation of something new with respect to a task at hand (Barron, 1955; Hennessey, 2015; J. C. Kaufman, 2002; Simon, 1990). Furthermore, several components of this definition have been identified, such as high quality (Sternberg, 1999), surprise (Boden, 2004; Bruner, 1962; Simonton, 2012), aesthetics, authenticity (Kharkhurin, 2014), and provoking innovation (Plucker, Beghetto, & Dow, 2004).

It is worth noting that since the 1920s, American psychology has been orientated by behaviorism. A series of classical experiments demonstrated that behaviors are learned and that subjects can be conditioned to learn, such as Pavlov's dogs and Skinner's pigeon. Behaviorists mainly focus on directly observable phenomena, on that which happens on the outside, on that which can be seen. In contrast, anything that happens on the inside, within the mind, cannot be directly observed, constituting an empirical no man's land behaviorism seeks to avoid. And it is for this reason that behaviorists do not produce much work on creativity. Until the 1950s, the heyday of behaviorism, the other remarkable approach in psychology was Freudian psychoanalysis (Thurschwell, 2009). For Freud, creativity was a subconscious activity that masked unexpressed or instinctive desires. The realm of art was in this view a creative arena in and through which repressed and unfulfilled sexual desires could be articulated and redirected (Fuss, 1993). Taken to the extreme, art is in essence the creation of hallucinations, the generation of fantasy worlds, an orderly instantiation of a range of disorderly neuroses (Gregory & Paidoussis, 1966).

After World War II, creativity was afforded increased scholarly attention, eventually bridging the divide between the individualistic and socialist approaches to the phenomenon. Modern creativity research manifested in three waves, each of which roughly cut into the timeline. The first wave emerged in the 1950s and 1960s, focusing particularly on the personalities of creators, on their individual characteristics. The second wave, in the 1970s and 1980s, introduced cognitive psychology to the study of creativity, accordingly shifting the attention of researchers to cognitive-based approaches.

More specifically, the second wave contributed *experimental* cognitive psychology, which is concerned with empirically assessing how people think, perceive, learn, and remember their creative process. Notably, this perspective considered the individual creator, acknowledging the personal journey as that which is constitutive of the structures and processes that together define what we call creativity. Consequently, new combinations of spirits and expressions in the world have been assigned the label of creativity.

The third wave of creativity research was one in which socio-cultural methodologies were applied, where creative people were examined with respect to their collaborations within discrete social and cultural systems. The empirical lens was adjusted to account for the ways in which groups effectively produce innovations amidst the diverse currents of social or cultural processes whose character and trajectories are themselves subject to the machinations of group dynamics. In such complex contexts, creativity is defined as that which is produced by a knowledgeable social group, the outcomes of which are at once novel, appropriate, useful, and valuable. Socio-cultural definitions of creativity require that certain products resonating social value must be created before actions or people can be termed "creative." Moreover, only solutions to immense problems or the generation of works of genius can be considered creative manifestations.

Such conceptions thus call for an interdisciplinary approach that incorporates scholarship from multifarious domains and combines the expertise of a diversity of researchers, from sociologists to anthropologists to historians. After decades of research, we are now closer than ever to a fully informed and well-charted exploration of creativity. That said, one especially intractable problem remains: each of the three waves of creativity research exists in "narrow isolation" (Greene et al., 2019)—conversely, the lack of multidisciplinary integration of these three waves might serve as much to explain creativity as it does to hinder such an explanation. Ultimately, what is truly needed is agreement on what constitutes creativity, which, thematically speaking, may represent one of the most challenging themes for social science as a whole. Therefore, in this chapter, we seek to illustrate individual approaches to the study of creativity—a traditional research area, and yet also a stepping stone for future creativity research.

4.2. Structure of Creativity

When creativity became a popular topic of research in the modern age, several studies proposed to reveal its structure, which, it was assumed, would also help to capture its essence. The theories and models that emerged in response to this proposal were aimed at shaping the structure of creativity from different angles. One basic model, proposed by Rhodes (1961), was named the 4P framework, as it classified all aspects of creative practice into Person, Product, Process, and Press (environment). The 4P framework corresponded to four crucial questions: What kinds of people are creative? What outcomes are considered creative? What is the creative process? How does the environment affect creativity? A research from Glăveanu (Glăveanu, 2013) promotes a different framework composed of 151 specific vocabularies and categorized into Actor, Audience, Action, Artifacts, and Affordance—i.e., the 5A framework (Glăveanu, 2013). This framework addresses contemporaneous concerns within the social and physical domains, problematizing and raising novel questions about the inter-relationships between different creative elements, such as the relationship between creator and audience, between socio-cultural forces and materials, and between new and existing artifacts.

The individual being and the social-culture domain are two fundamental components of creativity research. Besides framing the relationships between such components, distinguishing corresponding levels of creativity enriches the various dimensions of creativity research. In the 3C model (Feldman & Pentland, 2003), a vivid description of creativity is evoked using a piano keyboard as a metaphor. High-C means significant creativity, which generates a wide range of extraordinary inventions. Low-C connotes minor creativity, whereas Middle-C refers to the middle point between the two extremes of creativity. Extending the 3C model are the notions of Mini-C (small creativity) and Pro-C (professional creativity in a domain) (Barbot & Reiter-Palmon, 2019), in addition to Little-C (everyday creativity), and Big-C (excellent creativity). This model also connects to the theory of creative learning (J. C. Kaufman, Beghetto, & Watson, 2016), which suggests that creativity and the learning process are interdependent. Mini-C can progress with suitable guidance and feedback to Little-C. Intentional practice for several years in a given area can potentially make someone a creative professional in that area—a Pro-C (J. C. Kaufman & Beghetto, 2009). Finally, a talent person whose creative work continues to exert a substantive impact on others for many years would be considered a Big-C.

Similarly, various theories have taken into account how creativity manifests in many fields. According to the concept of *multiple intelligences* proposed by Gardner (1993) and (Cacioppo, Gardner, & Berntson, 1999; Gardner, 1993)intelligence is not a monolithic modality but is instead multifaceted, including interpersonal intelligence (the ability to interact with others), personal intelligence (self-insight), visual–spatial intelligence, natural intelligence, linguistic intelligence, logic-mathematical intelligence, body-kinesthetic intelligence (motor intelligence), and musical intelligence. Intelligence could potentially also be creative. In other words, the intelligence applied to connect all levels of creativity, from Mini-C to Big-C.

Another theory that focuses on the differentiation of modalities and how they relate to a holistic view of creativity is called the Amusement Park Theory (APT) Model of Creativity (Baer et al., 2004; Glaveanu & Baer, 2017; Kaufman et al., 2009). The APT model uses the metaphor of an amusement park to illustrate the extent to which people rely on creative ideas and expressions to respond to a diversity of choices, options, and requirements, such as those confronting visitors to an amusement park (e.g., attractions, rides, activities, tickets). According to this model, creativity may require a certain level of intelligence, motivation, and environment (Gajda, Karwowski, & Beghetto, 2017). And extending this metaphor, especially large amusement parks, such as Disney World, contain many smaller, thematically oriented zones (i.e., theme parks), in which there are also a great number of individual rides, attractions, and the like. These park divisions are hierarchically distinguished in terms of scale and complexity, and can in this way be likened to corresponding domains of creativity from which people can choose when engaging in all manner of life tasks. Likewise, some fundamental dichotomies, such as art and science (Snow & Nunn, 1959) or aesthetics and function (Cropley & Cropley, 2009), may also serve as indicators of creative domain differences.

The structural model described above covers many core issues in the creativity domain, each of which provides useful insights into specific creative behaviors. Notwithstanding the various models that have framed and been applied to questions of creativity, the fact remains that creativity is conceptually manifold and extraordinarily complex. Accordingly, to fully comprehend creativity, dynamic perspectives are essential.

More than dynamism, novel perspectives on creativity must possess a global character, as they are situated in a globalized world. Contemporary creativity research reflects this character (Mason, Gunst, & Hess, 2003; Reckwitz, 2017; Weiner, 2000), but in the same fashion also mirrors—and thereby reinforces— modern beliefs about, for example, the power of personality and the capability of bringing about novelty (Negus & Pickering, 2004). Rather than echoing the "normal" state of the world, our current interest in and desire for creativity must be scrutinized in terms of its *actual* social, cultural, scientific, technological, economic, and political dimensions and contexts. Just as our societies are persistently in flux, conceptions about creativity and creative people are neither fixed nor absolute. Admittedly, then, any effort to understand creativity must necessarily interrogate our own preconceptions and subjective limitations, reflexively asking ourselves such seemingly basic questions as why we consider creativity to play such a crucial role and how our viewpoints may shift in the future. In this sense, studying creativity and related theories with an exceedingly careful degree of caution is perhaps the best—if not only—recourse to meaningfully shedding light on our human identity, our society, our present, and our future.

4.3. Individual Approach

Like Guilford, many scholars became engaged in creativity research during World War II. Surprisingly, early research on creativity was linked to security intelligence and military training. Donald W. MacKinnon and Maurice Stein, both of whom worked for the Office of Strategic Services (OSS), the precursor to the Central Intelligence Agency (CIA), applied controversial theories on creativity to the assessment of the best candidates for irregular warfare overseas, including the selection of spies, counterespionage agents, and resistance leaders (Melosh & McKinnon, 1978). For his part, Guilford worked for the US Air Force, where he was charged with developing tests to identify essential knowledge and capabilities.

After World War II, these military psychologists established several research institutes to study creative individuals. In 1949, MacKinnon founded the Institute for Personality Assessment and Research (IPAR) at the University of California, Berkeley. In the early 1950s, Guilford founded the Qualification Research Program at the University of Southern California. Stein founded the Center for Creativity and Mental Health at the University of Chicago in 1952. Because of the creativity research is a high-stakes game during the nuclear arms, psychologist Carl Rogers and Morries Stein intended to believe that they were defending freedom from the nuclear annihilation(R. Keith Sawyer, 2017). Around that time, the US government has supported creativity research, including the development of tests to identify uniquely talented children. In this case, schools can recognize potential geniuses, nurture their gifts, and position them in highly creative careers in science and technology that finally reward the country (Parnes & Harding, 1963). The IPAR emerged in this period, describing a creative society as follows: "It has freedom of speech and action, no fear of dissent or conflict, a willingness to break conventions, and a spirit of entertainment and dedication to work"(Parnes & Harding, 1963, p.152).

In the 1950s and 1960s, the conception of creativity was nearly synonymous to that of scientific creativity. The US created the National Science Foundation (NSF) to support and fund large numbers of projects aimed at developing standardized creativity measurements. Because psychologists cannot directly observe the mind, mental structures and processes, such as motivation, personality, intelligence, memory, and emotion, are invisible and thus essentially hypothetical *constructs*. Although constructs cannot be directly observed, their existence can be inferred from observable behaviors. The operationalization of a construct is the first action taken by a psychologist after its proposal and definition. This is because operationalization is a methodological procedure designed to measure otherwise hypothetical constructs, such as the measurement of mental processes via their alleged observable behavioral corollaries.

Since creativity research was first incorporated as an academic discipline, more than 100 creativity tests have been developed (Hocevar & Bachelor, 1989). In the following, we focus on the most widely used creativity tests and on a series of remarkable tests based on divergent thinking.

4.3.1. Gough Adjective Check List (ACL)

An early example of a creativity test is the Gough Adjective Check List (ACL), a general personality assessment tool comprising 300 adjectives that was commonly used at Berkeley's IPAR in the 1950s and 1960s. To complete the test, participants select those adjectives that they believe best describe themselves (Gough, 1976). Of the 300 adjectives, Gough incorporated 30 into a subscale aimed at predicting creativity: the Creative Personality Scale (CPS). Moreover, Gough identified 18 adjectives that he believed were associated with creativity: capable, clever, confident, egotistical, humorous, informal, individualistic, insightful, intelligent, interests wide, inventive, original, reflective, resourceful, self-confident, sexy, snobbish, and unconventional (Gough, 1979). He also identified 12 adjectives that were negatively related to creativity: vulgar, discreet, stable, conservative, traditional, disgruntled, fewer interests, polite, sincere, submissive, and suspicious. The total score is derived from subtracting the number of negative items from the number of positive items. Then, a variant of the CPS was developed by Domino (1970): the Domino Creativity Scale (Cr). This scale referenced Gough's 300 adjectives to identify 59 associated with greater creativity.

Despite their value, these tests are susceptible to gender or cultural bias. For example, Gough (Gough, 1979) surveyed 1,121 female college students and 760 male college students, finding that the average score for male students was 5.03, whereas for female students the average score was 3.97. What is undeniable is that these adjectives are inevitably associated with gender stereotypes. Since then, a series of tests have been developed and continue to be improved. The individual approach in creativity research has become the most productive type, generating profound insights with broader applicability.

4.3.2. Remote Association Test

Associative thinking is a classical topic, one that dates back hundreds of years to philosophers like John Locke, Alexander Bain, and David Hume (Levine & Ross, 2002; Marx & Cronan-Hillix, 1987). Many creative cognition theories focus on associative processes, i.e., how ideas are generated and connected to other ideas. Hypotheses have occasionally been proposed in this area but have not been subjected to sufficient empirical testing. One exception is Mednick (1962), who put forth the association theory of modern psychology, particularly in the context of the creative process, and conducted empirical tests to verify the theory(Mednick, 1962). One of Mednick's main contributions was his assertion of the rarity of original ideas. Only when we have exhausted existing ideas, Mednick claimed, were original ideas accessible. In other words, insights appear late in the chain of associations.

Mednick was inspired by historical research that demonstrated that breakthrough innovations were most often the result of combining material from different disciplines (Simonton, 1999). For example, imagine a possible combination of tables and chairs. People might have a dining room table and chairs or a school desk and chairs. Making combinations from these pieces of furniture is easy because both chairs and tables belong to the same type of furniture. Ask people to combine a chair with a hippopotamus, however, and the results will vary tremendously. This is because chairs and hippos are obviously entirely different, and thus people must form a "remote" association. People tend to form strong connections between related concepts based primarily on their education and learning experiences. Mednick described this as a steep hierarchy of associations. He assumed that combining two significantly different concepts via association would be more creative than combining two very similar concepts.

FIGURE 4-1

Steep and flat associative hierarchies according to Mednick's theory.

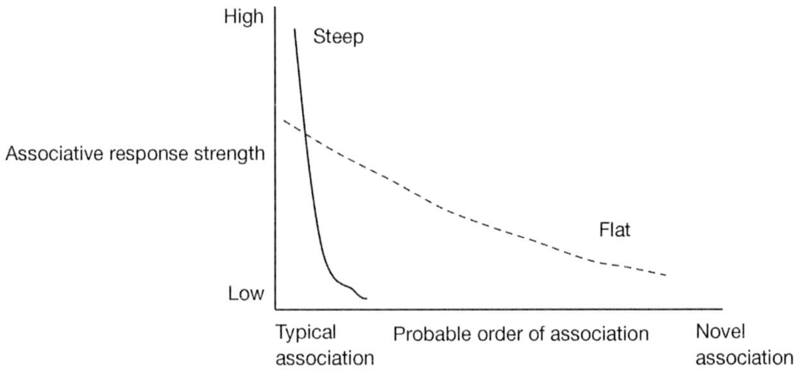

Note. This figure is redrawn based on *Origins of genius: Darwinian perspectives on creativity.* (Simonton, 1999) Oxford University Press. Inc.

Similarly, creative people may be better at making remote associations than others. Concerning this, Mednick (1962) developed the Remote Association Test (RAT) to assess creativity in terms of the frequency with which remote connections are made. Additionally, the RAT only requires people to create new combinations, and the score does not involve any requirements from social and cultural definition and the appropriateness of subjective judgment.

Because of these advantages, the RAT has been used as an indicator of creativity in several recent empirical studies (Ansburg & Hill, 2003) as well as in a series of cognitive neuroscience studies (Isen, Labroo, & Durlach, 2004; White & Shah, 2006). Unsurprisingly, then, the RAT has been adapted for different purposes (Jones et al., 2005). In one variation, for instance, participants were asked to write a short story in three words. Two variables were highlighted: (1) creative/not creative; (2) related/unrelated words. The results indicated that the stories based on unrelated words were more creative than those based on related words. The stories that were required to be creative were unconstrained compared to the stories that were not given this requirement. Even for those participants who were given unrelated words and instructed to not be creative, their stories were still better than those written by participants who were given related words and instructed to be creative. This variant RAT test provided evidence that combinations of unrelated concepts are more likely to inspire creativity.

While the RAT is useful, it has some notable drawbacks. First, its implementation is limited by language. The traditional RAT involves analogies between three given words and a blank space (e.g., water: blood: sky :). However, empirical investigations of the RAT have shown that the test lacks discriminative validity and that the resulting scores tend to be moderately correlated with scores from convergent thinking tests or language ability tests. This empirical bias was defined early on when IQ tests were discussed. Linguistic bias is a similar problem in that it shows that certain factors, such as language ability, have little to do with the tested target but significantly affect RAT results. This means that all individuals with moderate or high language ability will likely perform well on the RAT, whereas individuals with low language ability will likely perform poorly on the RAT, even though the RAT is designed to measure associations and creative potential rather than verbal ability.

Even though the RAT has limitations, several creativity surveys have empirically determined that the test can provide useful information about creative potential (Caraco, Martindale, & Whittam, 1980; J. Lee & Lee, 2009). On the other hand, some valuable studies have suggested that creative insights may not be derived from remote connections but instead from connections between closely related material (Gough, 1976; McKinnon, 1962; Perkins, 1983).

4.3.3. Divergent Thinking (DT) Test

The first divergent thinking (DT) test was an open-ended, multi-question test developed in 1896 by Binet, the originator of the IQ test (Barron & Harrington, 1981). Similar measurements of "imagination" proliferated in the early 20th century.

Many versions of the DT test have been developed by different researchers, such as Guilford, during the Aptitude Research Project at the University of Southern California. Another version is the Structure of Intelligence (SOI) model, which identifies DT as one of six operations (Frick, Guilford, Christensen, & Merrifield, 1959; Joy P Guilford, 1967). Other operations include cognition, memory recording, memory retention, convergent production, and evaluation (R. Keith Sawyer, 2017). Guilford proposed four capabilities—fluency, flexibility, originality, and elaboration—as essential components of the divergent production process. He and his team then developed a large number of influential tests to measure these four components, which were later adapted in two of the most famous DT tests: the Torrance Test (Raithby & Torrance, 1974) and the Wallach-Kogan creativity test (Wallach & Kogan, 1965). The participants are asked to list as many functions of objects with which they are familiar. Assessments are then carried out according to the four components mentioned above. The number of answers measures fluency; originality is measured by whether the responses were independently provided; flexibility is measured by the number of responses that could be classified in different categories; elaboration is a measurement of the description of each response.

Creatively psychometric process examinations have been widely used by researchers for decades and remain a popular measure of the creative process and creative potential. The assessment of the creative process is common in schools (Csikszentmihalyi & Sawyer, 2014). However, this assessment is different from most standardized achievement or ability tests, and the DT test requires an individual to provide several responses to a particular prompt. The emphasis on the responses is often referred to as thought fluency, which plays a vital role in ideation but is not the only part of the creative process. DT is contrasted with convergent thinking, in which cognitive processes are used to produce comprehensive or possible solutions to a given problem (as in most standardized tests). From a practical point, many scholars have claimed that it is unbelievable that so many researchers take so much time to conduct a single creativity assessment (J. C. Kaufman, Plucker, & Baer, 2008). But on the other hand, primarily DT tests are still widely used today in creativity research and education. These include the SOI (Joy P Guilford, 1967), the creative thinking test (TTCT) (Almeida, Prieto, Ferrando, Oliveira, & Ferrándiz, 2008a; Raithby & Torrance, 1974), and the DT task (Getzels & Jackson, 1962; Wallach & Kogan, 1965). However, one of the most apparent differences between intelligence and creativity is that intelligence requires convergent thinking in order to arrive at a single right answer. In contrast, creativity requires DT to come up with many possible answers.

Current research (Acar & Runco, 2015) has developed 13 dimensions based on Guilford's different originality conception. These responses to DT tests can be categorized (e.g., impractical, infeasible, playful) in the Literal Divergent Thinking (LIDT) test. The LIDT test differs from traditional flexibility assessments in that its dimensions are meant to be generalized across different DT projects. In contrast, traditional flexibility categories vary within the DT test (Runco & Albert, 1985). According to which polar directions they tend toward, the test dimensions are created to assess "divergent" responses in reality. This in turn helps to assess potential processes that may occur while developing the DT test answers. Although these dimensions are used to varying degrees, many are quite common and positively correlated with traditional originality and fluency scores. The LIDT test should be further explored to determine whether it is a more valuable predictor of creative thinking than the traditional DT.

The SOI model (Joy P Guilford, 1967) frames 24 different DT types, roughly classified into four elements —graphical, symbol, semantic, behavior—and six categories—unit, class, relation, system, transformation, and connotation. A well-known example of SOI is the matchstick problem (graphics transform), which has several versions, each of which uses 17 matchsticks to create two rows of a three-column grid (i.e., six squares). Participants were asked to remove three matches to form four squares. The other examples, like the sketch task, require participants to create the graphical units skillfully. Participants must draw many pictures of a particular shape in this task, such as a circle or a square. The SOI task is usually meant to inspire flexible thinking by countless trial and error. Guilford and his colleagues collected a large amount of data to validate the SOI model, and the results generally performed well (for example, (Gastl et al., 1993). Although this model is not perfect, even inspiring some criticism (Gao, Chen, Weber, & Linden, 1999; Horn & Knapp, 1973; Sternberg & Grigorenko, 2001), it has led to further developments in DT tests, such as the TTCT.

4.3.4. Torrance Tests of Creative Thinking (TTCT)

Torrance Tests of Creative Thinking (TTCT) (Almeida et al., 2008a; Torrance, 1972) is a well-known assessment that was inspired by the SOI model and has been widely used in countless creativity studies, even being translated into over 32 languages (Frasier, 1991). One of the primary purposes of the TTCT in the 1960s was to recognize geniuses when they were children and attempt to guide them toward occupations that benefit from creativity. Over several decades, the TTCT (Torrance, 1972) has continued to be improved in terms of management and scoring, which may be responsible for its enduring popularity.

The TTCT (Almeida, Prieto, Ferrando, Oliveira, & Ferrándiz, 2008b; Torrance, 1972)(Guilford, P. (1976 consists of two forms: oral and graphical. Each type of test contains form A and B, which can be used alternately. For instance, the graphical test has the following phases: picture structure: participants are asked to use a basic shape to create a picture based on the original pattern: picture completion: participants are required to draw an exciting object according to an incomplete figure (See Figure 4-2).

FIGURE 4-2

Three examples of incomplete figures are used in the TTCT

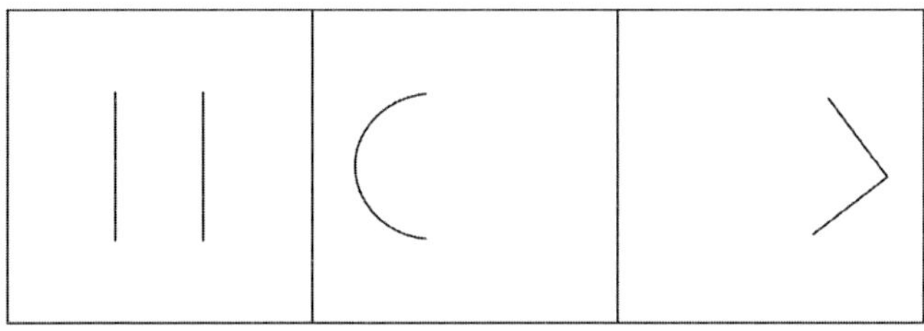

Note. It is redrawn from *Franck, K., & Rosen, E. (1949). Franck drawing completion test. Australian Council for Educational Research.*

Lines/circles: Subjects are asked to draw as many objects as possible, and each creation should start from a pair of vertical lines (e.g., forming A) or circles (e.g., forming B).

The other part of the TTCT is called the verb test, which has seven sub-questions. Participants answer three questions according to a picture at the beginning of the test. In form A, an elf looks at his reflection in the water (R. Keith Sawyer, 2017). Moreover, the questions should be considered as follows:

- Inquiring: Participants need to ask as many questions as possible about the picture.
- Guess the reason: Participants have to list the possible result of the action they have drawn.
- Guess the result: Participants are required to list possible outcomes of the actions they have drawn.
- Improve the product: Participants are asked to make changes to improve an object (such as a stuffed animal).
- Unusual function: Participants are asked to consider several possible uses for an ordinary object, such as a paper clip.
- Unusual questions: Participants are required to list as many questions as possible about an ordinary object (this item will not appear in a later version).

- Hypothesis: Participants are asked to imagine that an impossible situation has happened and then list the possible ramifications.

In its management, scoring, and final reports, the TTCT has adopted detailed specifications to standardize its measurements. Torrance recommended training the graders and found that even cursory training, like reading the grading manuals, allowed novice graders to generate scores related to acceptable reliability. However, he warned that untrained graders tended to rate the results based on their own judgment while deviating from the scoring system, particularly in evaluating originality. The initial tests that were produced combined four traditional DT areas: fluency, flexibility, originality, and elaboration. A significant change was made to the streamlined scoring system introduced in the revision, announced in 1984. Besides ratings, fluency, originality, and elaboration also yielded points for resistance to premature closure and title abstractness (K. Sawyer, 2017). The evaluation of flexibility was eliminated because ratings for this item did not differ much from those for fluency (Tang & Gero, 2002).

Creativity tests like the TTCT and various DT examinations primarily focus on creative process research. While the capability of idea generation is only one aspect of the creative process, how creativity works in problem solving in the real world is often inadvertently ignored. Some researchers have suggested that DT testing could be used to assess personal creative potential but should be used with careful consideration (Runco & Vega, 1990). Barron and Harrington (1981) reviewed hundreds of studies. They indicated that some DT tests have been adopted and scored under certain conditions and have provided evidence of creative capability in certain areas (Barron & Harrington, 1981). However, these results have not been consistent across domains because the requirements for DT tests vary from each file. In other words, creative achievement requires a combination of different thinking skills, critical assessments, and other complex competencies; moreover, creative persons are usually good at switching between different abilities to fulfill the creative process.

4.3.5. Cattell-Horn-Carroll (CHC) Theory

When creativity research was on the horizon, one topic was not ignored: intelligence. Is there any correlation between creativity and intelligence? IQ is usually considered to be an important measurement for assessing human potential, particularly during early creativity research. The first IQ test was developed in the late 19th and early 20th centuries; since then, psychologists have noticed that people who perform well on one test tend to perform well on the other. To integrate these phenomena, Spearman (1923) proposed two factors that would be central to all measurements: 'g' (general ability) and 's' (task-specific ability)(Spearman, 1923). Until World War II, most psychologists agreed that creativity was only a secondary product of intelligence, such that IQ was an accurate measure of creative potential. The advanced statistical technology of factor analysis has been refined, which has made it possible to measure performance on any specific test probably caused by 'g', general cognitive ability. Furthermore, many scholars have agreed that cognitive ability is virtually hierarchical. The general factor 'g' is at the top of the hierarchy, followed by broad capabilities like fluid thinking, working memory, and, at the bottom, particularly narrow abilities that are ordinarily relevant to a particular task (Carroll, 1993; KAUFMAN, COLE, & BAER, 2009).

A current study that was conducted among a group of gifted children implied that differences in IQ did not predict excellent creativity in adulthood. However, there seemed to be a minimum IQ requirement needed to achieve great success. Specifically, an IQ of 120 indicates excellence, but beyond this level, a higher IQ does not predict an increased likelihood of success (Barron & Harrington, 1981).

Researchers have shown that creative scientists, artists, and writers generally obtain high scores on the general intelligence test (Barron & Harrington, 1981). Nevertheless, one complicating factor in the debate over creativity and intelligence is that intelligence tests have changed dramatically since the 1960s. Moreover, most IQ tests are not based on psychological theory nor are they designed to measure 'g' or research-based ability (KAUFMAN et al., 2009). There is no single test that can accurately measure 'g', and each test as known contains both general and special abilities. At this point, the challenge is to integrate many specific tests and use all of their scores, combined with statistical techniques, to measure 'g'. Therefore, the focus has shifted since the 1960s, with the 10-factor theory being just around the corner. The 10-factor theory is known as the Cattell-Horn-Carroll (CHC) theory, which combines the Cattell-Horn theory of fluid and crystallized intelligence (Horn & Cattell, 1966) with Carroll's Three-Stratum Theory (McGrew, 2009). Today, all IQ tests are based on the CHC theory (Flanagan, Ortiz, & Alfonso, 2013).

Ten factors are involved in the CHC theory, each of which is further composed of two or more limited abilities, as outlined below:

- Gf (fluid intelligence; the ability to apply a variety of mental operations to solve novel
- problems that do not benefit from past learning or experience)
- Gq (quantitative knowledge)
- Gc (crystallized intelligence; the breadth and depth of a person's accumulated knowledge of culture and the ability to use that knowledge to solve problems)
- Grow (reading and writing)
- Gsm (short-term memory)
- Gv (visual processing)
- Ga (auditory processing)
- Glr (long-term storage and retrieval)
- Gs (processing speed)
- Gt (decision speed/reaction time)

Modern intelligence test measurements nearly all include these seven items. Gq and Grow are academic achievements, while Gt is not measured by any standardized test (Barbot & Reiter-Palmon, 2019). The various IQ tests usually measure between four and seven items. The most popular test, called the Wechsler Scale (WISC-IV and WAIS-IV), measures four abilities involving language understanding, perceptual reasoning, working memory, and processing speed (J. C. Kaufman & Beghetto, 2009). The relationship between intelligence and creative capacity has been debated since the last century. If creativity is a valuable research field, then it needs to be separated from other scientific fields. Of course, evidence was required to verify that creativity and intelligence were not the same thing. Some of the early research on creativity aimed to test the possibility that creativity was different from intelligence. If creativity depended on intelligence, then there was no sense focusing on it, i.e., intelligence should be explored, as creativity would follow. However, to be sure, earlier research confirmed that creativity did not depend on traditional intelligence.

4.3.6. Threshold Theory

Another theory that deserves discussion is threshold theory. Specifically, threshold theory states that IQ and creativity are correlated up to an IQ of 120, beyond which the score and the correlation become irrelevant.

Threshold theory (Getzels & Jackson, 1962) was proposed and rapidly elaborated by many investigations in the later decades (Fuchs-Beauchamp, Karnes, & Johnson, 1993). The theory fits with the common observation which indicates the creative people whose intelligence usually above the average level. However, once they beyond the average intelligence level, the higher intelligence no longer plays a role in higher creativity. Some scholars have even suggested that high intelligence may interfere with creativity (Simonton, 1999). However, most evidence does not support threshold theory (Runco & Albert, 1985; Sligh, Conners, & Roskos-Ewoldsen, 2005). The relationship between fluid intelligence and DT has been found at all levels of intelligence (Preckel et al., n.d.). After integrating several studies and finding different correlations between IQ and DT, different IQ ranges were observed (Kim, 2011). For instance, when an IQ is below 100, the correlation coefficient is 0.260; when an IQ is between 100 and 120, the correlation coefficient is 0.140; when an IQ is between 120 to 135, the correlation coefficient is 0.259; and when an IQ is above 135, the correlation coefficient is 0.215.

Although these results are not statistically significant, the standard view is that there is a minimum intelligence threshold for creative performance.

Precisely, this view refers to a traditional intelligence threshold, because intelligence often means different things to different people. Some people equate intelligence with academic achievement, while others equate it with verbal ability or wit. Furthermore, different tests focus on diverse skills.

Threshold theory states that there is a threshold below which people cannot be creative. However, there is no evidence to conclude that creativity and intelligence are either the same or completely different—threshold theory attempts to determine the likelihood that IQ and creativity are linked at specific levels only. An important implication of threshold theory is that intelligence is necessary for creative achievement but is not sufficient. Therefore, if a person falls below the threshold, they cannot think independently nor produce any creative work. Beyond the threshold, they have creative potential but there is no guarantee that they are creative. Note that no one is both highly creative and low in intelligence. Finally, all of the data come from creativity and intelligence tests, and threshold theory is based on tested abilities rather than on performance in a real environment.

Threshold theory is more applicable than other tests to intelligence (Runco & Albert 1986b; Sligh et al., 2005). It is consistent with both logic and empirical research and performs optimally with the general principle of creativity. Much research undertaken to improve threshold theory has used complex statistical methods, like piecewise regression of iterative computational algorithms, to support the initial theory, but only with potential creative measures (Jauk et al., 2013). However, the threshold does not exist when analyzing creative performance in active practice. Moreover, this reflects a big difference between creative achievement and creative potential (Runco, 2008). It also demonstrates that the threshold is most pronounced at an IQ around 100, and only when originality is loosely defined (Jauk, Benedek, Dunst, & Neubauer, 2013). Another result from Jauk et al. (2013) is that when there is a threshold (i.e., the relationship between general intelligence and creativity), personality has a significant impact on creative achievement. This may explain why above the intellectual level, some people are creative and others are not.

4.4. Motivation and the Creative Process

4.4.1. Motivation for Creativity

Based on studies of the relationship between intelligence and creativity, Amabile (1988, 1998) proposed three intrinsically interrelated components that are essential to creative individuals and organizations. At first, field knowledge, professionalism, and expertise play a crucial role in specific creative processes, such as tolerating ambiguity and taking risks. The second is intrinsic motivation—that is, a person who participates in practice because it facilitates the determination of meaning in this process. Then there are extrinsic incentives, such as financial rewards or fame. We should also note that the orientation of the work will also affect one's creative motivation, even their sense of mission and passion for a career (Pratt, Pradies, & Lepisto, 2013).

However, we know that creation is an exploratory activity that sounds magnificent but is fraught with difficulties in practice because it does not always lead to successful work. However, it is still at the core of human development. Gruber and Wallace's evolutionary systems approach treats the creative person as a whole system and creative activity as an interconnected network (Gruber & Wallace, 1999). The motivation is to answer questions that arouse the curiosity of the creator. This perspective provides an opportunity to consider the dynamic relationship between knowledge, emotions, and purpose in the creative process and to understand what makes creators passionate about the things they do.

Flow, a remarkable concept proposed by Csikszentmihalyi (2006), points out that when people are intensely engaged in a favorite but challenging activity, they may enter an exhilarating, enjoyable moment of total concentration. This experience is a reward for any creative individual. Thus, flow experiences are a form of immanence that allows people to have transcendent experiences through constant creation, without worrying too much about specific end goals or external causes.

At this point, how exactly do internal and external causes affect creativity? A matrix from industrial/organizational psychology (Unsworth, 2001) provides a perspective comprising four types of creativity:

- Responsive creativity: This involves completing a specific task for an external reason.
- Desired creativity: Here there is more freedom, which is required to be creative, but it is still driven by other people.
- Contributive creativity: This requires people to be engaged and interested but also focused on a specific and narrower problem.
- Positive creativity: This is created for personal reasons, which is probably the most familiar creative concept.

Having an internal, personal reason to be creative leads to better results. However, it should be noted that motivation potentially triggers creative action, and that once the creative action has been taken, attention should be placed on the creative process, which will be the focus of the next session.

Over the centuries, philosophers have developed two competing theories about the creative process. Idealist theorists say that once one has a creative idea, it does not matter whether the idea is ever realized or whether others ever know of it. Once an idea is fully formed in the mind, the creative work is done. This conception is often referred to as the "Croce-Collingwood" theory, which was developed by two philosophers in the 20th century (Robert Keith Sawyer et al., 2003). The theory manifests in the Western cultural model as the belief that the essence of creativity occurs suddenly in a single moment. On the other hand, action theorists believe that creative work is essential to the creative process. This conception rests on the observation that in real life, creative thinking often happens when one is processing material. Once one begins to execute an idea, it is often realized that it is not working as expected, and therefore it must be changed. Sometimes, the final product is entirely different from the original idea.

Early theoretical work on creativity attempted to answer the obvious question: What is the creative process exactly? In the book *The Art of Thinking*, the author deals with this question with a creative cognitive process (Wallas, 1926). The "Five-stage model," which was inspired by a previous investigation (Koenigsberger, 1902), is still in use at present and includes preparation, collection, incubation, enlightenment, and verification.

The creator experiences learning and collection, then continues thinking, after which incubation or a series of reflections occur, ultimately leading to a breakthrough. Finally, the validation phase is implemented to test, extend, and execute the idea. After the Five-stage model (Wallas, 1926) of creativity was developed, mostly since the cognitive revolution, there was a new interest in the mental processes that underpin the whole creative process (Lubart, 2001). Guilford's (1950, 1967) intelligence model was structurally influential. Although it is primarily a theory of intelligence, creativity plays an important role. Until the theory concerning cognitive style, intelligence, and personality (Sternberg, 1985), as well as its modified version, had been developed (Sternberg & Grigorenko, 1997), intelligence research had emphasized creativity (J. C. Kaufman, Plucker, & Russell, 2012).

The two thinking processes proposed by Guilford are DT and convergent thinking. DT is a kind of ability used to develop different solutions to a problem, while convergent thinking involves choosing the best idea or answer, i.e., that which is most worth pursuing. These two thinking processes are sometimes referred to as "idea generation" and "idea exploration." The notion of DT is the core concept behind most creativity tests, such as the TTCT (Almeida et al., 2008b; Raithby & Torrance, 1974)(Guilford, P. (1976.

Thereafter, a synthesis model was developed that implied a creative process involving preparation, idea generation, idea evaluation, and validation (S. M. Sawyer et al., 2012).

The most significant contribution was combined problem identification (Mumford & Connelly, 1991; Reiter-Palmon & Robinson, 2009), which requires people to understand the problem to be solved in the early stage of the creation process. This is because in practice or on a test, the question is often explicit—but in the real world, the problem is not always well defined. A well-defined problem will significantly influence one's choice of solution (problem definition and problem solving will be introduced in Chapter 6). It is possible to find a solution after a series of mental activities.

The theory of Blind Variation and Selective Retention (BVSR) (Campbell, 1960) was first proposed in 1960 and then expanded and refined some decades later (Simonton, 2011). The BVSR holds that ideas usually emerge blindly. Some may spontaneously emerge, whereas others have been preserved over time. Only preserved ideas can endure and have a real impact. Galenson (2009) distinguished two types of outstanding creative processes: The first is concept creation, which often starts with an idea, which is then repeatedly evaluated in terms of the best way to apply it in practice (Galenson, 2009). The second is practice creation, which involves continuous refinements of thought and practice to determine which solution is the best. However, empirical support for this theory is not exceptional (Durmysheva & Kozbelt, 2010). Moreover, in this chapter, an integrated model (R. Keith Sawyer, 2018) is illustrated to display the creative synthesis process. In short, the eight stages are as follows:

1. Define a problem
2. Acquire knowledge related to the problem
3. Collect information
4. Incubate the information
5. Generate ideas
6. Combine ideas
7. Select the best idea
8. Apply the idea

In the following section, each stage of the creative process will be explained in turn.

4.4.2. Eight Stages of the Creative Process

1) Define the Problem

Modern cognitive psychology has indicated that creativity is essentially a form of problem solving, and researchers have compared the creative process stages with the stages of problem solving (Blum et al., 2000; Flavell & Draguns, 1957; Joy P Guilford, 1967; Y. J. Kaufman & Sendra, 1988). In a seminal article from 1962, Newell et al. first proposed that creativity seems to be a special kind of practice within problem solving. Furthermore, Guilford even argued that creativity was very similar to problem solving.

When psychologists study how people solve problems, they present participants with well-defined problems, the solutions to which are obviously known. Newell et al. (1962) proposed that the general process of problem solving occurs in an imaginary solution space, which is like a map in one's mind. There is a starting point, and the challenge is to reach the end point, i.e., the solution. Various strategies must be adopted to arrive at the target since the whole map cannot be seen. However, no matter in art, science, or business, these problems are rarely accurately represented in real-world contexts. Perhaps the most real-world corollary are exams. Unfortunately, most creativity processes occur when people are in the midst of solving ambiguous problems rather than taking exams.

Therefore, ill-defined problems should be identified and better defined before proceeding toward their solution (Jay & Perkins, 1997). Because convergent thinking is primarily involved in solving well-defined problems, ill-defined problems likely require a high level of DT. The first—and only—step to creating a search space is to follow the problem that has been identified.

2) Acquire Knowledge Related to the Problem

The second stage involves acquiring knowledge related to the problem once it has been defined. This process requires the creator sufficiently familiar with their professional knowledge and internalize the knowledge within the domain because adequate background knowledge and profound accumulation are the foundation of creation. Creativity occurs when the existing elements have been effectively combined in some way to produce a new concept. Many researchers have found that a person needs to study a field for about 10 years before being capable of making a creative contribution (Gardner, 1993). The 10-year period demonstrates the importance of learning this field.

Excellent creators actively engage in unique learning during this period, which Anders Eriksson calls deliberate practice (Ericsson, 2006; Ericsson, Krampe, & Tesch-Römer, 1993). However, this intentional practice is undertaken not only to repeat the same process several times over but also to push a little further ahead than before, eventually culminating in mastery through commitment and constant feedback. The 10,000 hours of professional knowledge proposed by Ericsson et al. (1993) indicates that only a person who has consciously invested 10,000 hours of practice in a specific field can achieve world-class performance. This prediction is reliable in chess, medicine, programming, dance, and music. Similar figures have been highlighted by other researchers in biographical studies of prominent creators.

Also, domain knowledge is not entirely about passive internalization—on the contrary, field knowledge can be transformed creatively, even in the initial learning process. This is a natural process. When artists walk through galleries, they instinctively and selectively review the paintings or artworks that potentially inspire them to creatively solve the problems on which they are currently working.

Advanced research (Mumford, Baughman, Maher, Costanza, & Supinski, 1997) has shown how the information we encode virtually affects our ability to use that information for innovation. People cannot be creative if they do not know how to internalize domain knowledge, so formal learning is essential for creativity. Some studies have found that creativity has an inverted "U" function concerning education level (See Figure 4-3). However, overeducation also interferes with creativity.

Specifically, after receiving adequate education in the field, further training may oversocialize a person and lead to a rigid way of thinking. Researchers who have studied Nobel laureates for many years have found that highly creative people actively seek out a role model who is equally highly creative in the same field (Zuckerman, 1974). Furthermore, correlations have been found between having a mentor and the number of recognized creative contributions (Almeida et al., 2008b; Nakamura, Shernoff, & Hooker, 2009).

FIGURE 4-3

The relationship between formal education and ranked eminence for creators (Simonton, 1981).

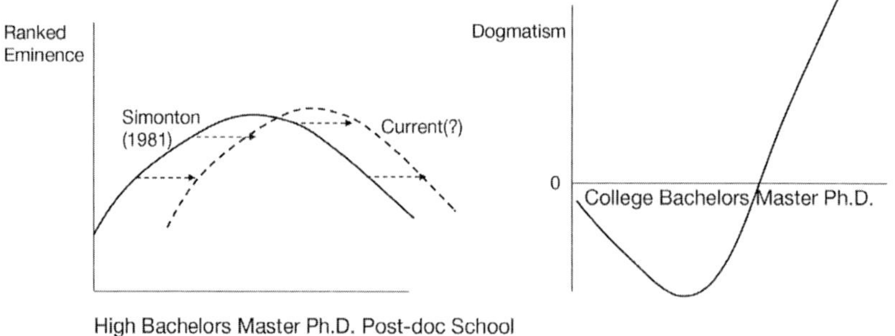

Note. It is redrawn from Simonton, D. K. (1981). Formal education, eminence, and dogmatism. *Journal of Creative Behavior*, 17, 149–162.

3) Collect Information

Creative thinking is a kind of perception that continually pays attention to environmental information of real or potential relevance to a problem. Our brains must process vast amounts of absorbed information into meaningful units from a variety of sources. This constitutes a mental process that involves both creativity and transformation. Rodolfo Linas, a physiologist and neuroscientist, believes that our view of the world is ultimately a projection created by our brains. Scientists have suggested that our eyes process visual data through the visual cortex and into the advanced regions responsible for thinking and creativity in the brain.

Further evidence generated by neuroscience over the past decade has shown that millions of neurons are responsible for sending information from high-level regions in the brain and to the visual cortex. Less than half of these connections to the visual cortex stem directly from the eyes, whereas the majority stem from the brain. These findings (Bakker & Niemantsverdriet, 2016) indicate that only 20% of our perception comes from external information—i.e., 80% of our perception is determined by our brains (Bakker & Niemantsverdriet, 2016).

Moreover, psychologists have identified many perceptual techniques associated with creative thinking. When people organize information, they become more creative and consciously retain useful information needed to promote understanding (Mobley, Doares, & Mumford, 1992). This requires being critical and evaluative when seeking information (Lonergan, Scott, & Mumford, 2004). In other words, creative people are better at finding gaps, identifying potential relationships, and exploiting opportunities to solve problems in conjunction with current information (Burger, Perkins, & Striegler, 1981).

4) Incubate the Information

Incubation is a critical part of the creative process. The emphasis here is on giving time to process all of the relevant information, finding new and appropriate combinations conducive to creative problem solving. Many great creators have claimed that their best ideas emerged from a non-oriented, unconscious process—called incubation.

Take the following story about the great mathematician Archimedes: One day, Archimedes was charged with proving that a new crown made for the king of Syracuse, Hieron, was not made from pure gold. Despite much thought and deliberation, Archimedes could not find a method for doing so. He decided to let the problem go for a while, giving himself a break by taking a long bath. Archimedes filled his bathtub and stepped in, but as he did, he suddenly realized that the water spilling over the edge of the tub was being displaced by his body, meaning that the water was equal to the weight of his body. As he knew that gold was heavier than other metals, Archimedes stumbled upon a method for determining that the crown was not pure gold.

Although this is only a story, it vividly depicts the role of the subconscious in incubating multiple projects simultaneously (Moneta & Csikszentmihalyi, 1996). Many creators use the metaphor of cooking food to describe the process of incubation. When faced with a challenging task, it is recommended to put it aside for a while, to let creativity—like food on a stove—simmer over time. During incubation, ideas rapidly combine and recombine in a disordered way. About this, Einstein wrote: "Mental entities seem to be elements of thought, the certain symbols and clear images that can more or less be combined... This combination seems to be a fundamental feature of creative thinking" (Defoe, Adams, Rogers, & Cowper, 1945). Accordingly, the study of incubation can be closely related to insight theory, in which preconscious process thinking is dominated by secondary process thinking. Consciousness is largely reactive to these underlying forces. Kris (1952) argued that the artist's consciousness should play a more active role in what is called a "return to self-efficiency." A successful creator is one who consciously absorbs the main processes of the unconscious mind.

Further, to understand incubation, we must also understand another concept, called fixation. One of the most important realizations is the recognition of being stuck, i.e., fixation, because that is the moment at which one should put the problem aside, at least temporarily.

For incubation, however, it is necessary to stop counterproductive actions even if there is no fixed effect. However, the question remains as to in which direction or what type of solution will be found. While there is no clear answer to this question, fixed questions can sometimes provide useful hints.

5) Generate Ideas

The associationist theory strongly supports behaviorism, which is a psychological paradigm that dominated American psychology in the early years of the 20th century. However, the Gestalt school rejected associationism and advocated instead that thought integrity was an irreducible phenomenon (Duncker, 1926). American psychologist William James believed that sudden insights result from having a large amount of information and being able to make connections between different factors. On the contrary, the gestalt scientist Duncker pointed out that some problems are solved suddenly, and that there is no evidence of gradual processes in this regard. To prove this, he designed 20 puzzles and claimed that the questions corresponding to these puzzles could not be solved by increasing association. One of the most famous of these questions is Duncker's (1945) radiation problem:

> *Suppose you are a doctor and you are confronted with a patient who has a malignant tumour in his stomach. Surgery is out of the question, but the tumour must be destroyed, or the patient will die. There is a kind of X-ray that can be used to destroy tumours. If the X-ray is powerful enough to destroy the tumour, it also destroys the stomach's healthy organs. However, the soft X-ray does not harm other organs but also any sense to remove tumours. So the question is, how do you use X-ray to cure the patient?*

When Dunker presented the question to 42 people, only two got the answer right, which was expected. However, many researchers have attempted to depict the thinking process by adopting the thinking aloud protocol, which claims that participants usually come up with an obvious solution. Then researchers have realized that it is not feasible even falls into a lock. Most of people are so focused on the solution that they cannot see the problem from any other perspective. As another example, the Nine-Dot Problem (Figure 4-4) requires the participant to connect the nine dots using four connecting lines but not releasing the pencil from the paper.

FIGURE 4-4

Nine-Dot Problem. Connect the nine dots with four straight lines without lifting the pencil from the paper (Maier, 1930).

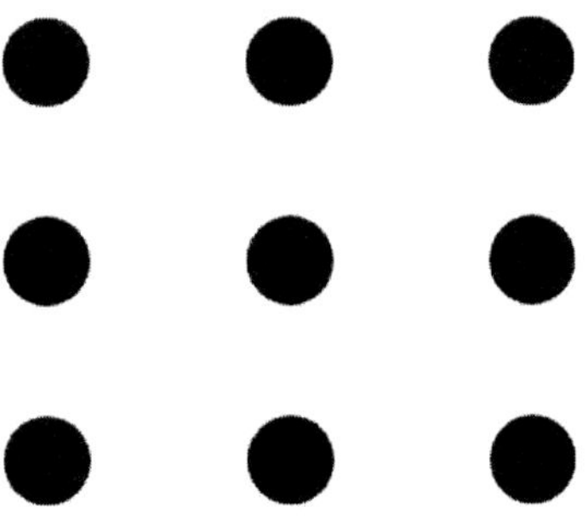

A lot of participants find that the task is difficult because they usually concentrate on connecting the dot with straight line, and always intended to write the Roman letters "VI". Why this problem is so difficult? One possible reason is that people make unfounded assumptions, but they rarely consider extending the line outside the box. Gestalt researchers have argued that insights emerge not because of an increasing chain of associations but instead because the fixation is broken. The problem can then be reorganized and thus resolved.

Many of Dunker's classic problems are still in use today, such as the candle problem (See Figure 4-5). Here, there is a box of thumbtacks, matches, and candles, and the task is to light a candle and stick it on the wall. The candle problem highlights another issue: functional fixation (Glucksberg, 1962). One does not realize that the box can be used as a shelf, not just a container.

Even the insights are easy to understand. However, people are still surprised that how the problem is being solved because of the rigidly ordered deduction cannot demonstrate the answer. But one thing is clear that the insight issues involves several cognitive abilities associated with creativity, such as DT, convergent thinking, and overcoming fixation (DeYoung, Flanders, & Peterson, 2008).

FIGURE 4-5

Using only the pictured items, mount the candle on the wall and light it.

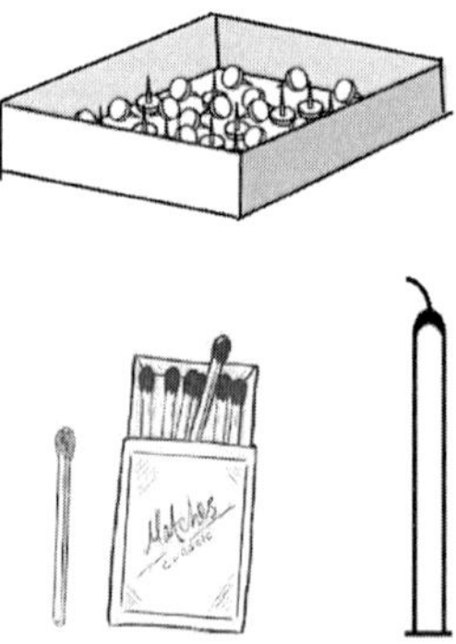

Note. It is redrawn from the Duncker's (1945) candle problem.

Fixation - Restructure

Most people will experience distress before receiving insights. As gestalt theory claims that the position taken by the insight problem is difficult because of "fixation" on the wrong solution, it results in a stalemate, one resolved only through a radical restructuring of the problem, not through a series of incremental associations (Weisberg & Alba, 1981). An everyday example of fixation is the tip of the tongue phenomenon (TOT), where one tries to remember, for instance, a name, which remains at once close to being recalled and yet entirely elusive (Roediger & Neely, 1982). In 1995, Smith researched design students and found that they and design professionals either saw an example of a design first or no example at all. Even when they were told to "create something as different from the example design as possible," they remained focused on the example.

In another experiment, people were asked to imagine and then draw pictures of animals that might exist on another "very Earth-like" planet (Ward, 1995). Interestingly, the participants expected the animals to have certain core traits, such as eyes, ears, and legs. Additionally, the bodies of the animals were always symmetrical as well. In a second experiment, Ward asked another group to imagine animals on a planet "very different from Earth." Nevertheless, the results of this experiment were nearly identical to those of the first. Experiments like this show that imagination is often highly structured, and that people tend to produce "new" things that are mostly similar to what they already know. These experiments show that fixed and structured imagination interferes with the ability to produce unusual and original solutions. Trying to overcome this limitation to generate a breakthrough is exceedingly challenging for the creative process.

6) Combine Ideas

For many decades, psychological research on insights has indicated that new ideas gradually emerge from the recombination of existing ideas rather than from the sudden, spontaneous emergence of entirely new conceptions. This is very much in line with association theory, which holds that creativity is the process of combining or recombining existing ideas—more precisely, familiar ideas and conventions that already exist in the field and have been internalized by the creator. In short, all ideas can be considered derivative. However, the association research of the 19th century never explained the mechanism of mental associations. Over the past few decades of cognitive psychology development, scholars have revealed a lot about how the brain combines ideas.

Insight is usually explained in terms of the concept of reorganization (Ohlsson, 1984). Of all the cognition process studies, concept combinations, metaphors, and analogies have been thought to be most relevant to creativity (Thompson et al., 1997; Ward, 1995). In this view, combinations of two or more different concepts into a new concept constitutes the act of creativity. For analogies, some attributes are transferred from one mental model to another. In a famous case, De Mestra came up with the idea for Velcro when thinking about how burrs stick to clothes (Hill, Fujii, Johnson, & Kawasaki, 1978). Thereby, it can be claimed that conceptual (re)combinations are the fundamental cognitive faculty of human beings. Nevertheless, Hampton (1987) found that when people combine familiar conjunctions (Hampton, 1987), such as pets and birds, they rarely come up with unexpected attributes because they are only recalling instances of that category—like parrots, such as talking. Accidental attributes are more likely to be combined to produce fictitious objects because they often require complex problems to be solved, and stories must therefore be composed to explain how they work.

Another explanation employs information theory to explain linear searches (Newell & Simon, 1972; Weisberg & Alba, 1981). This implies that problem solving is a progressive process that occurs in an alternative space until a sequence of actions is found that connect the problem to the solution (Ohlsson, 1984). However, expanded research into insights suggests that it may depend on both information and experience. Especially when an individual has rich experience in a field, insights can become difficult (Wertheimer, 1985) because such experience erects mental structures in the mind that prevent the discovery of new and original ideas. This phenomenon is similar to functional fixation, which occurs when an individual adheres to previous experience or traditional ways of thinking about a new problem (Duncker & Lees, 1945). Even experts, who possess a wealth of expertise (Rubenson & Runco, 1995) and substantial knowledge, most of which is domain-specific, have great difficulty with innovative thinking. Another interesting phenomenon is that experts often make too many assumptions because they know too much within a domain. Specific knowledge is automatically activated when solving field problems, such that although experts may perform better than novices in many arenas, they are also frequently hindered from exercising creative thinking. Therefore, many scholars have encouraged experts to explore multiple fields of knowledge in order to capture new perspectives (Skinner, 1956) and thereby bypass the saturation and rigidity of domain knowledge and excessive expertise (Martinsen & Helland-Hansen, 1995).

7) Select the Best Idea

Selecting the best idea means thinking about which problem is worth exploring, deciding what to study, determining what to consider, and confirming what should be given up. However, nothing can be carried out under a perfect plan. It is believed that cognition, memory, divergent production, convergent thinking, and evaluation are parallel forces in the creative process (Joy P Guilford, 1967), such that even evaluating which ideas to retain or surrender is itself a creative process. In other words, when people are asked to solve problems by choosing useful concepts, they perform loosely in the second and third stages (Mumford et al., 1997), and they care too much about long-term goals and the quality of solutions. The subconscious then decides on what in the external environment to focus, and this attention may be related to the work being undertaken. Moreover, when a new insight or combination appears in one's consciousness, the creator must evaluate and determine whether it is a good idea.

After all, not every idea is good; not every notion can successfully leap from incubation to awareness. Insights may prove to be inaccurate, and an innovation may not be implemented for technical reasons; An idea for a painting might sound good but look terrible. All such considerations usually evoke critical thinking or are referred to as convergent thinking. In other words, the evaluation stage of the creative process is fully conscious. To be effective, the creator must draw on a great deal of knowledge in the field or reflect deeply on the profession. Timely evaluation and modification will impact the creative outcome directly (Lonergan et al., 2004). In this respect, 12 kinds of attribute have been identified from a review of the relevant literature (Blair & Mumford, 2007):

1. Risky (high probability of incurring a loss)
2. Easy to understand
3. Original
4. Complete description (provides detailed steps needed to make the idea work)
5. Complicated
6. Consistent with existing social norms
7. High probability of success
8. Easy to implement
9. Benefits many people
10. Produces desired societal rewards
11. Time and effort required to implement
12. Complexity of implementation

Many studies have shown that people prefer ideas that conform to social norms and quickly produce desired results; moreover, it is better if the ideas are complex to implement but easy to understand and of benefit to many people. Although people may reject risky original ideas most of the time, they can become riskier when stressed and thus more receptive to creative ideas. In this case, people devote extra time to sifting through riskier and more creative ideas. Another study (Dailey & Mumford, 2006) showed that people often consider two issues when evaluating new ideas. The first are the resources required to implement the idea, and the second are the potential consequences of implementing the idea. For most creative work, many different evaluation criteria are related, and it is not clear which of the criteria is more crucial or how each relates to each other. Numerous studies have demonstrated that evaluation strategies are based on rapid assessment within a domain and field knowledge for novelty and suitability (Bink & Marsh, 2000). Simultaneously, technical expertise and specific materials are also considered in a general evaluation (Csikszentmihalyi & Sawyer, 2014). Furthermore, there is often tension between evaluating the correctness of an idea and determining its appropriateness. The field is continually changing, which requires a timely refinement of the evaluation criteria to stay relevant.

Most research on creativity has found that creative people are also good at critically evaluating their ideas and selecting the best idea from among the available options. Alternatively, a tight association between divergent and convergent thinking enhances creativity. Runco (2003) argued that creativity in the real world requires generating ideas and critical selection. In several studies, Runco revealed the relationship between DT scores and the accuracy of judging one's ideas. Later studies (Runco & Chand, 1995) found that the accuracy of a person who assesses their ideas is correlated with generating original ideas on different tasks (R s = 0.48, 0.61). Evaluation accuracy was shown to be associated with DT in both adults (Runco & Vega, 1990) and children. Moreover, people who possessed many original ideas were also better at rating them.

Another study asked participants to complete four DT tasks, including the unusual use of two objects—bricks and knives (Silvia et al., 2009)—and two practical tasks—round and something that make sounds—and then asked them to choose the two most creative ideas for each task. The raters then evaluated all of their responses on a scale of 1 to 5. The results showed that the participants with high openness had more creative responses to the DT tasks. Their evaluations were accurate, and the participants who were conscientious showed the opposite pattern. The ability to generate creative ideas is positively correlated with the ability to evaluate ideas. Specifically, people who come up with more ideas can accurately evaluate ideas. However, as these studies were conducted in laboratories and did not require expertise in any field, the extent to which the findings are applicable to real-world creative fields is difficult to determine. However, the findings are consistent with what we know about Big-C creativity. For instance, we know that creativity requires substantial domain knowledge, and that domain knowledge contributes to generating and evaluating ideas.

There is much evidence (Lonergan et al., 2004) to suggest that some evaluations precede DT in stage 5. The ability to accurately assess potential creativity is essential to be a productive creator. The above studies demonstrated a significant relationship between evaluation capability and other creative tests, such as the DT test, and the creative process.

8) Externalize Ideas

Studies of creativity are coincidentally focused on developing an idea—however, it would take far too much effort to make an idea a reality. Excellent creators are those who are good at executing their ideas, anticipating how others react to their ideas, and preparing reasonable responses. To identify the resources necessary to implement actualize these ideas, they create practice plans and improvise their work as new information emerges. The final stage of this creative process is primarily the consciousness-oriented stage, in which creators must utilize their knowledge to translate their idea into a complete creative product.

Many scholars adhere to the idealist theory that claims that this final stage is not truly "creative" but is instead simply the execution of the idea. Generating creative ideas is the core of the process, whereas executing the idea is a skillful process, but one devoid of creativity. However, putting an idea into practice often leads to other new views and subsequent insights as a comprehensive agreement, shown in many creative process studies. The most creative people intend to organize and externalize the primary idea before it is even fully formed. They intend to present any worldview since the idea or even the hunch initially emerged in their mind. If a person has an idea but never implements it, then the idea will be lost to history. In early research about the ideal problem-solving model, externalization was one of the five core elements of a practical solution (Stein, Littlefield, Bransford, & Persampieri, 1984).

Moreover, in another study, more than 70 prominent creators were interviewed and their diaries and notebooks were analyzed (Steiner, 1985). Steiner found that all of the interviewees across the domains commonly presented their early ideas and hunches in sketchbooks, notes, or quick prototypes. They did not come up with ideas overnight, but rather over time, as they worked with these external images.

The value of externalization has been recognized through a two-stage model (Finke, Ward, & Smith, 1992). The first stage is the structure of the cognition of the experience in the generation stage. Generative processes include memory extraction, association, mental synthesis, transformation, analogical interpretation, and category reduction. Then, the exploratory stage examines the meaning of cognitive structures, which include finding attributes, conceptual interpretation, functional reasoning, contextual shifts, hypothesis testing, and identifying limitations (Finke et al., 1992). Finke and colleagues argued that outstanding creators often invent structures before the generation and externalization of ideas and then explain their ideas in various ways, including via vague concepts, preliminary experiments, or prototypes.

A group of painters was recruited (Verstijnen, van Leeuwen, Goldschmidt, Hamel, & Hennessey, 1998) to conduct experiments, and it was found that they were more creatively externalized in their visual processes. However, for non-experienced artists, there was no difference. Mental visualization is a useful technique, but it only works for relatively simple problems. As the number of components increases, externalization becomes increasingly crucial, because the brain does not have the conscious and working memory needed to represent it internally in complex mechanical combinations (Finke et al., 1992).

The study of externalization shows that it is not a simple matter of execution to actualize an idea that has been formed in the mind. On the contrary, the process of rendering early ideas concrete and then manipulating them promotes a rich but uncertain creative process. This investigation revealed why experts always emphasize practice in design by accentuating "visualization," "materialization," and "spatial memory" (Fischer & Boynton, 2005). The Western cultural model endorses two traditional beliefs: (1) the essence of creativity is the moment of insight, and (2) creative ideas mysteriously appear from the unconscious mind. However, through several decades of empirical scientific research, many achievements have supported the theory of action and challenged these two beliefs.

4.4.3. Discussion of the Creative Process

The eight-stage model is an effective way to capture all of the cognitive processes involved in creativity. However, creativity rarely unfolds linearly, and many fields of creative process overlap or repeat with the mental processes related to all of these eight stages or appear in reverse order. This pertains to highly creative individuals. As the creativity study field continues to develop, we can confirm that creativity emerges in complex, nonlinear ways over time. Many innovative products take months or even years to incubate. Gruber (1974) analyzed Darwin's theory-developing process over 13 years by reviewing his diaries (Gruber & Barrett, 1974).

With the profound development of cognitive science, it has been shown that those who can develop a flexible understanding are more creative and use multiple understandings and active recombinatory elements in problem solving (Mumford & Gustafson, 1988). This sounds like our everyday life, like common ways to solve problems at hand. Indeed, early cognitive psychologists thought of creativity as problem solving based on the practice of cognitive ability. But it is the unique cognitive structure that leads to different creative behaviors. To study creativity by using the DG test that emerged in the 1950s and 1960s, we need a better framework to understand the creative behavior underlying cognitive processes, thereby enabling us to develop new assessments and to explore new combinations of skills and to even reinterpret skills within creativity.

Researchers are currently theorizing about long-term processes that retain countless practical questions that the experiments cannot answer. These researchers need more qualitative, biographical methods to study those individuals who might deal with many problems in most creative professions, and insights often create more questions than they answer. Moreover, creative insights that generate the appropriate questions are more valuable than those that only conclusively answer existing questions because solving a good problem may lead to a new one. In working, the creator frequently experiences small insights, which are often easily explained as efforts and conscious accumulations in the process. Even so, we still do not know exactly what is happening inside the brain.

4.5. Cognitive Neuroscience Approach

Cognitive neuroscience provides a distinguished methodology compared to the traditional cognitive approach in that it deploys three types of brain-imaging technology: positron emission tomography (PET), electroencephalography (EEG), and functional magnetic resonance imaging (fMRI). According to neuroscience, the brain comprises 100 to 150 billion neurons (R. Keith Sawyer, 2018). Each neuron is connected to from 1,000 to 10,000 other neurons through synapses. When the neurons receive signals through short tentacles called dendrites, on which the signals aggregate to determine the strength of the signals, they transmit them to individual axons. Each axon has at most 1,000 or more axon ends, each of which relays signals to the dendrites of other neurons (Brosch, 2018). Most of these axons are connected to neighboring neurons, and a small number of neurons have longer axons that can send signals throughout the brain (S. M. Sawyer et al., 2012).

However, each technology has its own strengths and weaknesses—a brief introduction of these three methods is provided below.

4.5.1. Positron Emission Tomography (PET)

Introducing a radioactive tracer into the bloodstream is the fundamental component of the PET procedure, which is based on the observation that the more blood flows, the more radiation there is. A radioactive isotope of oxygen is often adopted, one which decays rapidly and is essential to reducing radiation exposure. O-15 is the most commonly used oxygen isotope, as it has a half-life of 122 seconds. The participants was given a cognitive task in a PET experiment that could be finished in a given amount of time during the decay period of the oxygen isotope. Most of the O-15 isotope would have decayed in about 40 seconds, and the signal would have reached its peak as well. While the associated brain regions increase neuronal activation once they are engaged in the cognitive task, the increased radioactivity caused by regional cerebral blood flow was detectable by a PET scanner.

The results depicted a three-dimensional representation of the brain activity of those who engaged in cognitive tasks. Neuronal activation in this particular area was increased due to the neocortex firing faster and the neurons needing more oxygen and blood flow to this area. Moreover, the PET indirectly measures neuronal activity by detecting local cerebral blood flow (rCBF) (R. Keith Sawyer, 2018). However, the PET performed at a high quality at the spatial resolution but took more time to detect brain activity than the EEG (Goense & Logothetis, 2008; Logothetis, 2008).

4.5.2. Electroencephalography EEG

The electroencephalograph (EEG) utilizes scalp sensors to measure the electromagnetic fields generated by neural activity. The mechanization of the measurement is based on the transmission of signals from neurons to axons and dendrites through electrical impulses. EEG detects the electrical activity of dendrites (Goense & Logothetis, 2008). A small magnetic field is created if several neurons and their dendrites are aligned in parallel and receive signals simultaneously. Detectable electromagnetic fields will be generated in the cerebral cortex if the neurons and dendrites are aligned. If the neurons do not align in the brain's bottom area, then the electrical signals in the scalp are weaker than in parallel conditions. Therefore, the EEG technique normally used to study cortical activity.

EEG is outstanding in that it can detect the brain's response to an externally stimulating event instantaneously, even in microseconds, which is called high time resolution. But it still has the drawback of being incapable of determining where the primary neurons make the changes that emerge in the electromagnetic field, and as such it is also considered to have low spatial resolution. Even if there are 20 electrodes around the skull, an event-related potential (ERP) at any particular electrode does not necessarily mean that the neurons below the electrode caused the ERP. The electromagnetic field will expand throughout the brain. To identify brain regions associated with neuronal activity, other techniques with higher spatial resolution are needed, such as fMRI.

4.5.3. Functional magnetic resonance imaging (fMRI)

Functional magnetic resonance imaging (fMRI) has quickly become the most widely used brain imaging technique after PET. It is called "the most important brain imaging development since discovering x-rays in 1895" (Logothetis, 2008). fMRI mainly detects the ratio of oxygenated blood to deoxygenated blood. This ratio is called the blood oxygen level-dependent signal. When neuronal activity in a specific area of the neocortex increases, blood flow increases faster than neurons use oxygen, thereby increasing the signal. fMRI has been used more than PET because it is easier to obtain and has excellent spatial resolution. There is no need to inject a radioactive tracer for each test and it can allow hundreds of tests, the average of which can be taken. In comparison, PET experiments can do up to 30 experiments because the radioisotope must be injected before each experiment: 12 to 16 experiments are the typical range. The time resolution of fMRI is also high, and researchers can get an fMRI image every two seconds. As with EEG, due to the complexity of the brain's response, changes in any single event are impossible to detect. So when the researcher averages the responses of 50 trials involved in irrelevant brain activity and fluctuations, they will get signals related to the event that they can study (S. Lee & Care, 2011).

To explain common changes in the human brain, cognitive neuroscientists do not study individual people. Instead, they perform the same experiment on many people. The statistical images they make average all of the brains and then use statistical algorithms to identify average brain activity in an experiment. The brain images of all subjects are averaged to generate a single "average" brain image, just like each of us has slightly different fingerprints, even though they all look like fingerprints. Likewise, everyone's brain is slightly different, although the overall organization of all brains is very similar. However, the shape and size of heads are different, which means that researchers must mathematically adjust the size of all brains to compare two brains so that they are the same. There is currently no way to make a standard detailed structure of each brain.

Cognitive neuroscience is a fantastic field for explaining creativity (Greene, Freed, & Sawyer, 2019). These studies have shown that creativity is not limited to a particular area of the brain; on the contrary, creativity is produced by a complex network of neurons throughout the brain (S. M. Sawyer et al., 2012). These findings paint a complicated picture of the relationship between neuroscience and creativity. But creativity is not limited to a specific area of the brain. Many studies have shown that creativity involves a variety of cognitive abilities. Each cognitive ability itself is a complex and emergent characteristic of the biological brain; each involves many brain areas simultaneously, and each requires continuous time. Therefore, creativity cannot be reduced to a single brain area to which insights at a specific time can be attributed.

4.6. Conclusion

Creativity is a multifaceted structure that has been with us since the beginning of our species (S. B. Kaufman et al., 2016). The debate about its nature and roots is ancient (Afhami & Mohammadi-Zarghan, 2018). In the past few decades, the field of creativity has expanded in many different fields. In this chapter, we sought to introduce the individual approach, which has a crucial effect on creativity research, after which we introduced the synthesis model of the creative process. The 4P model (Rhodes, 1961) is a solid framework that distinguishes people, processes, products, and pressure (environmental factors). However, there are still many components that need to be explored. The study of creative personality is an independent unit, and there are also biological perspectives based on genetics and neuroscience (GrandPré, Nakamura, Vartanian, & Strittmatter, 2000). However, it mainly focused on the cognitive perspective to explain creativity, and the relationship between creativity and IQ.

Concerning creativity in different fields, from business to education, from psychology to neuroscience, further interdisciplinary cooperation is warranted. Today, such goals seem to be easier to achieve than ever before. Our networks and virtual interactions allow us to travel, meet new friends, and share new ideas on an unprecedented scale. However, the fact that people can communicate with each other does not mean that they can overcome all of the obstacles like culture and languages. With this situation, we should have a standard consensus in the field. Many scholars are interested in creativity but may not be familiar with specific creativity research. With the vast amount of information we know about creativity, it is challenging to develop a set of universally accurate tools even with a common language. Some criticisms of current assessments concern the predominance of tests. IQ tests can help determine which students are gifted or have learning disabilities (J. C. Kaufman et al., 2016; J. C. Kaufman, Cole, & Baer, 2009).

Standardized group tests determine which students enter university or graduate school (Regier et al., 2013) and which people are more likely to get well-paid and influential jobs. However, these indicators consistently show significant differences between different races, usually gender differences (Bleske-Rechek & Browne, 2014). These differences are problematic. Even affordable, fast, and accurate creativity tests will only promote the field's development to a limited extent and will not intrinsically improve positive creativity.

As Sternberg and Kaufman(2012) claimed, empathy is the core of wisdom. Recognizing the role of empathy in creative practice and actively using this process to understand and respond to the needs of others requires an in-depth analysis of the creative process and, at the same time, the ability to obtain psychological representations of the needs, intentions, and beliefs of others. There is growing evidence that empathy can regulate individuals and groups (Cross, Laurence, & Rabinowitch, 2012). These ideas arise when we go beyond our position and consider what other people might say or do, whether a specific audience or the general public. This process can open up new possibilities for creative practice and develop active, creative forms.

Of course, this model does not mean that immediately or automatically accepting others' opinions will increase creativity, nor does it necessarily mean becoming more concerned about others' needs. But it is a way for us to gain insight into pro-social creative possibilities without participating in these activities and cultivating our ability to reflect on different perspectives.

Creativity, be it ordinary to revolutionary, requires the interaction of multiple elements. Many components comprise the creative individual and the material world, social life, and culture. Therefore, from a methodological standpoint, questions and methods should aim to identify and maintain this complexity instead of reducing the various levels of creativity through analysis (Barbot & Reiter-Palmon, 2019). It should also be the primary motivation to reveal creative performance by applying inter-disciplinary approaches, which would promise a bright future for creativity research.

4.7. Discussion and assignment

4.7.1. Group discussion in classroom

1) Individual task (15 min)

Think of a time when you made something that you thought was particularly creative—a school project, a written report, a mechanical device, a block tower, a painting, or a musical performance.

- What mental process led to its creation?
- Did you have a lot of training and expert knowledge in the domain? If not, what prepared you to make this creative product or idea or how did this idea develop?
- Did you have the idea all at once, fully formed, such that all you had to do was make it? If so, what preceded the insight—what preparations did you make, and was there an incubation period?
- Think of a time when you had an idea that, upon closer examination, turned out to be not such a good idea. What evaluative process made that clear? Why did you not see it right away?
- We are often required to present our new ideas for our study or career. And our ideas are typically evaluated by the criteria of "creativity" or "innovativeness." When you became an evaluator, how did you evaluate others' ideas based on the criteria of "creativity" or "innovativeness"?

2) Group task

Share your thoughts of the individual task above with classmates.
Group size: 3–5 (depending on the class size and its diversity)

Time: The group discussion is 10 minutes, preparation for the presentation is 5 minutes, presentation is 5 minutes per group, and all group Q&As are 5 minutes.

Presentation: All group members should contribute to the group discussion and preparation for the presentation. The presenter will be randomly selected by the instructor.

4.7.2. Assignment

Review the academic literature on the topic of creative cognitive process and use this knowledge to make recommendations for how to apply it in your field of interest.

REFERENCES

✦ ✦ ✦

Acar, S., & Runco, M. A. (2015). Thinking in multiple directions: Hyperspace categories in divergent thinking. *Psychology of Aesthetics, Creativity, and the Arts, 9*(1), 41.

Afhami, R., & Mohammadi-Zarghan, S. (2018). The Big Five, aesthetic judgment styles, and art interest. *Europe's Journal of Psychology, 14*(4), 764–775. https://doi.org/10.5964/ejop.v14i4.1479

Almeida, L. S., Prieto, L. P., Ferrando, M., Oliveira, E., & Ferrándiz, C. (2008a). Torrance Test of Creative Thinking: The question of its construct validity. *Thinking Skills and Creativity, 3*(1), 53–58.

Almeida, L. S., Prieto, L. P., Ferrando, M., Oliveira, E., & Ferrándiz, C. (2008b). Torrance Test of Creative Thinking: The question of its construct validity. *Thinking Skills and Creativity, 3*(1), 53–58. https://doi.org/10.1016/j.tsc.2008.03.003

Amabile, T. M. (1998). *How to kill creativity* (Vol. 87). Harvard Business School Publishing Boston, MA.

Ansburg, P. I., & Hill, K. (2003). Creative and analytic thinkers differ in their use of attentional resources. *Personality and Individual Differences, 34*(7), 1141–1152.

Baer, J., Kaufman, J. C., & Gentile, C. A. (2004). Extension of the Consensual Assessment Technique to Nonparallel Creative Products. *Creativity Research Journal, 16*(1), 113–117. https://doi.org/10.1207/s15326934crj1601_11

Bakker, S., & Niemantsverdriet, K. (2016). The interaction-attention continuum: Considering various levels of human attention in interaction design. *International Journal of Design, 10*(2), 1–14.

Barbot, B., & Reiter-Palmon, R. (2019). Creativity assessment: Pitfalls, solutions, and standards. *Psychology of Aesthetics, Creativity, and the Arts, 13*(2), 131–132. https://doi.org/10.1037/aca0000251

Barron, F. (1955). The disposition toward originality. *The Journal of Abnormal and Social Psychology, 51*(3), 478.

Barron, F., & Harrington, D. M. (1981). Creativity, intelligence, and personality. *Annual Review of Psychology, 32*(1), 439–476.

Bink, M. L., & Marsh, R. L. (2000). Cognitive regularities in creative activity. *Review of General Psychology, 4*(1), 59–78.

Blair, C. S., & Mumford, M. D. (2007). Errors in idea evaluation: Preference for the unoriginal? *The Journal of Creative Behavior, 41*(3), 197–222.

Bleske-Rechek, A., & Browne, K. (2014). Trends in GRE scores and graduate enrollments by gender and ethnicity. *Intelligence, 46*, 25–34.

Blum, J., Wurm, G., Kempf, S., Poppe, T., Klahr, H., Kozasa, T., ... Schräpler, R. (2000). Growth and form of planetary seedlings: Results from a microgravity aggregation experiment. *Physical Review Letters, 85*(12), 2426.

Boden, M. A. (2004). *The creative mind: Myths and mechanisms*. Psychology Press.

Brosch, R. (2018). What we 'see' when we read: Visualization and vividness in reading fictional narratives. Cortex, 105, 135–143. https://doi.org/10.1016/j.cortex.2017.08.020

Bruner, J. S. (1962). The conditions of creativity. *Contemporary Approaches to Creative Thinking, 1958, University of Colorado, CO, US; This Paper Was Presented at the Aforementioned Symposium*. Atherton Press.

Burger, E. D., Perkins, T. K., & Striegler, J. H. (1981). Studies of wax deposition in the trans Alaska pipeline. *Journal of Petroleum Technology, 33*(06), 1–75.

Cacioppo, J. T., Gardner, W. L., & Berntson, G. G. (1999). The affect system has parallel and integrative processing components: Form follows function. *Journal of Personality and Social Psychology, 76*(5), 839.

Campbell, D. T. (1960). Blind variation and selective retentions in creative thought as in other knowledge processes. *Psychological Review, 67*(6), 380.

Caraco, T., Martindale, S., & Whittam, T. S. (1980). An empirical demonstration of risk-sensitive foraging preferences. *Animal Behaviour, 28*(3), 820–830.

Carroll, J. B. (1993). *Human cognitive abilities: A survey of factor-analytic studies*. Cambridge University Press.

Cropley, A. J., & Cropley, D. (2009). *Fostering creativity: A diagnostic approach for higher education and organizations*. Hampton Press Cresskill, NJ.

Cross, I., Laurence, F., & Rabinowitch, T.-C. (2012). *Empathy and creativity in group musical practices: Towards a concept of empathic creativity*. na.

Csikszentmihalyi, M. (2006). A systems perspective on creativity. *Creative Management and Development, Third Edition*, 3–17. https://doi.org/10.4135/9781446213704.n1

Csikszentmihalyi, M., & Sawyer, K. (2014). Shifting the focus from individual to organizational creativity. In *The systems model of creativity* (pp. 67–71). Springer.

Dailey, L., & Mumford, M. D. (2006). Evaluative aspects of creative thought: Errors in appraising the implications of new ideas. *Creativity Research Journal, 18*(3), 385–390.

Defoe, D., Adams, W. H. D., Rogers, W., & Cowper, W. (1945). *The life and strange surprizing adventures of Robinson Crusoe, of York, mariner*. Peter Pauper Press.

DeYoung, C. G., Flanders, J. L., & Peterson, J. B. (2008). Cognitive abilities involved in insight problem solving: An individual differences model. *Creativity Research Journal, 20*(3), 278–290.

Domino, G. (1970). Identification of potentially creative persons from the Adjective Check List. Journal of Consulting and Clinical Psychology, 35(1p1), 48.

Duncker, K. (1926). A qualitative (experimental and theoretical) study of productive thinking (solving of comprehensible problems). *The Pedagogical Seminary and Journal of Genetic Psychology, 33*(4), 642–708.

Duncker, K., & Lees, L. S. (1945). On problem-solving. *Psychological Monographs, 58*(5), i.

Durmysheva, Y., & Kozbelt, A. (2010). The creative approach questionnaire: Operationalizing Galenson's finder-seeker typology in a non-expert sample. *The International Journal of Creativity & Problem Solving*.

Ericsson, K. A. (2006). The influence of experience and deliberate practice on the development of superior expert performance. *The Cambridge Handbook of Expertise and Expert Performance, 38*(685–705), 2.

Ericsson, K. A., Krampe, R. T., & Tesch-Römer, C. (1993). The role of deliberate practice in the acquisition of expert performance. *Psychological Review, 100*(3), 363.

Feldman, M. S., & Pentland, B. T. (2003). Reconceptualizing organizational routines as a source of flexibility and change. *Administrative Science Quarterly, 48*(1),

94–118.

Fink, K. S. (2009). Understanding rating systems when interpreting evidence. *American Family Physician, 80*(11), 1206–1207.

Finke, R. A., Ward, T. B., & Smith, S. M. (1992). *Creative cognition: Theory, research, and applications.*

Fischer, B., & Boynton, A. (2005). Virtuoso teams. *Harvard Business Review, 83*(7), 116.

Flanagan, D. P., Ortiz, S. O., & Alfonso, V. C. (2013). *Essentials of cross-battery assessment* (Vol. 84). John Wiley & Sons.

Flavell, J. H., & Draguns, J. (1957). A microgenetic approach to perception and thought. *Psychological Bulletin, 54*(3), 197–217.

Franck, K., & Rosen, E. (1949). Franck drawing completion test. *Australian Council for Educational Research.*

Frasier, M. M. (1991). Disadvantaged and culturally diverse gifted students. *Journal for the Education of the Gifted, 14*(3), 234–245.

Frick, J. W., Guilford, J. P., Christensen, P. R., & Merrifield, P. R. (1959). A factor-analytic study of flexibility in thinking. *Educational and Psychological Measurement, 19*(4), 469–496.

Fuchs-Beauchamp, K. D., Karnes, M. B., & Johnson, L. J. (1993). Creativity and intelligence in preschoolers. *Gifted Child Quarterly, 37*(3), 113–117.

Fuss, D. (1993). Freud's Fallen Women: Identification, Desire, and" A Case of Homosexuality in a Woman". *The Yale Journal of Criticism, 6*(1), 1.

Gajda, A., Karwowski, M., & Beghetto, R. A. (2017). Creativity and academic achievement: A meta-analysis. *Journal of Educational Psychology, 109*(2), 269.

Galenson, D. (2009). *Conceptual revolutions in twentieth-century art.* National Bureau of Economic Research.

Gao, Z., Chen, T., Weber, M. J., & Linden, J. (1999). A2B adenosine and P2Y2 receptors stimulate mitogen-activated protein kinase in human embryonic kidney-293 cells: cross-talk between cyclic AMP and protein kinase C pathways. *Journal of Biological Chemistry, 274*(9), 5972–5980.

Gardner, J. (1993). *On leadership.* Simon and Schuster.

Gastl, G. A., Abrams, J. S., Nanus, D. M., Oosterkamp, R., Silver, J., Liu, F., ... Bander, N. H. (1993). Interleukin-10 production by human carcinoma cell lines and its relationship to interleukin-6 expression. *International Journal of Cancer*, 55(1), 96–101.

Getzels, J. W., & Jackson, P. W. (1962). *Creativity and intelligence: Explorations with gifted students.*

Glăveanu, V. P. (2013). Creativity development in community contexts: The case of folk art. *Thinking Skills and Creativity, 9*, 152–164. https://doi.org/10.1016/j.tsc.2012.11.001

Glucksberg, S. (1962). The influence of strength of drive on functional fixedness and perceptual recognition. *Journal of Experimental Psychology, 63*(1), 36.

Goense, J. B. M., & Logothetis, N. K. (2008). Neurophysiology of the BOLD fMRI signal in awake monkeys. *Current Biology, 18*(9), 631–640.

Gough, H. G. (1976). Studying creativity by means of word association tests. *Journal of Applied Psychology, 61*(3), 348.

Gough, H. G. (1979). A creative personality scale for the adjective check list. *Journal of Personality and Social Psychology, 37*(8), 1398.

GrandPré, T., Nakamura, F., Vartanian, T., & Strittmatter, S. M. (2000). Identification of the Nogo inhibitor of axon regeneration as a Reticulon protein. *Nature, 403*(6768), 439–444.

Greene, J. A., Freed, R., & Sawyer, R. K. (2019). Fostering creative performance in art and design education via self-regulated learning. *Instructional Science, 47*(2), 127–149. https://doi.org/10.1007/s11251-018-9479-8

Gregory, R. W., & Paidoussis, M. P. (1966). Unstable oscillation of tubular cantilevers conveying fluid II. Experiments. *Proceedings of the Royal Society of London. Series A. Mathematical and Physical Sciences, 293*(1435), 528–542.

Gruber, H. E., & Barrett, P. H. (1974). *Darwin on man: A psychological study of scientific creativity*. EP Dutton.

Gruber, H. E., & Wallace, D. B. (1999). The case study method and evolving systems approach for understanding unique creative people at work. *Handbook of Creativity, 93*, 115.

Guilford, Joy P. (1967). Creativity: Yesterday, today and tomorrow. *The Journal of*

Creative Behavior, 1(1), 3–14.

Guilford, Joy Paul. (1950). *Fundamental statistics in psychology and education.*

Hampton, J. A. (1987). Inheritance of attributes in natural concept conjunctions. *Memory & Cognition, 15*(1), 55–71.

Hennessey, B. A. (2015). Creative Behavior, Motivation, Environment and Culture: The Building of a Systems Model. *Journal of Creative Behavior, 49*(3), 194–210. https://doi.org/10.1002/jocb.97

Hill, K. O., Fujii, Y., Johnson, D. C., & Kawasaki, B. S. (1978). Photosensitivity in optical fiber waveguides: Application to reflection filter fabrication. *Applied Physics Letters, 32*(10), 647–649.

Hocevar, D., & Bachelor, P. (1989). A taxonomy and critique of measurements used in the study of creativity. *Handbook of Creativity*, 53–75.

Horn, J. L., & Cattell, R. B. (1966). Age differences in primary mental ability factors. *Journal of Gerontology*, 21(2), 210–220.

Horn, J. L., & Knapp, J. R. (1973). *On the subjective character of the empirical base of Guilford's structure-of-intellect model.*

Isen, A. M., Labroo, A. A., & Durlach, P. (2004). An influence of product and brand name on positive affect: Implicit and explicit measures. *Motivation and Emotion, 28*(1), 43–63.

Jauk, E., Benedek, M., Dunst, B., & Neubauer, A. C. (2013). The relationship between intelligence and creativity: New support for the threshold hypothesis by means of empirical breakpoint detection. *Intelligence, 41*(4), 212–221.

Jay, E. S., & Perkins, D. N. (1997). Problem finding: The search for mechanism. *The Creativity Research Handbook, 1*, 257–293.

Kaufman, J. C. (2002). Narrative and paradigmatic thinking styles in creative writing and journalism students. *Journal of Creative Behavior, 36*(3), 201–219. https://doi.org/10.1002/j.2162-6057.2002.tb01064.x

Kaufman, J. C., & Beghetto, R. A. (2009). *Beyond Big and Little : The Four C Model of Creativity. 13*(1), 1–12. https://doi.org/10.1037/a0013688

Kaufman, J. C., Beghetto, R. A., & Watson, C. (2016). Creative metacognition and self-ratings of creative performance: A 4-C perspective. *Learning and Individual Differences, 51*, 394–399. https://doi.org/10.1016/j.lindif.2015.05.004

Kaufman, J. C., Cole, J. C., & Baer, J. (2009). The construct of creativity: Structural model for self-reported creativity ratings. *The Journal of Creative Behavior, 43*(2), 119–134.

KAUFMAN, J. C., COLE, J. C., & BAER, J. (2009). The Construct of Creativity: Structural Model for Self-Reported Creativity Ratings. *The Journal of Creative Behavior, 43*(2), 119–134. https://doi.org/10.1002/j.2162-6057.2009.tb01310.x

Kaufman, J. C., Glaveanu, V. P., & Baer, J. (2017). *Cambridge Handbook of Creativity Across Domains Creativity.*

Kaufman, J. C., Plucker, J. A., & Baer, J. (2008). *Essentials of creativity assessment* (Vol. 53). John Wiley & Sons.

Kaufman, J. C., Plucker, J. A., & Russell, C. M. (2012). Identifying and assessing creativity as a component of giftedness. *Journal of Psychoeducational Assessment, 30*(1), 60–73. https://doi.org/10.1177/0734282911428196

Kaufman, S. B., Kozbelt, A., Silvia, P., Kaufman, J. C., Ramesh, S., & Feist, G. J. (2016). Who finds Bill Gates sexy? Creative mate preferences as a function of cognitive ability, personality, and creative achievement. *The Journal of Creative Behavior, 50*(4), 294–307.

Kaufman, Y. J., & Sendra, C. (1988). Algorithm for automatic atmospheric corrections to visible and near-IR satellite imagery. *International Journal of Remote Sensing, 9*(8), 1357–1381.

Kharkhurin, A. V. (2014). Creativity. 4in1: Four-criterion construct of creativity. *Creativity Research Journal, 26*(3), 338–352.

Kim, K. H. (2011). The creativity crisis: The decrease in creative thinking scores on the Torrance Tests of Creative Thinking. *Creativity Research Journal, 23*(4), 285–295.

Koenigsberger, L. (1902). *Hermann von Helmholtz.*

Kris, E. (1952). *Psychoanalytic explorations in art.*

Lee, J., & Lee, K. (2009). Evidence and Tools by Cross-Cultural Study. *International Journal of Design, 3*(1), 17–28.

Lee, S., & Care, P. (2011). Service Design in Healthcare: Patient-centered care. *International Journal of Design, 5*(2), 61–71. Retrieved from www.ijdesign.org

Levine, S., & Ross, F. (2002). Perceptions of and attitudes to HIV/AIDS among young adults in Cape Town. *Social Dynamics, 28*(1), 89–108.

Logothetis, N. K. (2008). What we can do and what we cannot do with fMRI. *Nature, 453*(7197), 869–878.

Lonergan, D. C., Scott, G. M., & Mumford, M. D. (2004). Evaluative aspects of creative thought: Effects of appraisal and revision standards. *Creativity Research Journal, 16*(2–3), 231–246.

Lubart, T. I. (2001). Models of the creative process: Past, present and future. *Creativity Research Journal, 13*(3–4), 295–308.

Maier, N. R. (1930). Reasoning in humans. I. On direction. *Journal of comparative Psychology, 10*(2), 115.

Martinsen, O. J., & Helland-Hansen, W. (1995). Strike variability of clastic depositional systems: Does it matter for sequence-stratigraphic analysis? *Geology, 23*(5), 439–442.

Marx, M. H., & Cronan-Hillix, W. A. (1987). *McGraw-Hill series in psychology. Systems and theories in psychology*. Mcgraw-Hill Book Company.

Mason, R. L., Gunst, R. F., & Hess, J. L. (2003). *Statistical design and analysis of experiments: with applications to engineering and science* (Vol. 474). John Wiley & Sons.

McGrew, K. S. (2009). *CHC theory and the human cognitive abilities project: Standing on the shoulders of the giants of psychometric intelligence research*. Elsevier.

McKinnon, R. I. (1962). Wages, capital costs, and employment in manufacturing: a model applied to 1947-58 US data. *Econometrica: Journal of the Econometric Society*, 501–521.

Mednick, S. (1962). The associative basis of the creative process. *Psychological Review, 69*(3), 220–232.

Melosh, H. J., & McKinnon, W. B. (1978). The mechanics of ringed basin formation. *Geophysical Research Letters, 5*(11), 985–988.

Mobley, M. I., Doares, L. M., & Mumford, M. D. (1992). Process analytic models of creative capacities: Evidence for the combination and reorganization process. *Creativity Research Journal, 5*(2), 125–155.

Moneta, G. B., & Csikszentmihalyi, M. (1996). The effect of perceived challenges and skills on the quality of subjective experience. *Journal of Personality, 64*(2), 275–310.

Mumford, M. D., Baughman, W. A., Maher, M. A., Costanza, D. P., & Supinski, E. P. (1997). Process-based measures of creative problem-solving skills: IV. Category combination. *Creativity Research Journal, 10*(1), 59–71.

Mumford, M. D., & Connelly, M. S. (1991). Leaders as creators: Leader performance and problem solving in ill-defined domains. *The Leadership Quarterly, 2*(4), 289–315.

Mumford, M. D., & Gustafson, S. B. (1988). Creativity syndrome: Integration, application, and innovation. *Psychological Bulletin, 103*(1), 27.

Nakamura, J., Shernoff, D. J., & Hooker, C. H. (2009). *Good mentoring: Fostering excellent practice in higher education.* John Wiley & Sons.

Negus, K., & Pickering, M. J. (2004). *Creativity, communication and cultural value.* Sage.

Newell, A., Shaw, J. C., & Simon, H. A. (1962). The processes of creative thinking. *Contemporary Approaches to Creative Thinking, 1958, University of Colorado, CO, US; This Paper Was Presented at the Aforementioned Symposium.* Atherton Press.

Newell, A., & Simon, H. A. (1972). *Human problem solving* (Vol. 104). Prentice-hall Englewood Cliffs, NJ.

Ohlsson, S. (1984). Restructuring revisited: II. An information processing theory of restructuring and insight. *Scandinavian Journal of Psychology, 25*(2), 117–129.

Parnes, S., & Harding, H. F. (1963). A SOURCE. *BOOK FOR CREAVIE THINKING NEW YORK: Scribner & Sons.*

Perkins, M. R. (1983). *Modal expressions in English* (Vol. 123). Ablex Publishing Corporation Norwood, New Jersey.

Plucker, J. A., Beghetto, R. A., & Dow, G. T. (2004). Why isn't creativity more important to educational psychologists? Potentials, pitfalls, and future directions in creativity research. *Educational Psychologist, 39*(2), 83–96.

Pratt, M., Pradies, C., & Lepisto, D. A. (2013). *Doing well, doing good and doing with: Organizational practices for effectively cultivating meaningful work.*

Preckel, F., Holling, H., Weise, M., Richards, R., Kinney, D. K., Benet, M., ... Roskos-

Ewoldsen, B. (n.d.). Creativity: Theories and Themes: Research, Development, and Practice by Mark A. Runco, Elsevier Academic Press, 2007, 492 pp. ISBN 13: 978-0-12-602400-5. $74.95 (hardback). *Human Physiology, 26*, 516–522.

R. Keith Sawyer. (2018). EXPLAINING CREATIVITY. In *Oxford University Press*. https://doi.org/10.4324/9781351199797

Raithby, G. D., & Torrance, K. E. (1974). Upstream-weighted differencing schemes and their application to elliptic problems involving fluid flow. *Computers & Fluids, 2*(2), 191–206.

Reckwitz, A. (2017). Practices and their affects. *The Nexus of Practices: Connections, Constellations, Practitioners*, 114–125.

Regier, J. C., Mitter, C., Zwick, A., Bazinet, A. L., Cummings, M. P., Kawahara, A. Y., ... Davis, D. R. (2013). A large-scale, higher-level, molecular phylogenetic study of the insect order Lepidoptera (moths and butterflies). *PloS One, 8*(3), e58568.

Reiter-Palmon, R., & Robinson, E. J. (2009). Problem identification and construction: What do we know, what is the future? *Psychology of Aesthetics, Creativity, and the Arts, 3*(1), 43.

Rhodes, M. (1961). An analysis of creativity. *The Phi Delta Kappan, 42*(7), 305–310.

Roediger, H. L., & Neely, J. H. (1982). Retrieval blocks in episodic and semantic memory. *Canadian Journal of Psychology/Revue Canadienne de Psychologie, 36*(2), 213.

Rogers, C. R. (1977). *Carl Rogers on personal power*. Delacorte.

Rubenson, D. L., & Runco, M. A. (1995). The psychoeconomic view of creative work in groups and organizations. *Creativity and Innovation Management, 4*(4), 232–241.

Runco, M. A. (2003). Education for creative potential. *Scandinavian Journal of Educational Research, 47*(3), 317–324.

Runco, M. A. (2008). *Commentary: Divergent thinking is not synonymous with creativity.*

Runco, M. A., & Albert, R. S. (1985). The reliability and validity of ideational originality in the divergent thinking of academically gifted and nongifted children. *Educational and Psychological Measurement, 45*(3), 483–501.

Runco, M. A., & Chand, I. (1995). Cognition and creativity. *Educational Psychology*

Review, 7(3), 243–267.

Runco, M. A., & Vega, L. (1990). Evaluating the Creativity of Childern's Ideas. *Journal of Social Behavior and Personality, 5*(5), 439.

Sawyer, K. (2017). *Group genius: The creative power of collaboration*. Basic books.

Sawyer, R. Keith. (2017). Teaching creativity in art and design studio classes: A systematic literature review. *Educational Research Review, 22*, 99–113. https://doi.org/10.1016/j.edurev.2017.07.002

Sawyer, Robert Keith, John-Steiner, V., Csikszentmihalyi, M., Moran, S., Feldman, D. H., Gardner, H., ... Nakamura, J. (2003). *Creativity and development*. Oxford University Press, USA.

Sawyer, S. M., Afifi, R. A., Bearinger, L. H., Blakemore, S.-J., Dick, B., Ezeh, A. C., & Patton, G. C. (2012). Adolescence: a foundation for future health. *The Lancet, 379*(9826), 1630–1640.

Silvia, P. J., Kaufman, J. C., & Pretz, J. E. (2009). Is Creativity Domain-Specific? Latent Class Models of Creative Accomplishments and Creative Self-Descriptions. *Psychology of Aesthetics, Creativity, and the Arts, 3*(3), 139–148. https://doi.org/10.1037/a0014940

Simon, H. A. (1990). Invariants of human behavior. *Annual Review of Psychology, 41*(1), 1–20.

Simonton, D. (1981). Formal education, eminence and dogmatism: the curvilinear relationship. *The Journal of creative behavior, 17*(3), 149-162.

Simonton, D. K. (1999). *Origins of genius: Darwinian perspectives on creativity*. Oxford University Press.

Simonton, D. K. (2011). Creativity and discovery as blind variation: Campbell's (1960) BVSR model after the half-century mark. *Review of General Psychology, 15*(2), 158–174.

Simonton, D. K. (2012). Foresight, Insight, Oversight, and Hindsight in Scientific Discovery: How sighted were galileo's telescopic sightings? *Psychology of Aesthetics, Creativity, and the Arts, 6*(3), 243–254. https://doi.org/10.1037/a0027058

Skinner, B. F. (1956). A case history in scientific method. *American Psychologist, 11*(5), 221.

Sligh, A. C., Conners, F. A., & Roskos-Ewoldsen, B. (2005). Relation of creativity to fluid and crystallized intelligence. *The Journal of Creative Behavior, 39*(2), 123–136.

Snow, R. G., & Nunn, J. F. (1959). Induction of anaesthesia in the foot-down position for patients with a full stomach. *BJA: British Journal of Anaesthesia, 31*(11), 493–497.

Spearman, C. (1923). *The nature of" intelligence" and the principles of cognition.* Macmillan.

Stein, B. S., Littlefield, J., Bransford, J. D., & Persampieri, M. (1984). Elaboration and knowledge acquisition. *Memory & Cognition, 12*(5), 522–529.

Steiner, J. (1985). The training of psychotherapists. *Psychoanalytic Psychotherapy, 1*(1), 55–63.

Sternberg, R. J. (1985). Implicit theories of intelligence, creativity, and wisdom. *Journal of Personality and Social Psychology, 49*(3), 607.

Sternberg, R. J. (1999). *Handbook of creativity.* Cambridge University Press.

Sternberg, R. J., & Grigorenko, E. L. (1997). Are cognitive styles still in style? *American Psychologist, 52*(7), 700–712. https://doi.org/10.1037/0003-066X.52.7.700

Sternberg, R. J., & Grigorenko, E. L. (2001). *Unified psychology.*

Sternberg, R. J., & Kaufman, J. C. (2012). When your race is almost run, but you feel you're not yet done: Application of the propulsion theory of creative contributions to late-career challenges. *Journal of Creative Behavior, 46*(1), 66–76. https://doi.org/10.1002/jocb.005

Tang, H., & Gero, J. (2002). A cognitive method to measure potential creativity in designing. *Workshop*, 47–54. Retrieved from http://cs.gmu.edu/~jgero/publications/2002/02TangGeroECAI.pdf

Thompson, S. K., Halbert, S. M., Bossard, M. J., Tomaszek, T. A., Levy, M. A., Zhao, B., ... D'Alessio, K. J. (1997). Design of potent and selective human cathepsin K inhibitors that span the active site. *Proceedings of the National Academy of Sciences, 94*(26), 14249–14254.

Thurschwell, P. (2009). *Sigmund Freud.* Routledge.

Torrance, E. P. (1972). Predictive validity of the torrance tests of creative thinking.

The Journal of Creative Behavior.

Unsworth, K. (2001). Unpacking creativity. *Academy of Management Review, 26*(2), 289–297.

Verstijnen, I. M., van Leeuwen, C., Goldschmidt, G., Hamel, R., & Hennessey, J. M. (1998). Sketching and creative discovery. *Design Studies, 19*(4), 519–546.

Wallach, M. A., & Kogan, N. (1965). A new look at the creativity-intelligence distinction 1. *Journal of Personality, 33*(3), 348–369.

Wallas, G. (1926). *The art of thought.*

Ward, T. B. (1995). What's old about new ideas. *The Creative Cognition Approach,* 157–178.

Weiner, B. (2000). Attributional thoughts about consumer behavior. *Journal of Consumer Research, 27*(3), 382–387.

Weisberg, R. W., & Alba, J. W. (1981). *Gestalt theory, insight, and past experience: Reply to Dominowski.*

Wertheimer, M. (1985). A Gestalt perspective on computer simulations of cognitive processes. *Computers in Human Behavior, 1*(1), 19–33.

White, H. A., & Shah, P. (2006). Uninhibited imaginations: creativity in adults with attention-deficit/hyperactivity disorder. *Personality and Individual Differences, 40*(6), 1121–1131.

Zuckerman, M. (1974). *The sensation seeking motive.*

C H A P T E R

05

Topic 4 Types of Innovation

Topic 4

Types of Innovation

Nilima Haque Ruma and Eunyoung Kim

This chapter portrays the types of innovation (ToI) from different angles to help us relate to the innovation concept in diverse fields. Before discussing the ToI, this chapter provides brief details about how innovation is understood and how it originated in the academic and market contexts.

5.1. Review of the Study of Innovation

Innovation refers both to ideas that are commercialized in the marketplace and to ideas that have already been successfully marketed (Dziallas & Blind, 2019). It is often misunderstood as applying and commercializing new ideas to the products, processes, or any other aspects of a firm's economic activities. However, the concept 'innovation' has further meaning and it has been defined by various researchers in diverse fields. Fagerberg and Mowery (2009) contended that innovation mostly takes place in firms, although it may also occur in other types of organizations, such as universities or public hospitals. Morris (2006) viewed "innovation" as evoking images of inventors, new technologies, and new products. Numerous definitions of the innovation concept have been developed since the 1990s, when Schumpeter (1983) first drew attention to it. Most of these definitions, however, are isolated and fragile because of their limited focus on certain products, processes, or technological innovations.

The list of innovations is endless, and the manifestations of innovative products and services in daily life are immeasurable. Nowadays, we cannot imagine life without cell phones, computers, the internet, SNS, televisions, and airplanes, to name a few. Schumpeter (1983) anticipated that innovation plays the role of a changing drive. Traditional concepts, products, and business models are continuously replaced by brand-new innovations, which led Schumpeter to characterize "capitalism" as a means of "creative destruction." Previous works have suggested that innovation is a critical force by which firms pursue the utilization of technological advancement, sustainable management, coping with gradual changes in the marketplace, and meeting customers' needs and requests, ultimately resulting in the attainment of sustainable competitive advantages in terms of business performance (Morris, 2006). Many scholars have supported the notion that innovation occurs after the introduction and cultivation of some noble, fresh, and original ideas regarding new products, processes, or services. One critique of this viewpoint is that noble or new ideas alone are inadequate for properly realizing an innovation; rather, such ideas must also meet market criteria: purposeful, commercially valuable, desired by customers, and resilient. Drucker (1987) asserted that innovation is most acceptable and adaptable in practical and academic debate. To him, successful innovation results from a conscious, purposeful search for opportunities for innovation, which exist in only a few situations.

Purposeful innovation comprises the analysis, system, and hard work that can be discussed and presented as the practice of innovation.

5.1.1 The genesis of innovation

Historically, in the thirteenth century, the word "Novation," which means *reviving* an obligation by altering an agreement, emerged in the field of law (Benoit, 2008; Kaihan Krippendorff, 2017)Tommy Hilfiger, etc.. In the fields of arts and sciences, however, the term was barely used before the twentieth century. To Benoit (2008), there was controversy about "innovation" in the religious environment of mid-seventeenth-century England. This is because almost all debates and writings of the time depicted the term as connoting change, not creativity. Before the twentieth century, the concept of "innovation" played critical roles in meaning both in religion and politics. In politics, it was received negatively due to traditions, whereas it was considered unorthodox due to religious belief. Moreover, in the eighteenth century, inventors began earning money from their inventions, that put projectors (as innovators were called then) troublesome because of insufficient science, poor management, and fraud. In the nineteenth century, and up until World War II, the "innovation" term was not popular. However, it was widely used in the science and technology product fields, where it was tied to the idea of economic growth and competitive advantage. The concept of innovation was also discussed in the abundant scientific literature and in the social sciences, including sociology, management, and finances, as well as in the arts and humanities (Benoit, 2008). In the mid-twentieth century, innovation took center stage in the widespread imaginary, in mass media, and in public policy, as well as in economic development. Innovation became the fundamental driver of competitiveness for economic activities and actors, whom Schumpeter (1983) called "entrepreneurs."

According to the Global Innovation Index (GII), innovation is pivotal to the Economic Policy Strategies and Sustainable Development Goals (SDGs) of a country. In 2019, the UN General Assembly recognized innovation, parallel with science and technology, as a means for achieving SDGs. The appeal of innovation is as well accepted as it is ubiquitous. It has become commonplace for marketers to stress the significant role of creative thinking in the strategies and future growth potentials of a firm, or any organization. Harvard University professor Joseph A. Schumpeter is often regarded as the first economist to draw attention to the role of innovation in social and economic change. He argued that economic development had to be a process of qualitative change fueled by innovation taking place over many years. In his theory of "Circular Flow" (or the German word *Kreislauf*),

Schumpeter defined "innovation" as "carrying out new amalgamations" of current resources by entrepreneurs. To him, entrepreneurs neither accumulate any kind of goods, nor they design creative methods of production; however, they use the current way of production differently, more properly, and more efficiently. Examples of innovation, according to Schumpeter, are introducing innovative goods, innovative procedures, new marketplace entrances, new sources of supplies, and innovative approaches in industrialized organizations (Schumpeter, 1983, 1989).

There is a general, essential difference between invention and innovation. An invention is the first manifestation of a concept for a new creation or procedure. On the contrary, an innovation is a leading endeavor undertaken to transform innovation itself into practice (Fagerberg, 2003). Despite this difference, it is hard to distinguish invention from innovation to some extent as both terms are so closely linked. There is no doubt that the term "innovation" has influenced the business activities of micro- to macro-level firms and of the local to global economy, so much so that it has become a taken-for-granted prerequisite for competitive economic performance in the eyes of entrepreneurs. In contemporary times, the success of an organization is considered in direct relationship to its capacity to commercialize new ideas or formulas. As Fargerberg (2003) noted, to transform an invention into an innovation, an organization must combine numerous unique forms of expertise, talent, and supplies. This transformation is inherently linked to the process of commercializing or extracting value from ideas. On the contrary, an invention alone does not need to be directly associated with commercialization (Rogers, 1998).

5.1.2 The significance of innovation

Market competitiveness and rapid technological advancements have put corporate managers in the troublesome position of having to make the right decisions when confronting new challenges. Tackling business uncertainties in an era of market volatility and social problems means that firms will respond in varying ways in terms of their economic activities, innovativeness, and corporate behaviors. More specifically, variations will occur in a firm's integrated product-, process-, market-, or technology-driven innovations, or even in its customer-oriented and human-centered approach, as an adaptive mechanism.

Many multinational firms have been shaping their innovation commitments from several contingency factors for many years, many of which also appear in Schumpeter (1934). He believed that firms intended to be innovative for the following reasons:

- The high degree of uncertainties.
- Moving forward and reaping economic potentials.
- Acknowledging the fundamental challenge to new ideas.

Schumpeter's (1934) speculation on entrepreneurship went beyond the boundary of firms, whereas Drucker (1987) highlighted innovation in the context of firms, noting that the success of firms in the innovation process relies heavily upon how they assess the areas of opportunities related to the innovation both within and outside of the company. Such areas of opportunities can be divided into two categories: internal (within the firm's internal environment) and external (outside the firm's internal environment). These areas influence the extent to which firms are innovative, which Drucker (1987) called "sources of innovation." The internal sources include unpredictable circumstances, incompatibilities, procedural needs, and industrial changes. On the other hand, demographic changes, changes in perception, and new knowledge are considered external sources of opportunities. These sources often appear as outcomes of increasing a firm's market shares and its branding as an iconic image across the globe. It can be inferred that firms' strategic orientation concerning product and process innovation, such as technological adaptations in production systems, would lead them to be consistent in their economic performance. Many companies have stood out from their competitors and created market value as pioneers in product innovation. Their organizational strategies made them innovators, which is consistent with an innovation orientation.

Boston Consulting Group (BCG) evaluates the performance of companies along four dimensions and publishes a list of the most innovative companies for the last 14 years. The BCG's assessments have revealed that over the past 14 years, 162 companies have been at the top of the list: almost 30% appeared just once, whereas 57% have appeared three times or fewer. Only eight companies have continuously been at the top of the list for the last 14 years, i.e., companies demonstrating the capacity for serial innovation. Therefore, the BCG experts have argued, serial innovation is difficult (Ringel et al., 2020). The most obvious challenge for firms in this regard is how to continuously nurture and boost innovation practices. Although innovation is increasingly crucial for firms to maintain competitive advantage, it remains extremely difficult for firms to actually and consistently achieve.

Hambrick (1983) tested four types of organizations with regard to innovation operationalization: prospectors, defenders, reactors, and analyzers. As Hambrick explained, a prospector organization is one that tends to rapidly offer alternating product lines and competes primarily by promoting and meeting market demands. On the contrary, defender organizations conduct little or no new product-market development but instead concentrate on improving the efficiency of their existing products and operations. Reactor organizations also do not respond to changes in the product-market environment but rather manage extant environmental pressures when pressured to do so. Analyzer organizations, on the other hand, follow a hybrid path that combines approaches taken by both prospectors and defenders. Compared to prospector organizations, analyzer organization pursue slower changes in product-market development; compared to defender organizations, analyzer organizations are less inclined toward managing stability and efficiency (Hambrick, 1983).

Investigations by the BCG have also identified three types of firms in terms of their innovative nature: committed, skeptical, and confused innovators (Ringel et al., 2020). According to a BCG survey, committed and skeptical innovators constituted approximately 45 to 30 percent of 1,000 surveyed firms worldwide. Innovation was found to be a priority among committed innovators/committed firms, which allocate significant resources and a large portion of their budget for continuous improvement. On the contrary, skeptical innovators neither consider innovation to be a strategic priority nor situate innovation as a crucial target for increased investment. So-called "confused innovators" comprised 25 percent of the total firms surveyed by the BCG. These firms were found to follow a seemingly incompatible— hence confused— approach in terms of innovation, one in which the strategic importance given to innovation was incommensurate with the level of funding allocated for it. Therefore, the data showed that almost one-quarter of companies were not interested in pursuing innovation.

5.2 Types of Innovation

Innovation has no ubiquitous classification, and it can manifest in myriad forms. However, innovation may be categorized according to "types," as Schumpeter (1989) demonstrated: new product orientation, new production method, new supply sources, new market entry, and new changes to organizing the business. However, this classification pertains only to the firm's operational context, which welcomes changes, and its focus is almost exclusively on "product" and "process" innovations. Many other types of innovation, however, have also been identified and practiced in the academic and business arena. Morris (2007) described six distinct views on innovation in his book *Permanent Innovation: The Definitive Guide to the Principles, Strategies, and Methods of Successful Innovators*. These views can be divided into three outsider and three insider perspectives. To Morris, the outsider perspectives include *Knowledge Channel Innovation, Peer-to-Peer Innovation, and Outside-in Innovation*, whereas the insider views consist of *Technology-Driven Innovation, Bottom-Up Innovation*, and *Top-Down Innovation*. Arguably, in the prior mentioned literature, there are the four types of innovation process—incremental innovations, product and technology breakthroughs, business model innovations, and new ventures—are evident in the firm's innovation orientation. Figure 5-1 depicts all four types of innovation based on their extension.

FIGURE 5-1

Types of innovation (Morris, 2006)

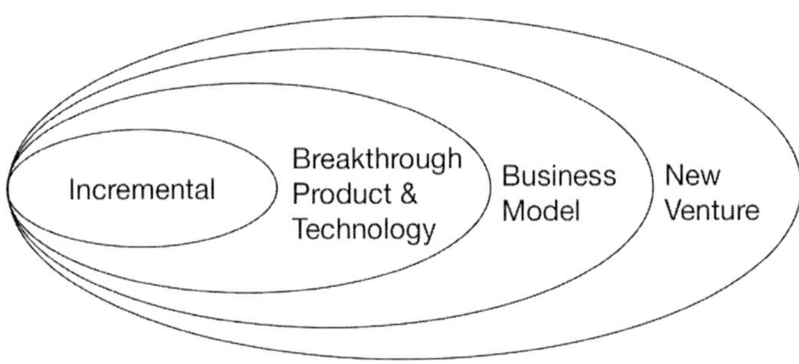

Note. It is redrawn from Morris (2006), Permanent Innovation: The Definitive Guide to the Principles, Strategies, and Methods of Successful Innovators.

5.2.1 Incremental innovation

Incremental innovation refers to continuous innovations that proceed through gradual changes or improvements within existing products and services. The key function of incremental innovations is to improve cost leadership, ensure quality control, and manage changes in production processes. In modem times, continuous improvements in existing products and services is taken for granted, meaning that companies always pursue upgrades to their products and services. For instance, contemporary automobiles, cell phones, computers, or other home appliances are constantly updated in terms of their design, shape, quality, functions, recyclability, and reusability. Morris (2006) asserted that incremental innovation can also be a compelling, effective, and even aggressive strategy in and of itself. As an example, he discussed Sony, which manufactured a total of 160 different versions of its Walkman, averaging 25 days for each new model, in the 1990s. Toyota's production system, headed by legendary engineer Taiichi Ohno, is another good example of incremental innovation. Toyota focuses on continuous improvements (Kaizen) in its manufacturing and assembling plants, and accordingly it is considered one of the most efficient and highest-quality automotive companies. Incremental improvements in its assembly processes have helped Toyota to create a lean process throughout its enterprise. This lean production system has cut changeover times, which were initially required in the development from one model to another (Ledbetter, 2018). Incremental innovation is easy to understand, and is less risky, and as such most companies invest resources in incremental projects. Doing so balances organizational capabilities over resource allocation and control in continuous innovation projects. As Kahn (2018) explained, it is by pursuing small wins that big wins can be achieved. However, proponents of the other forms of innovation have claimed that the incremental innovation orientation is not solely adequate for sustaining the long-term future of a firm; rather, many other forms of innovation, like breakthrough products and technology, innovative business models, and new venture are also crucial to the long-term success of a firm.

5.2.2 Breakthrough innovation

Breakthrough innovation, also referred to as "discontinuous innovation" or "rupture innovation," is named as such because it disrupts the marketplace to produce a desired effect. A breakthrough innovation resolves existing problems significantly better than previous innovations, and it is precisely through disruptions that such innovations can be distinguished from incremental innovations (Morris, 2006). Most companies push breakthrough innovation projects as strategic priorities because derivative projects influence existing competencies more effectively (Dyer et al., 2011). To realize a breakthrough innovation, the firm must pursue a risk-taking strategy. Mistakes are to be expected in such efforts, and employees must therefore be granted autonomy or authority to take quick actions when necessary. It is for these reasons, i.e., high risk and need for immediate decision making, that breakthrough ideas are often disregarded. Additionally, previous research has also argued the breakthrough innovations require special resources that incremental innovations do not (Kahn, 2018). Dyer et al. (2011) produced several examples of world-leading innovative companies that have successfully handled failures while taking risks. Again, for those firms that truly pursue innovation, employee failures must not only be allowed but also be perceived as an opportunity to learn and to distinguish good from bad failures. For instance, a "good" failure at Google has been defined by two characteristics: (1) the reasons for the failure are known and incorporated as relevant knowledge for next projects; (2) good failures occur fast enough, and these are not big enough to compromise your brand (Dyer et al., 2011).

5.2.3 Business model innovation (BMI)

Another popular concept, business model innovation (BMI) or innovative business model has flourished across industrial sectors and in academic writing. Proponents of BMI argue that it is a simple and more feasible model for coping with a firm's existing products and process innovations. Moreover, BMI generates outcomes that can change the industry (Kahn, 2018). BMI requires neither new technologies nor the creation of brand-new markets; rather, it is all about the delivery methods of the existing products produced by existing technologies to existing markets. Successful innovative companies, whether they be a new venture or an established player, need to choose a good business model to deliver their products and services to existing markets. The business model of a firm must answer Peter Durker's age-old questions: "Who is the customer? and "What does the customer value?" (Drucker, 1987). Moreover, the business model must also answer every corporate manager's queries concerning a product's distribution channels, profit streams, value delivery to customers, and expenditures (Joan Magretta, 2019).

IBM Institute for Business Value gave exemplary definitions based on the robustness and intricacy of BMI (Edward Giesen et al., 2009). Their critical review of 35 best practice cases, as shown in Table 5-1 below, generated a framework consisting of three key types of business models: the industry model, the revenue model, and the enterprise model.

TABLE 5-1 Types of Business Model Innovations

Category	Characteristics	Examples
Industry model	Innovates "industry value chain" by transforming new industries, redefining current industries, or creating completely new ones, and by identifying distinct assets.	Dell's direct to customers approach, which eliminates intermediaries; Apple's iTunes, which delivers music direct to customers; and the launch of Google and Facebook with the advent of the internet.
Revenue model	Innovating on how companies yield income through offering re-configuration (product/service/value mix) and pricing models.	Netflix's movie rental option, and Gillette's strategy of underpricing razors.
Enterprise model	Innovating the roles played in the value chain by changing the extended enterprise and relationship with employees, suppliers, customers, and others, including capability/asset configuration.	Japanese *keiretsu* framework or clothing retailers like Zara and H&M and Bharti Airtel. All of these companies focus on the marketing, sales, distribution, and outsourcing of much of their products for external parties.

Note. This table is created by authors explanations, partially sourced from IBM (2009)

5.3. Tech-driven vs. Human-centered Innovation

5.3.1 Technology-driven innovation

Nowadays, technology-driven innovation is significant and influential in industrial revolutions.

Since the first industrial revolution, tech-driven innovation has been shifting in its appeal to the manufacturing sector as the speed of economic activities and productivity has increased. Referring to the Business Dictionary, the term "technology-driven" can be defined as follows:

> *Management philosophy that pushes for development of new goods or services based on firms' technical abilities instead of proven demand: to make keys first and then look for locks to open. Practically every breakthrough innovation is based on a technology-driven orientation.* (Rosenzweig, 2015, pp. 71-72)

Schumpeter's (1983) first two categories, new products and new processes, greatly rely on the technological capabilities of a firm. Almost two decades before Schumpeter's (1983) postulates, Schmookler (1966) distinguished between "product technology" and "production technology" in his classic work, "Invention and Economic Growth." He stated that the difference between "product" and "production" innovation was critical for one's comprehension (Fagerberg, 2003; Oliveira & Von Hippel, 2011). Thus, the first concerns the *creation or improvement* of products, while the latter concerns knowledge about *know-how skills* to produce them. These two important elements of "new product creation" and "production process improvement" have been emphasized over the decades with regard to innovation orientation. Both terms could be used to characterize the innovation of new goods or services as well as improvements in the ways these goods and services are manufactured., respectively (Drucker, 2015; Fagerberg, 2003; Manu & Sriram, 1996).

Previous studies showed that innovation orientation is broadly based on a technology-driven strategy. For Morris (2006), tech-driven innovation begins in scientific discoveries and develops over years of accumulated technical know-how. The combined forces of science and technology are inspired and accepted by entrepreneurs in a wider application. Every industry, nowadays, is becoming a technology industry to some extent, and this kind of breakthrough is becoming ever more essential (Ringel et al., 2020). The percentage of new product introductions or process improvements differs based on technological capabilities. Generally, technology-driven companies are strong users of technologies in order to bring new products to market or to generate new ways of production. These groups are often considered as product or process innovators from a marketing perspective, and they adopt upgraded technologies more swiftly than their competitors do. Manu and Sriram (1996) claimed that product innovators could be described by their high promotion and advertising costs, as well as unique product quality, but with a few varieties in customer types. In contrast, process innovators spend moderately high marketing expenditures, have relatively broad product-market scopes, and produce relatively high-quality products, but at a low level of services and with a very poor image. The emphases on research and development (R&D) and its expenditures are more crucial to product innovators than to process innovators. This finding suggests that even expenditures in achieving technological capabilities may vary according to organization type, innovation environment, and economic performance. The environment has a strong association with each innovation type, as Manu and Sriram (1996) found, as the environments of product innovators are influenced by a high degree of dynamism.

Tech-driven innovation is central to the competitive position for high-tech manufacturing (Morris, 2006). High-tech is associated with high, medium, and low R&D strength in production (or value-added). This occurs either directly (in the industry itself) or with the inclusion of R&D-intensive machinery and other types of input (Fagerberg, 2003). Industrial R&D has an immense influence on advancing technologies significantly and the consequent results for innovative products. Schumpeter (1989) claimed that modern firms equipped with R&D laboratories have become the central innovative entity. Berkhout et al. (2010) explained that industrial R&D had a strong influence on technology-driven innovations, such radar, rocket technology, and wireless communications as well as weaponry, for the military during World War II. To date, many developed countries and their multinational firms have substantially increased their expenditures on R&D to adopt technological changes and to subsequently meet market needs.

FIGURE 5-2

Diagram of the linear models of innovation

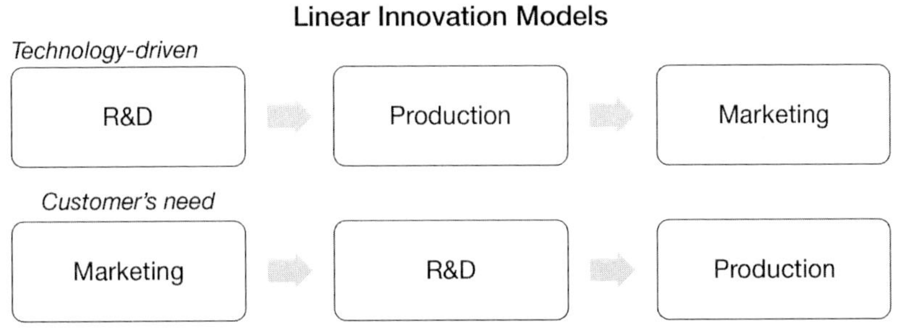

Note. It is modified by authors from Michelini, L. (2012), *Social Innovation and New Business Models, Social Innovation and New Business Models*. doi: 10.1007/978-3-642-32150-4, and from Kline and Nathan Rosenberg (1986).

According to Berkhout et al. (2010), technology advancement is often dominated by R&D-intensive industries, and consequently the technology platforms are mediating new knowledge creation (KC) to be commercially realized according to market desires. They presented a model of how new KC by science-based societies or educational institutions could contribute to technology development that further mediates new product and service innovations with respect to customers' needs. This model was also replicated in the preceding concept of "linear process" (see Figure 5-2) by Kline and Nathan Rosenberg (1986), who defined the holistic view of innovation by criticizing the misinterpretation of innovation. To them, models that depict innovation as a smooth, well-behaved linear process badly unspecify the nature and direction of the causal factors at work.

Tech-driven firms always pursue discovering and deploying useful new technologies for product and process innovation commitment. Global firms often consider tech-driven innovation as a source of competitiveness. Gartner, who publishes an annual report of the hype cycle[1] for emerging technology,

1 https://www.gartner.com/en/newsroom/press-releases/2020-08-18-gartner-identifies-five-emerging-trends-that-will-drive-technology-innovation-for-the-next-decade

identified the technologies that facilitate a composable enterprise of 2020 (Gartner, 2020). Brian Burke, research vice president of Gartner, claimed that almost all new technologies are disruptive. However, these technologies are not well known or proven in market competitions, and most will take more than five years, and some more than 10 years, to reach the productivity plateau. In 2020, as a result of the COVID-19 pandemic, related technologies, such as health passports and social distancing equipment, became two of the most relevant emerging technologies and are taking the fast track through the hype cycle with a high impact on the market. According to Gartner (2020), technologies rarely position the hype cycle at the point where social distancing technologies have entered it, but this technology has received remarkable attention in the media due to privacy concerns.

5.3.2 Human-centered innovation

Aside from technology-driven innovation, human-centered innovation has drawn attention in solving users' specific needs and desires in the innovation paradigm over the years. Human-centered innovation focuses on creating new solutions rooted in actual human needs (Determann, 2015). Because of human desires for user-specific products, marketers are rethinking aspects of new market creation, development of sourcing, and internal changes within their organization. Innovation practices are applicable not only in technology disruption but also in meeting people's needs by propelling the business and society forward. Innovation helps to improve the quality of human life by adding different values such as competitive advantages, differentiations, knowledge creation and so on. Traditionally, innovation is a linear process that starts from fundamental inquiry and proceeds to the development of technology and its evaluation, demonstration, deployment, commercialization, and market penetration. However, market saturation, obsolescence, and finally replacement depends on its success (Perelman, 2007). On the contrary, human-centered innovation entails human and social aspects, such as needs, desires, demands, and behaviors, which are considered either not at all or instinctively, anecdotally, unintentionally, and often reactively. Determann (2015) posited that human-centered projects invariably comprise their contours and character. Human-centered design and innovation does not replace the simple linear model of innovation but instead augments it with a more detailed web of the innovation ecosystem. The innovation priority should concern human and social imperatives. Moreover, human factors are not limited to ergonomics and economic utility but also envelope culture, meaning, and behavior, which as such should be given intense consideration. Several leading commercial design firms, such as IDEO.org, RKS, and 4DProducts, are recent examples of human-centered innovation. They usually start projects with a comprehensive study of human and social factors before any technical designs are outlined. IDEO innovates many products and services that focus on human desires and actual needs—for instance, *"Vroom"* for early child development, *"Moneythink mobile"* for digital financial literacy, and *"Smartlife"* for water and hygiene business are some key human-centered innovations (see www.designkit.org). Another example is Opti Desktop PC and its American design partner, ZIBA Design, which won a gold award for China's Lenovo Group in the latest annual industrial design excellence competition co-sponsored by Business Week and the Industrial Designers Society of America. "Human-centered" has an absolute implication of humaneness— i.e., it requires some value standards to sort out "good" from "bad" innovation (Perelman, 2007).

5.3.3 Toward a strategy of human-centered innovation

The management-by-exception approach has considered developing workshops to emphasize human-centered innovation. The following challenges have been identified to be overcome in these workshops (Perelman, 2007):

- Blatant barriers to human-centered innovation: policies, programs, and practices that discourage detailed attendance to human and social requirements.
- Methods that force innovation efforts toward wasteful or destructive outcomes.
- Warning signs that innovation endeavors are heading toward unplanned, adverse consequences.

Identifying the worst practices is easier than recognizing the best practices. It could be feasible to discover and pursue certain crucial features of human-centered innovation. One of such method is ZIBA program, which fund ethnographers, anthropologists, and other social and behavioral analysts to study user desires, expectations, behaviors, and needs first, and then channel technical designs based on the resulting insights. Such programs would seem to be more likely to respond successfully to human requirements than programs that simply engineer products in a vacuum of social disinterest. Thus, a positive consequence of management-by-exception may be to identify some of the essential "habits" of highly effective, human-centered innovators, as in the approach taken by Jim Collins in his research for Built to Last (Perelman & Group, 2014).

The globalization and fast growth of the Internet of Things (IoT), artificial intelligence (AI), and robotics technologies have significantly impacted societal changes and people's desires. The values of community, society, and environment are becoming increasingly diverse and difficult. According to Fukuyama (2018), there are numerous activities that focus on modern technologies throughout the world, such as "4th Industrial Revolution," the Industrial Internet, and Made in China 2025. Digital transformation has become a driving force and key pillar of industrial policy in many countries (Fukuyama, 2018). However, the world is facing many pressing issues concerning global warming, natural resource scarcity, climate-based risks, inequality, and terrorism, each of which must be confronted on a global scale. During this period of rapid uncertainty and complexity at every stage, the maximum utilization of ICT must be pursued to gather new knowledge and create new values through connecting "people and things" as a valuable and useful means to resolve the problems facing global society and thereby lead to better lives for people and sustainable growth of the economy.

The Japanese government adopted the "Society 5.0" policy in the 5th Science and Technology Basic Plan by the Council for Science, Technology, and Innovation, which was approved by Cabinet decision in January 2016. This policy refers to an "intelligent society" in which physical and cyberspaces are interconnected (Salgues, 2018). To the Cabinet Office of the Japan Government, Society 5.0 focuses on the "human-centered" aspects of society that will lead to an equilibrium in terms of economic prosperity concerning societal issues through a fusion of both physical and cyberspaces. The Society 5.0 policy was designed as a purposeful event to devise a new social contract and economic function, one that combines the 4th Industrial Revolution and technology-driven innovation (Harayama, 2017). The country has proactively taken initiatives by valuing humanity and machines to resolve the greatest issues that society is encountering in the twenty-first century. Society 5.0 considers many issues, such as healthcare, finance, infrastructure, distributions, and AI (Mark Minevich, 2019). The evolution of human history has occurred in several stages, which social and cultural theorists have termed primitive society, agrarian society, and industrialized society. At present, primitive society is recognized as Society 1.0, and it involves a reliance on a hunting and gathering economy in harmony with nature. The livelihood of agrarian society, which is classified as Society 2.0, mainly depends on agricultural farming, collective organization, and nation-building; Society 3.0 is defined by the age of industrialization through the industrial revolution and mass production. The explosion of digital technologies, automation, robotics, and AI at the beginning of the twenty-first century has transformed industrialized society rapidly into a data- and information-driven economy. These transitions are often recognized as "Industry 4.0," on which 'Society 4.0' stands, where increased added value is pursued by connecting intangible assets, such as information networks. In this evolution, Society 5.0 is an information society built upon Society 4.0 that aims for a prosperous human-centered society (Harayama, 2017; Minevich, 2019). To Salgues (2018, p. 3), the goal of Society 5.0 is to guide Japan toward "the most favorable country for innovations."

The goal of Society 5.0 is to create a human-centric society in which to achieve both economic development and the resolution of societal challenges and where people can enjoy a fully active and comfortable life having all the necessary items and services fulfilled (Harayama, 2017). The fusion of cyberspace and the real world (physical space) is essential to produce valuable data and to establish new values and solutions to overcome challenges. Japan has raised this public vision to endeavor for a new, human-centered society as well as to resolve multiple societal issues. However, Japan's growth strategy,

Society 5.0, is not limited to Japan, because its goals are similar to SDGs. Japan faces challenges, such as an aging population, a birthrate decline, a decreasing population, and an aging infrastructure, that eventually many other countries will face. As soon as these challenges have been resolved through Society 5.0, the solutions will be shared with the whole world. In this respect, Japan can contribute to overcoming national problems while also meeting global SDGs (Fukuyama, 2018).

5.4. Social and Regional Innovation

5.4.1. Social innovation

Social innovation is often referred to as sustainability-driven innovation (Little, 2006; Trifilova et al., 2013) or "catalytic innovation" (Christensen et al., 2006), terms which refer to a solution to a social problem (Kearney & Ashoka, 2017). Social innovations consider integrating social, environmental, or sustainability drivers to create new ways of working, new products, new services, and a new marketplace. To Christensen et al. (2006), it is called catalytic innovation because it challenges organizational incumbents by offering simpler, "good-enough" solutions aimed at underserved groups. He characterized catalytic innovators by five distinct qualities based on their actions (Christensen et al., 2006):

- *First, they build social change through scaling and replication.*
- *Second, they meet either an observed need (that is, the existing solution is more complex than necessary for many people) or not served at all.*
- *Third, they offer simpler and cheaper products and services than alternatives, but recipients view them as good enough.*
- *Fourth, they bring in resources that initially seem distasteful to incumbents; and*
- *Fifth, they are often ignored, put down, or even discouraged by existing organizations, which do not see the catalytic innovators' solutions as viable.*

Over the decades, social innovation has emerged as an indispensable part of firms' corporate strategies with regard to their social responsibility. International organizations, policymakers, state heads of many countries, and business communities have become increasingly interested in tackling the social and environmental risks with regard to the planet, its people, and product agendas. Multi-national corporations (MNCs) are starting to implement environmental, social, and governance (ESG) business practices in their long-term strategies.

The OECD has defined social innovation as a solution to social market failures in the provision of vital public goods. This definition includes references to the process dimensions of social innovation. Corporate social responsibility (CSR) has become increasingly popular for organizations focused on scaling the social impacts generated from their business operations. Firms have long implemented a range of tools to acknowledge and contribute to their citizenship in society, including corporate governance, corporate philanthropy, and CSR. Much social entrepreneurship has emerged in the recent past that particularly rests on implementing social agendas that value cooperation and collaboration with big corporations. These social enterprises have gained immense social business scope by absorbing societal problems as opportunities. As the President of the European Commission in 2011 asserted, "social innovation should be at the core of our social market economy and also contribute to making our social market economy more competitive" (Schmitt, 2015, p. 1).

The European Union has emphasized the social innovation strategy to integrate the needs of society into business processes to design a social market economy for long-term competitiveness. Peter Brabeck-Letmathe, Chairman of Nestle, addressed the social challenges ad hoc to resolve issues in future business prospects. He expressed, *"It is a society that gives us the right to be active, our license to operate. A business leader has to think about how to solve the societal challenges of today because if we don't solve them, we will not have a business"* (Jennifer & Milligan, 2016, p. 5).

Above all, these factors each greatly influence MNCs to rethink beyond the business-as-usual (BAU) model. Many MNCs, or even iconic global brands, are investing time and resources to shifting BAU practices (top-down) to bottom-up practices, involving their key stakeholders, including social entrepreneurs, social activists, non-governmental organizations, and education institutions. Many MNCs perceive CSR activities and contributions to societal issues as philanthropic endeavors that rarely yield effective corporate social innovation practices. Critiques of CSR have argued that the practices embedded in CSR have, over the decades, rarely captured underlying societal and environmental issues. Since the inception of corporate social innovation (CSI), CSR activities have become obsolete and are often called "traditional CSR." The more inclusive CSI has become imperative to strategies in which co-creation, cooperation, collaboration, and a mutual relationship are given priority among stakeholders to drive social change.

CSI can be differentiated from traditional CSR in many respects, as shown in Table 5-2 below. Education institutes, such as the "Lewis Institute," have focused on "breakthrough interactions" to yield social innovations by solving social problems. These institutes believe that a distinctive set of corporate strengths is required for CSI (Marc Violo, 2018). CSI can involve collaborations with other sectors and the co-creation of innovative solutions to complex economic, social, and environmental issues that have bearing on the sustainability of both business and society (Marc Violo, 2018). Another example can be drawn from Social Innovation Exchange (SIX).

TABLE 5-2 Differences Between Traditional CSR and Inclusive CSI

Characteristic	Traditional CSR	Inclusive CSI
Organizational intent	Philanthropic	Strategic
Strengths	Money, manpower	R&D, corporate assets
Autonomy	Employee volunteerism	Employee development
Partnership	Contracted service providers	NGO/Government partners
Offerings/Contributions	Social and eco-services	Social and eco-innovations
Outcomes	Social good	Sustainable social change

Note. Adapted from Marc Violo (2018). see https://socialinnovationexchange.org/insights/25-companies-carrying-out-corporate-social-innovation)

Michelini (2012) argued that social innovation can be classified by how it spreads from ideas to values to software to tools and lastly to habits. She proposed a framework for new product development that describes the social product development process to target the low-income market. The framework consists of six elements, beginning with idea generation, as outlined in Table 5-3 below.

TABLE 5-3 Elements of New Social Product Innovation

Phase	Activities
Ideation	Development of new concepts begins from customers' needs or is derived from tech inputs or from restrictions and limitations of the ecosystem.
Testing	Laboratory tests and field studies.
Social and Economic Analysis	Considers enterprise's economic benefits and the societal impacts of the projects on the society and local communities.
Marketing Plan	Marketing strategy, such as objectives, targeting customers, positioning, and the evolution of the social marketing mix, such as product, price, distribution, promotion, and packaging.
Monitoring and Evaluation	Audit of social and economic outcomes of the projects.
Scaling up	Possibility of quantitative and functional applications.

Note. This table is adapted from Michelini (2012), *Social Innovation and New Business Models.*

Michelini (2012, p. 47) listed the four best practices in social product innovation that MNCs have implemented to resolve specific social issues:

- *PuR developed by Procter and Gamble (P&G) – water purifier project for the household level that reduces illness of children.*
- *Plumpy' nut, owned by Nutriset – a ready-to-use product for the treatment of severe acute malnutrition.*
- *Shakti Doi, by Grameen Danone – a yogurt enriched with calcium, protein, and micronutrients for children's growth; and*
- *Interceptor, by BASF – an insecticide-treated mosquito net to eliminate insect-borne diseases, such as malaria.*

5.4.2 Level of social innovation

According to Nicholls et al. (2015), social innovation can be divided into three types: incremental, institutional, and disruptive. First, *incremental* innovation in goods and services involves addressing social needs more realistically or competently, such as the objective of contributing to charities and non-profit organizations. Second, *institutional* innovation aims to utilize the current social and economic structures to devise new social values and outcomes. Examples of this are Fair Trade or mobile banking, which typically restructures the existing market by offering additional social value. Finally, *disruptive* social innovation aims at system-wide changes. These innovations constitute social movements and self-consciously "political" actors, groups, and networks aimed at changing power relations and social hierarchies and at reframing issues for the benefit of marginalized groups.

5.4.3 Regional innovation

Regional innovation is often referred to as "local innovation" in that it addresses issues in local areas. In an era of techno-globalism, the capacity of regional innovations is of heightened importance because it includes a knowledge-based economy by creating and sharing knowledge among industries, local institutions, and educational organizations. Regional innovations may adopt the micro-level perspective in technology development or technical skills to improve the local economy. Regions are deemed as growing members of multi-level governance systems. Moreover, regions play a vital role in synchronizing innovation practices. Many previous studies on emerging economics have highlighted the concentration of product technologies and production process development on regional or local economic needs.

Prior research has argued that regions are a critical component in the new age of global, knowledge-based capitalism. Regions have become focal points for KC and learning in the new era of capitalism and have become progressively more important sources of innovation and economic growth, as well as vehicles for globalization (Florida, R. 1998). Peter Drucker and Ikujiro Nonaka asserted that capitalism has shifted into a new age of KC and continuous learning. This new system of knowledge-intensive capitalism comprises a synthesis of intellectual and physical labor—a melding of *innovation* and *production* (Drucker, 2015; Nonaka & Nishiguchi, 2001).

A knowledge-based economy or society is more technologized and commercialized, as it is also used across the whole spectrum of human activity to yield important benefits (Rooney, 2005; Rooney et al., 2005). Knowledge-based management is much deeper and more fundamental to social, cultural, and communication processes that condition KC and use and that predispose groups to different levels and kinds of outcomes in terms of quality of life, learning, creativity, and innovation.

An emerging economy like that of China has been shifting its knowledge-based economy over the decades. The local economy in Chinese big cities has become more knowledge-intensive, and local firms are increasingly emphasizing technology development by combining intellectual and physical labor. According to the 2019 Future Health Index, China is leading the way in the adoption of digital health technology. However, global health technology innovators are confronting continuous challenges because of China's entrance into the medical and digital infrastructure. Chinese health technology is vastly different from that of other countries considering its unique regulatory demands and lack of affordability of existing solutions for more widespread use in rural or impoverished regions. From giant corporations to new startups, all firms acknowledge the importance of digital technologies, such as *telehealth* and *artificial intelligence*, to alleviate China's overstretched healthcare professionals and to help in providing better care. Chinese government policies and companies' quick adaptations to regional needs help to innovate new health technology, such as medical and digital infrastructure. The key to successful innovation lies in having a deep understanding of market-specific needs and challenges and the ability to forge local partnerships—while also keeping an eye on best practices in other healthcare systems. According to the 2019 Future Health Index, China spent 60% of its global total investment and financing in the field of AI between 2013 and Q1 2018, followed by the US (29%) and India (5%). This has led China to become more experienced concerning the benefits of AI (Phillips, 2019).

Many regional innovation projects (see Table 5-4) have been organized by the European Commission to improve competitiveness, increase growth, and promote jobs in many parts of Europe. Danuta Hübner, who is responsible for Regional Policy of the European Commission, explained the trigger point of regional innovation in Europe. To her, Europe's regions already have a wealth of experience in this area, and sharing this experience is one of the most effective ways of helping us to understand the mechanisms of regional innovation (Veronica Gaffey, 2007). To promote and motivate the regional innovation system, the EU Commission launched the innovative project award, named "RegioStars," to evaluate the most regional innovative projects. The goal of this recognition is to develop and share good practices across the European Union.

TABLE 5-4 Examples of Regional Innovation Projects

Project Theme	Projects	Location	Main Objectives
Clustering and business networking	InnoEnvi: Environmental mini clusters	South Finland	This project generated sustainable cooperation, which is now being extended nationally and internationally
	Manufacturing Excellence Club	East England	The main objective of this project was business-to-business exchanges of experience and the development of new business partnerships
Creating links between research and enterprises	Food Logistic	South Finland	In this project, SMEs in the food sector found common logistics solutions when transporting their produce into the capital
	COOPERA	Aragon, Spain	Cooperation projects launched between companies and technology providers that developed strategic research structures

Source. Adapted from Veronica Gaffey (2007), *Examples of Regional Innovation Projects.* Available at: http://ec.europa.eu/regional_policy/cooperation/interregional/ecochange/index_en.cfm

5.5. Discussion and Assignment

5.5.1 Group discussion in classroom

Think about cases of innovations (products, services, inventions, etc.) you are aware of. What type of innovation are they?

- Who, when, and how was it created?
- Is it human-centered or technology-centered?
- Is it market-based or non-market based?
- Is it network-based or created individually?
- Is it fundamental science-based or real life based?
- Can you suggest a new type of innovation other than the ones introduced in the class?

Group size: 3–5 (depending on the class size and its diversity)

Time: The group discussion is 25 minutes; preparation for the presentation, 5 min.; presentation 5 min. per group; all group Q&A, 5 min.

Presentation: All group members should contribute to group discussion and preparation for the presentation. The presenter will be randomly selected by the instructor.

5.5.2 Assignment

Review the academic literature on the topic of innovation studies and management and use this knowledge to suggest further development for application in your research area.

Key conceptual words

Tech-driven innovation, hype cycle, human-centered innovation, regional innovation, social innovation

REFERENCE

Benoit, G. (2008) *Innovation: the History of a Category, Project on the Intellectual History of Innovation Working*. Montréal, Québec. Available at: http://www.csiic.ca/PDF/IntellectualNo1.pdf.

Berkhout, G., Hartmann, D. and Trott, P. (2010) 'Connecting technological capabilities with market needs using a cyclic innovation model', *R and D Management*, 40(5), pp. 474–490. doi: 10.1111/j.1467-9310.2010.00618.x.

Christensen, C. M. et al. (2006) 'Disruptive innovation for social change', *Harvard Business Review*, 84(12), pp. 1–10.

Determann, L. (2015) *The Field Guide to Human-Centered Design*. 1st edn, *Determann's Field Guide To Data Privacy Law*. 1st edn. IDEO.org. doi: 10.4337/9781789906196.00009.

Drucker, P. (1987) 'The Discipline of Innovation ':, *Harvard Business Review*, 2(4), pp. 484–485. doi: 10.20801/jsrpim.2.4_484_2.

Drucker, P. F. (2015) *Innovation and Entrepreneurship:Practice and Principles*. First publ. New York, NY 10017 , USA: Routledge, 2 Park Square, Milton Park, Abingdon, Oxon OX14 4RN.

Dyer, J., Gregersen, H. and Christensen, C. M. (2011) *The Innovator's* DNA. HARVARD BUSINESS REVIEW PRESS, BOSTON, MASSACHUSETTS.

Dziallas, M. and Blind, K. (2019) 'Innovation indicators throughout the innovation process: An extensive literature analysis', *Technovation*. Elsevier Ltd, 80–81(May 2018), pp. 3–29. doi: 10.1016/j.technovation.2018.05.005.

Edward Giesen et al. (2009) *Paths to success, IBM Corporation*. doi: 10.1007/BF00736639.

Fagerberg, J. (2003) 'Innovation: A Guide to the Literature', in Fagerberg, J., And, D. M., and Nelson, R. R. (eds) *Oxford Handbook of Innovation*. doi: 10.1007/BF02944915.

Fagerberg, J. and Mowery, D. C. (2009) 'The Oxford Handbook of Innovation', *The Oxford Handbook of Innovation*, pp. 1–680. doi: 10.1093/

oxfordhb/9780199286805.001.0001.

Fukuyama, B. M. (2018) 'Society 5 . 0 : Aiming for a New Human-Centered Society', *Japan SPOTLIGHT*, (August), pp. 47–50. Available at: https://www.jef.or.jp/journal/.

Gartner (2020) *Gartner Identifies Five Emerging Trends That Will Drive Technology Innovation for the Next Decade, Gartner Newsroom*. Available at: https://www.gartner.com/en/newsroom/press-releases/2020-08-18-gartner-identifies-five-emerging-trends-that-will-drive-technology-innovation-for-the-next-decade.

Globaltimes (2020) *Huawei R&D spending surpasses that of each of 25 provinces in China -*

Hambrick, D. (1983) 'Some Tests of the Effectiveness and Functional Attributes of Miles and Snow's Strategic Types', *Academy of Management Journal*, 26(1), pp. 5–26.

Harayama, Y. (2017) *Society 5.0: Aiming for a New Human-centered Society - Japan's Science and Technology Policies for Addressing Global Social Challenges, Hitachi Review*.

Jennifer, B. and Milligan, K. (2016) *Social Innovation: A Guide to Achieving Corporate and Societal Value*. Geneva, Switzerland. Available at: www.weforum.org.

Joan Magretta (2019) 'Why Business Models Matter', in *HBR'S 10 MUST READS On Business Model Innovation*. Boston, Massachusetts 02163: Harvard Business School Publishing Corporation, pp. 1689–1699. Available at: http://publications.lib.chalmers.se/records/fulltext/245180/245180.pdf%0Ahttps://hdl.handle.net/20.500.12380/245180%0Ahttp://dx.doi.org/10.1016/j.jsames.2011.03.003%0Ahttps://doi.org/10.1016/j.gr.2017.08.001%0Ahttp://dx.doi.org/10.1016/j.precamres.2014.12.

Kahn, K. B. (2018) 'Understanding innovation', *Business Horizons*. 'Kelley School of Business, Indiana University', 61(3), pp. 453–460. doi: 10.1016/j.bushor.2018.01.011.

KAIHAN KRIPPENDORFF (2017) *A Brief History of Innovation ... and Its Next Evolution - Kaihan Krippendorff, KAIHAN KRIPPENDORFF'S BLOG*. Available at: https://kaihan.net/brief-history-innovation-next-evolution/ (Accessed: 5 January 2021).

Kearney, A. and Ashoka (2017) *Social Innovation Offers Five Golden Opportunities to the Apparel Industry, Ashoka and A.T. Kearney Limited*. Ashoka and and A.T. Kearney Limited. Available at: www.atkearney.com.

Ledbetter, P. (2018) *The Toyota Template: The Plan for Just-In-Time and Cultural Change beyond Lean Tools*. Boca Raton, FL 33487-2742: CRC Press, Tylor and Francis Group.

Little, A. D. (2006) 'The innovation high ground: Winning tomorrow's customers using sustainability-driven innovation', *Strategic Direction*, 22(1), pp. 35–37. doi: 10.1108/02580540610635942.

Manu, F. A. and Sriram, V. (1996) 'Innovation, marketing strategy, environment, and performance', *Journal of Business Research*, 35(1), pp. 79–91. doi: 10.1016/0148-2963(95)00056-9.

Marc Violo (2018) *25 companies carrying out corporate social innovation | socialinnovationexchange.org, Social Innovation Exchange*. Available at: https://socialinnovationexchange.org/insights/25-companies-carrying-out-corporate-social-innovation (Accessed: 6 February 2021).

Mark Minevich (2019) *Japan's 'Society 5.0' initiative is a road map for today's entrepreneurs | TechCrunch*. Available at: https://techcrunch.com/2019/02/02/japans-society-5-0-initiative-is-a-roadmap-for-todays-entrepreneurs/ (Accessed: 28 March 2021).

Michelini, L. (2012) *Social Innovation and New Business Models, Social Innovation and New Business Models*. doi: 10.1007/978-3-642-32150-4.

Morris, L. (2006) *Permanent Innovat!on: The Definitive Guide to the Principles, Strategies, and Methods of Successful Innovators*. Edited by L. Morris. Web. Available at: www.permanentinnovation.com.

Nicholls, A., Simon, J. and Gabriel, M. (2015) 'Dimensions of Social Innovation', in Nicholls, A., Simon, J., and Gabriel, M. (eds) *New Frontiers in Social Innovation Research*, pp. 1–26. Available at: https://scholar.google.nl/scholar?cluster=11413936125424182930&hl=en&oi=scholaralrt#0.

Nonaka, I. and Nishiguchi, T. (2001) *Knowledge emergence: Social, technical, and evolutionary dimensions of knowledge creation, Oxford University Press.Inc.*

Oliveira, P. and Von Hippel, E. (2011) 'Users as service innovators: The case of banking services', *Research Policy*. Elsevier B.V., 40(6), pp. 806–818. doi: 10.1016/j.respol.2011.03.009.

Perelman, L. J. (2007) *Toward Human-Centered Innovation*. Washington.

Phillips (2019) 'Future Health Index. Transforming healthcare experiences', p. 43. Available at: https://images.philips.com/is/content/PhilipsConsumer/Campaigns/CA20162504_Philips_Newscenter/Philips_Future_Health_Index_2019_report_transforming_healthcare_experiences.pdf?_ga=2.162057849.494004155.1612645567-581374906.1612645567.

Salgues, B. (2018) 'Society 5.0 Its Logic and Its Construction', in *Society 5.0*. First. ISTE Ltd. and John Wiley & Sons, Inc. doi: 10.1002/9781119507314.

Schmitt, J. (2015) *Social Innovation for Business Success: Shared Value in the Apparel Industry, Acta Universitatis Agriculturae et Silviculturae Mendelianae Brunensis*. Edited by J. Schmitt. Springer Gabler. Available at: www.springer-gabler.de.

Schumpeter, J. A. (1983) *The Theory of Economic Development: An inquiry into Profits, Capital, Credit, Interest, and the Business Cycle*. English Ed. Edited by REDVERS OPIE. Transaction Publishers. Available at: http://library1.nida.ac.th/termpaper6/sd/2554/19755.pdf.

Schumpeter, J. A. (1989) *Business Cycles*. Edited by Joseph A. Schumpeter. McGRAW-HiLL BOOK COMPANY, INC.

Trifilova, A. *et al.* (2013) 'Sustainability-driven innovation and the Climate Savers' programme: Experience of international companies in China', *Corporate Governance (Bingley)*, 13(5), pp. 599–612. doi: 10.1108/CG-06-2013-0082.

Veronica Gaffey (2007) *Examples of regional innovation projects*. Available at: http://ec.europa.eu/regional_policy/cooperation/interregional/ecochange/index_en.cfm.

WEF (2019) *Why social innovation matters to business, World Economic Forum*. Available at: http://www3.weforum.org/docs/WEF_Social_Innovation_Guide.pdf.

CHAPTER 06

Topic 5 Disruptive Innovation

Topic 5

Disruptive Innovation

Eunyoung Kim

This chapter introduces the concept of disruptive innovation, one of the most influential keywords of innovation study, and discuss how we can generate disruptive innovations.

6.1. Disrupt to overcome the difficulties for innovation

Despite great efforts and investment, many business entities have failed to innovate, and innovation is regarded as something difficult to achieve. In the field of business management, many studies have researched why companies fail to innovate. Prof. Christensen of Harvard Business School has given clear answers to the questions of why innovation is difficult and what kind of approach we can take to innovate by introducing the concept of *overshooting*, which means providing too much performance to the customers, and suggesting a focus on *disruptive innovation*, contrasted with *sustaining innovation*.

Here, we need to understand overshooting more concretely to identify what overshooting is and what makes an overshot customer. According to Anthony et al. (2008), "overshooting occurs when a product or service has performance that a customer doesn't need, and therefore doesn't value" (p. 89). Let's take an example from television (see Figure 6-1). The solid line in Figure 6-1 signifies the sustaining innovation of TV, which provides better performances over time with the advances in technology. The dotted lines represent the performance required to satisfy the customers. It is controversial to divide consumers into two groups based on their income levels; however, in the disruptive innovation theory, *low-end* usually refers to the bottom of the pyramid, which accounts for 2.7 billion people, out of the world population of 7 billion, whose daily income is less than 2.5 USD. On the other hand, the market segmentation of *high-end* varies depending on the characteristics of the industry; however, it is almost standardized in developed countries' television markets. We need to consider the cross-points that the arrows in Figure 6.1 indicate. When color television started to be widely available in the '70s and '80s, consumers were happy with its new performance. They continued to feel happy with replacing their thick TVs with slim and wide-screen TVs in the 2000s. Consumers still feel happy with the bigger TVs that can connect to wireless home networks to access personalized content based on individual taste. It seems like consumers have wanted the slim and wide TVs that show personalized content with vivid color before those kinds of TVs appeared on the market at affordable prices. However, at certain point of time, consumers do not feel happier as they did before with replacing their TVs with higher-performing technologies such as a rollable screen. Simply imagine how many times you might use 3D or the rolling function of a TV in your home. This overshooting can be applied to many tech-based devices, such as memory-storage devices for general consumers. Now, a 64 gigabyte USB flash drive is not as attractive as when we first obtained 8 megabyte flash drives in 2000.

FIGURE 6-1

Sustaining Innovation Through Technology-Driven Innovation

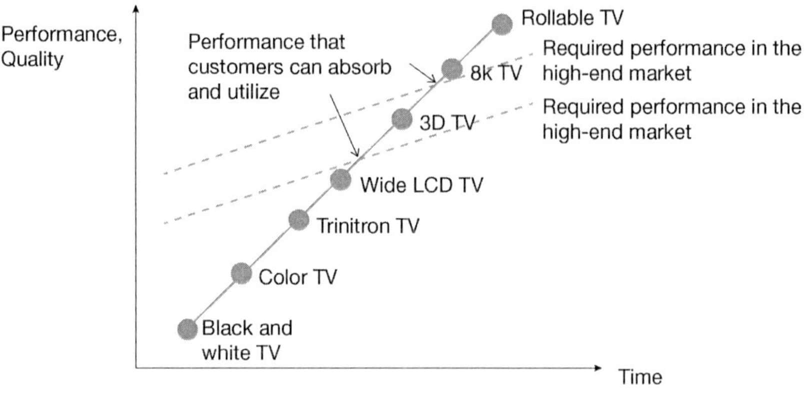

Overshooting explains why consumers are saturated with the new functionalities provided by products. Why are technologies developed over our demand?

Let's see Figure 6-2, which shows how the technology of a dense integrated circuit (IC) has developed over time. As you can see in Figure 6-2, the number of transistors in a dense IC has doubled every 18–24 months since 1970. Dr. Hwang, the former CEO of Samsung Electronics, proposed Hwang's Law in 2002, stating that the density of the memory chip doubles every year, not every two years. Samsung Electronics proved Hwang's law by developing 256 Mb NAND flash memory in 1999, 512 Mb in 2000, 1 Gb in 2001, 2 Gb in 2002, 4 Gb in 2003, 8 Gb in 2004, 16 Gb in 2005, 32 Gb in 2006, and 64 Gb in 2007. Although Hwang's Law has not been effective since 2008 because Samsung did not present 128 Gb in 2008, we could assume that information technology will be rapidly developed beyond the actual needs of our daily life.

FIGURE 6-2

Moore's Law: The Number of Transistors on Microchips Doubles Every Two Years (Roser & Ritchie, 2020)

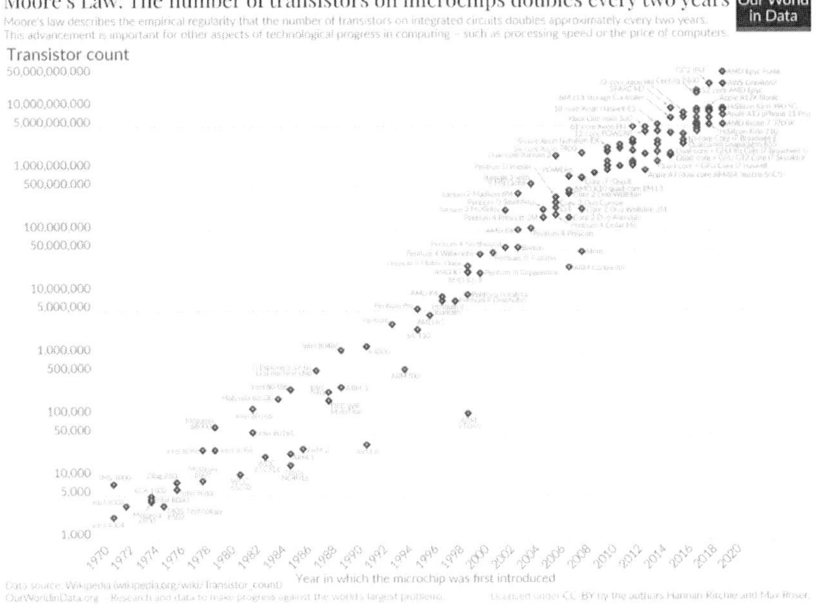

Note. This figure shows a logarithmic graph showing the timeline of how transistor counts in microchips are almost doubling every two years from 1970 to 2020; Moore's Law (https://ourworldindata.org/uploads/2020/11/Transistor-Count-over-time.png). CC BY 4.0

This kind of technology development, which produces higher-performing products, is also regarded as *innovation*—Prof. Christensen (2013) termed it *sustaining innovation* because it sustains itself by offering better-performing products to the high-end customers or existing customers. This perspective of continuously increasing technology and knowledge development is similar to Popper's (1959) paradigm of accumulation of knowledge.

However, Popper's (1959) accumulation of knowledge was criticized by Kuhn's (1962) idea of paradigm shift (see Figure 6-3). To this point, we need to rethink the structure of innovation by an analogy from *The Structure of Scientific Revolutions*, which is regarded as one of the most innovative theories in science philosophy.

FIGURE 6-3

Popper's Accumulation of Knowledge vs. Kuhn's Paradigm Shift

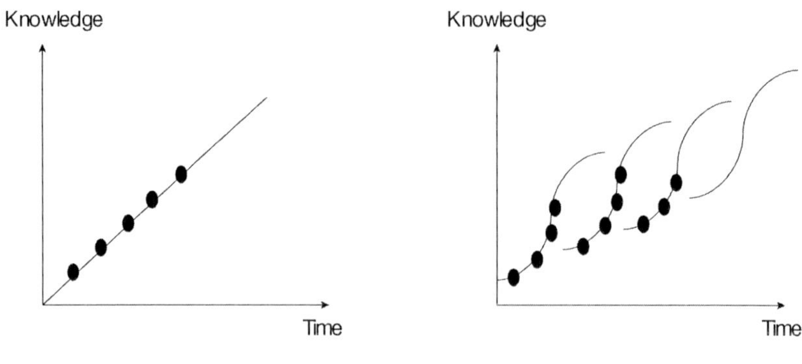

If technology continuously advances regardless of our actual needs, we should find an opportunity to create innovation not by continually advancing the technological performance and bringing better products into the established market but by shifting our paradigm to bring a whole new perspective and value proposition to the consumers and the market. This kind of innovation was named *disruptive innovation* by Prof. Christenson (2013). The reason we need to focus more on disruptive innovation is because it broadens the market, creates jobs, and attracts and utilizes capital investment in a short- to mid-term time frame, while gradual sustaining innovation makes little use of capital investment and does not create many jobs. Christenson suggested two approaches to create disruptive innovation: (1) create a new market for the nonconsumers, and (2) target the existing customers with a lower-cost business model.

6.2. Case study: New-market footholds

There have many methods, principles, and case studies on how to disrupt. Anthony et al. (2008) identified four barriers that might prevent the nonconsumer from becoming a consumer: skills, wealth, access, and time. They proposed three principles on how to approach the nonconsumers: simplifying, persevering against the criticisms of mainstream consumers, and not forcing but continually innovating.

This subchapter takes several examples of well-known businesses that successfully created a new market by shifting the target consumers, discovering a demand with a specific purpose, and gaining a foothold with the new technology.

6.2.1. Shifting the target consumers: Professional to layman, group to individual

Shifting the target consumer is the most common approach to attract nonconsumers. This subchapter introduces three Japanese cases of changing the target consumers to disrupt the market.

One-person karaoke

In East Asian culture, karaoke has long been a place for social gathering or strengthening bonds among friends and coworkers. Most karaoke bars are designed for group entertainment, so audiences are seated on a sofa to watch the singers in front of them, and the room is equipped with high-powered speakers and tambourines for cheering up the singers. This setting makes introverts and people who need to practice their singing skills feel uncomfortable, and they may be reluctant to go to karaoke.

Koshidaka Holdings spotted this constraint on consumption and started a new business of single-person karaoke called One Kara. They shifted the main target from a group of people to individuals by redesigning their karaoke rooms decorated as two meter squares spaceship, replacing the speaker with a headset and rental microphone, and equipping the space with a powder room for the ladies to fix their makeup after singing.

Home-visiting tutor Kumon

Excessive competition for entrance exams is a common issue in Asian countries. Especially in Japan, the competition starts early, often from kindergarten. This has created a huge private education market; many students go to a couple of private institutes for group study or hire a personal teacher to visit their house. They can select the level and the subject based on individual needs to pass or to achieve a better grade on their tests. However, many people prefer personal teaching services but cannot afford it or find it difficult to hire a personal teacher and manage the improvement of their learning.

Toru Kumon developed an educational method for math and languages called the Kumon Method to assess the level of students and present a new self-learning and coaching method based on the home visiting of a trained instructor to manage a student's improvement in specific skills at an affordable price. The Kumon Method and its business model have attracted numerous consumers because they do not need to study together in groups, they can progress at their own pace, and they can level up to a higher stage when they pass a test at each specific level. All their progress in learning is managed by a professional coaching system at a lower price than its substitutes.

Monthly scale model kit

Scale model kits used to be consumed by users with high skills in building and painting techniques. Tamiya is the company targeting the users of scale model kits with high prices and quality. It sells scale models with such intricate details that they are often described by modeling connoisseurs as "museum items." However, this approach is not easy for beginners who are interested in starting scale modeling as a hobby.

DeAgostini is targeting newcomers to scale model kits with periodicals, which cost about one-thirtieth compared to the high-end models. Anyone can easily buy an issue of their monthly magazine series of specific model kits such as R2-D2 from *Star Wars*, Iron Man, Godzilla, aircraft, famous castles, etc. It offers promotional pricing for the first issue, and each model consists of a magazine that explains how to build each part in detail to complete the scale model. The consumers can try their first issue lightly, and they can decide whether they want to continue by buying the next issue.

6.2.2. Discovering the neglected demand with a specific purpose

Shifting the target consumer from a group to an individual or from a high-end professional to a new entrant is a simple way to find a nonconsumer. There is another way to create a new market: by discovering the neglected or untold demand with a specific purpose. It is hard to catch what consumers need because they never explicitly express what they need. To illuminate their hidden needs, businesses should pay attention to human nature; the lifestyles of contemporaries, diverse social tribes, and generations; and micro-trends.

Let us look at an example of online social network services and smartphones that many of us depend on. Before those services and devices appeared in the market, no consumers explicitly said to any developer or businessperson that they needed an online social networking service or handy devices that they could use to post their personal information, feelings, opinions, and photos and interact with online friends. However, our underlying needs and traits of *fear of missing out* (FOMO), *pleasure of receiving messages* (PORM), *seeing work as priority* (SWAP), and the *urge to seem important* (UTSI) have made us obsessed with smartphones (Toyama, 2015).

This subchapter introduces a couple of interesting Japanese business cases of creating a new market by appealing to the consumers' specific needs.

***Shunsoku* for children's athletic relay**

Sports days (play days) are some of the biggest events for elementary schoolchildren in Japan. All the students participate in this event as a team, and they invite parents and grandparents to spend the day together by having lunch in the schoolyard, taking photos of their child or grandchild, cheering them up, and enjoying the group performance of the children. It is a full-day event, and the highlight of the day is the athletic relay race. However, school playgrounds are not big, and running tracks have sharp curves that hinder speeding up and might cause injuries from falling.

Achilles Corporation developed a new type of shoes called Shunsoku, literally meaning *flash feet*, with an asymmetric sole that helps runners keep their balance while running around the left-hand curve of a track. Children can run faster without falling with these shoes, so they gained huge popularity among children.

Shunsoku created a new market of special shoes for the children's athletic relay since its first release in 2003. And this market has grown rapidly year by year and expanded its business internationally.

***Nintendo's brain-training game* for preventing dementia**

The game industry has long been criticized by older generations who are afraid of their child(ren) spending too much time on games. On the other hand, many game companies have launched games that might help with learning or enhancing linguistic, mathematical, or coding skills. However, there have been controversies that learning through games cannot improve fundamental skills for learning such as critical thinking, creativity, and reading comprehension. Yet it is possible that we can train some skills related to short-term memory through games.

Learning through game devices is not only for children. In terms of enhancing short-term memory or repetitive training, it could be useful for the elderly. Dementia is a big problem in an aging society such as Japan. Nintendo, one of the biggest game companies in Japan, developed a new portable game device and launched a game software for the elderly to prevent dementia. Dr. Ryuta Kawashima, a neuroscientist in the medical school of Tohoku University in Japan, supervised a series of brain-training games with a variety of puzzles such as Stroop tests, mathematical quizzes, and Sudoku puzzles based on his expertise in preventing dementia. The game not only had great success in the global market but also received awards from industry and academia.

6.2.3. New-technology-and-trends foothold

Not all newly introduced technologies will be successfully adopted by the targeted users. However, when a technology's penetration rate reaches a certain level, it can create a new market. Thus, periods of technological transition could present great opportunities for creating a new market. Many prestigious research institutes or national think tanks have announced the expected technology for the upcoming years. For example, Nikkei Business Publications published a report titled *Most Expected New Technologies* based on a survey given to businesspeople (NikkeiBP, 2017), and other business research organizations, including Deloitte[1] and Gartner[2], have published annual reports on technology trends.

TABLE 6-1 Most Expected and Recognized Technologies

Rank	Most Expected Technologies in 2017	Most Expected Technologies in 2022	Most Recognized and Interesting Technologies
1	Regenerative Medicine	Regenerative Medicine	Drone
2	IoT (Internet of Things)	AI (Artificial Intelligence)	3D Printer
3	AI (Artificial Intelligence)	Post Lithium-ion Battery for EV	AI (Artificial Intelligence)
4	Machine Learning	IoT (Internet of Things)	Automatic Driving
5	Infrastructure Monitoring	Machine Learning	IoT (Internet of Things)
6	Immune Checkpoint Inhibitor	Infrastructure Monitoring	VR (Virtual Reality)
7	Liquid Biopsy	Automatic Driving	Observant Care System for the Elderly
8	Disaster Information Use by SNS	Immune Checkpoint Inhibitor	Regenerative Medicine
9	Observant Care System for the Elderly	Liquid Biopsy	Machine Learning
10	3D Printer	Next-generation Operation Assistant Robot	AR (Augmented Reality)

Source. reformatted from http://www.nikkeibp.com/news/2017/170314.html

Note. The survey was conducted from November 29 to December 16, 2016, with the online users of Nikkei BP, and valid respondents numbered 792.

1 https://www2.deloitte.com/us/en/insights/focus/tech-trends.html

2 https://www.gartner.com/smarterwithgartner/gartner-top-10-strategic-technology-trends-for-2020/

New technologies have derived numerous social and market trends. These new technologies and trends can be footholds for attracting new consumers and creating new markets. There have been numerous start-ups and large tech companies utilizing new technologies and trends to create disruptive innovations.

Let's take Netflix as an example. When it first launched in 1997, it was a newcomer in the movie-rental market. Its competitor, Blockbuster, was the undisputed champion until the early and mid-2000s, when every household subscribed to high-speed internet service. Netflix's early business model was rentals by postal mail delivery based on a monthly membership subscription, which meant it had to compete with other major players in the already existing market. However, new information technology allowed Netflix to shift to streaming video, and it changed its main platform to online streaming and started to produce original content. This path from the fringe of an existing market to successfully becoming the mainstream of the new market helps us understand disruption as a process.

6.3. Case study: Low-end footholds

One of the most influential scholars and global health statisticians H. Rosling gave a lot of invited talks[3] and published a couple of books to help the public realize how much we, especially well-educated people, are ignorant about our global society (Rosling et al., 2018). As he proved with the results from a set of quizzes given to numerous audiences of his talks, a majority of us are not well aware of the underprivileged as the target of a new market.

This subchapter introduces how we can approach the most-demanding consumers with low prices.

6.3.1. Appropriate technology

As many influential people or companies have founded nonprofit foundations, such as the Bill & Melinda Gates Foundation, there have been

3 https://www.ted.com/speakers/hans_rosling

numerous projects to solve the problems of the underprivileged.

A German-British economist, E.F. Schumacher, established the Intermediate Technology Group (changed to Practical Action[4] in 2005) with 20 technologists, fundraisers, and professors in 1965 to develop appropriate technologies in the fields of energy, food, water, sanitation, business, shelter, disaster, etc. His book *Small is Beautiful: Economics as if People Mattered* (Schumacher, 1989) introduced the concept of appropriate technology for the first time, and it influenced a number of designers, educators, technologists, and economists to create a movement of applying small-scale and affordable technology to support the lives of people in need. Prestigious higher educational institutes, including MIT, Stanford, and Harvard, also launched education programs—such as the Lemelson-MIT Program[5], MIT D-lab[6], D.school projects, and Humanitarian Design Projects—in cooperation with underserved local communities to create social innovations.

Tangible solutions of appropriate technology were widely introduced to the public by the exhibition titled *Design for the Other 90%* of the Cooper Hewitt National Design Museum in New York (Smith, 2007). It attracted huge attention and success through a series of further exhibitions all around the world and an official website to share the ideas for solutions[7].

---

4 https://practicalaction.org/

5 https://lemelson.mit.edu/

6 http://d-lab.mit.edu/

7 https://www.designother90.org/solutions/

TABLE 6-2 Representative Solutions of Appropriate Technology

Better Access to	Solution Examples	Description
Food	Pot-in-pot refrigerator	It cools by evaporation of water from the sand between the inside clay pot and the larger clay pot outside by pouring the water into the sand between the pots.
Water	Q-Drum	It is a wheel-shaped water container that rolls easily to transport a maximum of seventy-five liters from a clean water source to a house.
Sanitation	Life straw	It is a portable water filter that can remove bacteria, microplastic, and parasites in the water.
Transportation + Sanitation	Bicycle washing machine	It is a human-pedaling-powered washing machine used by placing the drum of a washing machine as the wheel of a bicycle.
Health	Self-adjustable glasses	Users can adjust the focus using a dial on the fluid-filled temples so that the fluid can be injected or removed into lenses.
Education	Kinkajou projector	It is a solar-powered projector to teach during nighttime for those who need to work during daytime.
Energy + Food	Solar cookers	It concentrates the heat from the sunlight and uses its geometrical-shaped surface to cook.

Although the movement of appropriate technology brought us numerous affordable products that can solve the real-life problems of the low-income classes, it has declined under the new trend of sustainable development, which includes broader perspectives of environment, economics, politics, and culture.

6.3.2. Information and Communication Technologies for Development (ICT4D)

As information and communication technology (ICT) advance, almost all the people who need to use it can access the mobile network such as wi-fi, 3G, 4G or 5G. As shown in Figure 6-4, the penetration rate of mobile network subscription reached close to 80% all over the world. In this regard, the importance of ICT has been increased dramatically in solving various problems to create innovations for fulfilling sustainable development goals (see Table 6-3).

FIGURE 6-4

Penetration Rate of Users Covered by at Least a 3G Mobile Network (Unit: %)

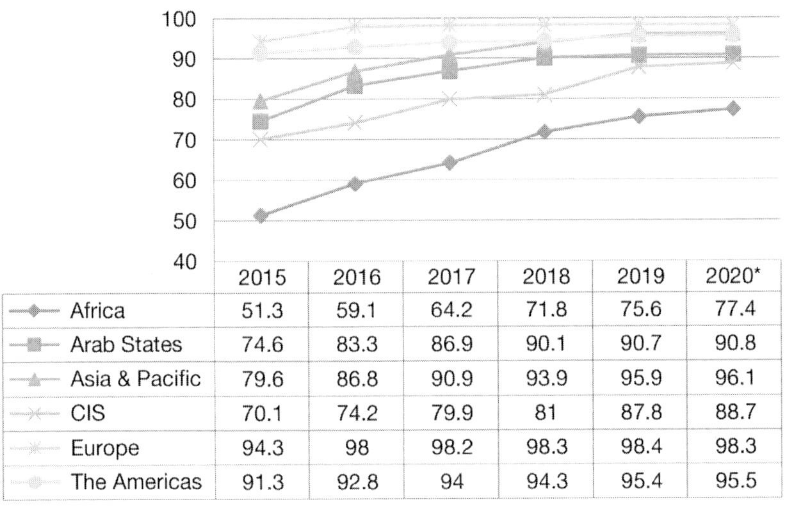

	2015	2016	2017	2018	2019	2020*
Africa	51.3	59.1	64.2	71.8	75.6	77.4
Arab States	74.6	83.3	86.9	90.1	90.7	90.8
Asia & Pacific	79.6	86.8	90.9	93.9	95.9	96.1
CIS	70.1	74.2	79.9	81	87.8	88.7
Europe	94.3	98	98.2	98.3	98.4	98.3
The Americas	91.3	92.8	94	94.3	95.4	95.5

Note. This figure is drawn by author and sourced from "Measuring digital development: Facts and figures 2020," Telecommunication Development Bureau, International Telecommunication Union (ITU).

TABLE 6-3 Sustainable Development Goals (SDGs)

GOAL 1	No Poverty	End poverty in all its forms everywhere.
GOAL 2	Zero Hunger	End hunger, achieve food security and improved nutrition, and promote sustainable agriculture.
GOAL 3	Good Health and Well-being	Ensure healthy lives and promote well-being for all at all ages.
GOAL 4	Quality Education	Ensure inclusive and equitable quality education and promote lifelong learning opportunities for all.
GOAL 5	Gender Equality	Achieve gender equality and empower all women and girls.
GOAL 6	Clean Water and Sanitation	Ensure availability and sustainable management of water and sanitation for all.
GOAL 7	Affordable and Clean Energy	Ensure access to affordable, reliable, sustainable and modern energy for all.
GOAL 8	Decent Work and Economic Growth	Promote sustained, inclusive and sustainable economic growth, full and productive employment and decent work for all.
GOAL 9	Industry, Innovation and Infrastructure	Build resilient infrastructure, promote inclusive and sustainable industrialization, and foster innovation.
GOAL 10	Reduced Inequality	Reduce income inequality within and among countries.
GOAL 11	Sustainable Cities and Communities	Make cities and human settlements inclusive, safe, resilient, and sustainable.
GOAL 12	Responsible Consumption and Production	Ensure sustainable consumption and production patterns.
GOAL 13	Climate Action	Take urgent action to combat climate change and its impacts by regulating emissions and promoting developments in renewable energy.
GOAL 14	Life Below Water	Conserve and sustainably use the oceans, seas and marine resources for sustainable development

GOAL 15	Life on Land	Protect, restore and promote sustainable use of terrestrial ecosystems, sustainably manage forests, combat desertification, and halt and reverse land degradation and halt biodiversity loss.
GOAL 16	Peace and Justice Strong Institutions	Promote peaceful and inclusive societies for sustainable development, provide access to justice for all and build effective, accountable and inclusive institutions at all levels.
GOAL 17	Partnerships to achieve the Goal	Strengthen the means of implementation and revitalize the global partnership for sustainable development

Source. https://sdgs.un.org/goals

The United Nation's Commission on Science and Technology for Development (UNCSTD) was launched in 1996, and it claimed the term ICT4D as a program in 2001. Since then, numerous projects have been implemented and many research papers have been published. Heeks (2017) defined ICT in ICT4D as a digital ICT, which means "any entity that processes or communicates digital data using smartphones, laptops, computer software, apps, internet, etc." (Heeks, 2017, p. 9).

ICT4D has been utilized in various fields such as HCI (human-computer interaction), education, health, finance, environment, disaster, politics, foods, etc. It created subfields, and related projects have been implemented as shown in Table 6-4.

TABLE 6-4 Sub-Fields of ICT4D and Their Representative Projects

	Description	Projects
HCI4D	Understanding how people and computers interact in developing regions, it designs systems and products in those contexts including hardware, software, interface, and content (Ho et al., 2009)	Text-free user interfaces for illiterate users (Medhi, Sagar, & Toyama, 2006)
		Designing an alternative approach of mobile phone and social media use in the slum area of Nairobi, Kenya (Wyche, 2015)
ICT4 Education/ Education 4ICT	In regard to SDG 4, quality education, the desire for education is top priority in developing regions (Gomez, 2014). ICT4E includes teaching and learning support systems and their content. E4ICT is education to teach ICT competencies, such as training digital literacy skills and pedagogic design (Kimaro, 2006).	The One Laptop Per Child Initiative http://www.laptop.org
		Hole-in-the-wall Kiosks (Dangwal et al., 2005)
		The iHub Kids Hacker Camps in Kenya (Ndaiga & Salim, 2015)
ICT4 Health	In regard to SDG3, good health and well-being, ICT4H aims to improve health in developing regions through public health information systems, diagnostics and treatment support systems, practitioner knowledge systems, health operation information systems, and health management / policy information systems (Heeks, 2017) .	The IKON tele-radiology project in Mali (Khanal et al., 2015)
		SMS for Life in Burundi and Zimbabwe (Dimaguila, 2015)
		District Health Information Software 2(DHIS2) in 50 countries in sub-Saharan Africa and South Asia (Karuri et al., 2014)
ICT4 Finance	In regard to SGD1, no poverty, the poor can utilize ICT for financial gain and to save/transfer money.	Kiva www.kiva.org
		M-pesa (Jack & Suri, 2011)
		M-Shwari (Cook & McKay, 2015)

Apart from the subfields and related projects introduced in Table 6.4, there are more various subfields (e.g., ICT4ClimateChangeAdaptation, ICT4DisaterMitigation) and numerous projects (e.g., University of Manchester's Resilience Assessment Benchmarking and Impact Toolkit, Map Kivera in Kenya) utilizing ICT for human and social development in line with SDGs, and there will be more research and investment as ICT advances over time in terms of technology itself. The ICT industry has great influence on global society.

Recently, data-intensive development has become mainstream in associating with 4Vs: *volume*—big data; *velocity*—real-time data; *variety*—diverse data; and *visibility*—open data (Dumbill, 2012). Accordingly, there are opportunities to initiate data-related innovative projects as shown in Table 6-5.

TABLE 6-5 Data-Intensive Innovation

Big data for development	Using mobile phone data and social media records as sources to build a system	Tracking population movement for transportation planning
Real-time data for development	Auto sensing without human intervention	Monitoring vaccine cold chain (Chaudhri et al., 2012)
	Participatory sensing by deliberate human action	Alerting residents in developing regions the status of local water supplies via SMS (Tsega et al., 2015)
	Opportunity sensing as a by-product of human action through mobile apps such as recording speed of movement, health data, etc.	A movement-tracking app for monitoring elderly people in case they fall

Diverse data for development	Predictive data, often extracted from social media data with a combination of data on health, location, economic, traffic, etc.	Tracking the displacement of people after the 2010 earthquake in Port-au-Prince, Haiti, via mobile phone records (Bengtsson et al., 2011)
	Sentiment data to measure opinion of public toward specific issues based on social media data	Analysis of sentiment via tweets regarding the vaccination during outbreak (Du et al., 2018)
Open data for development	Empowering the decision makers using open data	Helping parents make better decisions for their children using education performance data from Kenya's Open Data Portal (Mutuku & Mahihu, 2014)
	Open data economy benefitting enterprises and stimulating them to create service innovations	Gramener visualizes open government data and creates stories based on it https://gramener.com/

In almost all cases, ICT4D and its subfields aim for enhancing the quality of life for the underprivileged; however, the core ideas of those projects can also be applied to benefit any users or consumers by reducing the cost. For example, big data can be used in various industries to attract more customers with a low price or a free trial period and establish a database for developing better service or using those data for commercial purposes in another enterprise.

6.4. Discussion and assignment

6.4.1. Group discussion in classroom

To discover the nonconsumers, we need to train ourselves to seize an opportunity by shifting our perspective. Changing a viewpoint enables us to find another level of competitors of any specific brand that we consume.

1) Individual task (15 min)

Shifting a competitive landscape: How to discover a new market or shift a nonmarket to be a new market

- Select a couple of firms that you think are innovative, and search for the mission statements of those companies on their official webpages or in interviews with the founders.
- Think about what kinds of products, services, and brands could be their ultimate competitors. You should not consider candidates from the same or similar industry.

FIGURE 6-5

Mission Statements of Innovative Firms and Their Competitors from Broad Viewpoints

Company	Mission statement	Competitor
Coca Cola Company	To *refresh the world in mind, body and spirit. To inspire moments of optimism and happiness* through our brands and actions.	" *Water* is our ultimate competitor"
Peach LCC	Peach exist *to eliminate the war.* – CEO. Inoue Peach serves as a *bridge promoting the exchange of ideas, information, and cultural understanding between people.*	" *?* is our ultimate competitor"
Netflix	To *entertain the world*.	" *?* is our ultimate competitor"
?	?	" *?* is our ultimate competitor"

2) Group task

Share your ideas of the individual task above with classmates.

Group size: 3–5 (depending on the class size and its diversity)

Time: The group discussion is 10 minutes, preparation for the presentation is 5 minutes, presentation is 5 minutes per group, and all group Q&As are 5 minutes.

Presentation: All group members should contribute to the group discussion and preparation for the presentation. The presenter will be randomly selected by the instructor.

6.4.2. Assignment

Review the academic literature on the topic of disruptive innovation, and use this knowledge to make recommendations for generating disruptive innovations in your field of interest.

Key conceptual words

Innovation models, sustaining innovation, gradual innovation, disruptive innovation, new-market footholds, low-end footholds

REFERENCE

Anthony, S. D., Johnson, M. W., Sinfield, J. V., & Altman, E. J. (2008). *The innovator's guide to growth: Putting disruptive innovation to work: Harvard Business Press.*

Chaudhri, R., Borriello, G., & Anderson, R. (2012). Pervasive computing technologies to monitor vaccine cold chains in developing countries. *IEEE Pervasive Computing. Special issue on Information and Communication Technologies for Development, 10.*

Cook, T., & McKay, C. (2015). How M-Shwari works: The story so far. *Consultative group to assist the poor (CGAP) and financial sector deepening (FSD).*

Christensen, C. M. (2013). *The innovator's dilemma: when new technologies cause great firms to fail.* Harvard Business Review Press.

Dangwal, R., Jha, S., Chatterjee, S., & Mitra, S. (2005). A model of how children acquire computing skills from hole-in-the-wall computers in public places. *Information Technologies & International Development, 2*(4), pp. 41-60.

Dimaguila, G. L. (2015). *SMS for Life in Burundi and Zimbabwe: A Comparative Evaluation.* Paper presented at the International Conference on Health Information Science.

Dumbill, E. (2012). *Planning for big data:* Sebastopol.

Gomez, R. (2014). When you do not have a computer: Public-access computing in developing countries. *Information Technology for Development, 20*(3), 274-291.

Heeks, R. (2017). *Information and Communication Technology for Development (ICT4D):* Taylor & Francis.

Ho, M. R., Smyth, T. N., Kam, M., & Dearden, A. (2009). Human-computer interaction for development: The past, present, and future. *Information Technologies & International Development, 5*(4), pp. 1-18.

Jack, W., & Suri, T. (2011). *Mobile money: The economics of M-PESA.* Retrieved from

Karuri, J., Waiganjo, P., Daniel, O., & Manya, A. (2014). DHIS2: the tool to improve health data demand and use in Kenya. *Journal of Health Informatics in Developing Countries, 8*(1).

Khanal, S., Burgon, J., Leonard, S., Griffiths, M., & Eddowes, L. A. (2015). Recommendations for the improved effectiveness and reporting of telemedicine programs in developing countries: results of a systematic literature review. *Telemedicine and e-Health, 21*(11), 903-915.

Kimaro, H. C. (2006). Strategies for developing human resource capacity to support sustainability of ICT based health information systems: a case study from Tanzania. *The Electronic Journal of Information Systems in Developing Countries, 26*(1), 1-23.

Kuhn, T. S. (1962). The Structure of Scientific Revolutions.

Medhi, I., Sagar, A., & Toyama, K. (2006). *Text-free user interfaces for illiterate and semi-literate users.* Paper presented at the 2006 international conference on information and communication technologies and development.

Ndaiga, W., & Salim, A. (2015). *Kids hacker camps in Kenya: hardware hacking effectiveness in skills transfer.* Paper presented at the Proceedings of the Seventh International Conference on Information and Communication Technologies and Development.

NikkeiBP. (2017). *Nikkei Technology's Outlook 2017: 100 Technologies to Change the World:* Nikkei Business Publications.

Popper, K. (1959). *The Logic of Scientific Discovery.*

Roser, M., & Ritchie, H. (2020). A semi-log plot of transistor counts for microprocessors against dates of introduction, nearly doubling every two years. In: Our World in Data.

Rosling, H., Rosling, O., & Rönnlund, A. (2018). Factfulness: Ten reasons we're wrong about the world–And why things are better than you think: Sceptre. In: London.

Schumacher, E. F. (1989). *Small is beautiful : economics as if people mattered.* New York: HarperPerennial.

Smith, C. E. (2007). *Design for the Other 90%:* Cooper-Hewitt Museum of.

Toyama, K. (2015). *Geek heresy: Rescuing social change from the cult of technology:* PublicAffairs.

Wyche, S. (2015). *Exploring mobile phone and social media use in a Nairobi slum: a case for alternative approaches to design in ICTD.* Paper presented at the

Proceedings of the Seventh International Conference on Information and Communication Technologies and Development, Singapore, Singapore. https://doi.org/10.1145/2737856.2738019

CHAPTER 07

Topic 6 Thinking Skills

Topic 6
Thinking Skills

Qianang Sun and Eunyoung Kim

This chapter introduces different ways of thinking about problem-solving and discusses potential methods and processes of creative solutions from different perspectives.

7.1 Introduction

Around 2,500 years ago, Socrates pursued the truth by asking probing questions that incubated the thinking skill that we call rational criticism. The purpose of inquiring is to investigate the truth behind contradictory ideas beyond words. In this way, authoritative judgments cannot be recognized as reasonable, and an ideal individual should be independent in spirit rather than a credulous authority or a whimsical, irrational creature.

However, many facets of human consciousness and thinking are mysterious, including how humans make decisions in dynamic environments. Most people believe that they should be objective when facing diverse conditions and strive to make rational decisions. Many studies have been conducted to investigate how humans think and make decisions. The results of this research indicated that humans think they should be objective about many crucial issues and draw conclusions about them carefully, but they do not do much thinking about thinking. Even though we use our brains to understand how everything works, we still know next to nothing about exactly how the brain itself works. Under the rational thought model, perception and memory are neurological activities that maximize the likelihood of finding solutions to problems.

Rational thought refers to, among other things, the objective consideration of a range of possible options for the purpose of making the best possible choice. Social scientist Herbert A. Simon modified the rational thought model with the concept of "bounded rationality" (Simon, 1990). The underlying assumption of this concept is that, as the world is exceedingly complex, we seek to account for as much information as possible, but as there are limits on how much information we can absorb, process, and store, our capacity to make informed, rational decisions is correspondingly limited—or bounded—as well. Thus, human decision making occurs within an environment of bounded rationality. Because of this limitation, our mental models do not always match reality, especially when under pressure or in high-stakes situations. There is an advantage to bounded rationality, however, insofar as it simplifies the management of otherwise overwhelming amounts of information.

What is interesting is that most types of thinking require little to no conscious effort. In other words, we think without thinking, at least when it comes to making simple choices like whether to add milk or sugar to coffee. Similarly, if someone is asked a practical question, expresses a preference, or states a fact, that in and of itself is not a thinking skill. It may involve language and communication skills, but it is not so much a thought as it is an instinctual basis or trigger for what we would call "thinking."

Experts in different fields have made valuable contributions to the exploration of the mind, including the establishment of general categories or orders of thinking. Higher-order thinking, for instance, is applied when engaging in complex activities that require aggregate analysis, empirical evaluation, problem definition, and informed decision making, whereas lower-order thinking is associated with more basic aspects of understanding, identification, and learning. Higher-order thinking also manifests in the nuanced application of knowledge and in flexible adaptations necessary to accomplish various purposes. Such thinking, however, requires the independent identification and assessment of problems in corresponding scenarios and the judgment needed to determine which skills to employ to generate optimal solutions. When we talk about skills in this regard, we refer primarily to (1) specialized knowledge or expertise, and (2) the capacity to bring such knowledge and expertise to bear on challenging problems in the pursuit of effective, well-informed solutions. Further, the articulation of these skills must be balanced and controlled. Say, for instance, that two potters are making coffee cups, with one exerting intense effort, while the other proceeds in a gentle and measured fashion. Knowing which of the two produces a coarse and cumbersome cup and which produces a delicate and useful cup means one understands the value of balance and control in the exercise of skills.

It can be challenging to assess whether a person is expressing higher-order thinking skills because we cannot directly observe what or how they are thinking. As a consequence, we must rely on representations to evaluate the correspondence between real-world problems and the ways in which these problems are cognitively perceived. One person may, for instance, make reasoned guesses about how to solve real-world problems, while another may employ imagination or creativity for the same purpose.

In this chapter, we discuss thinking skills that focus on problem-solving, including design thinking, creative thinking, analogical thinking, and reflective thinking. First, of course, we need to define the problem. Defining the problem is sometimes more important than actually solving it, since problems should not be approached blindly, especially in increasingly complex environments from which problems are constantly emerging. Problems are rarely comprehensible at surface level, and many require some combination of rational thought and imagination to be perceived correctly (Yanagisawa & Takatsuji, 2015).

In Topic 3, we discussed creativity theories with a macro-perspective focus on the individual and for the purpose of evaluating the relationship between creative achievement and intelligence. From the perspective of multiple disciplines, creativity constitutes an important bridge between human beings and their surroundings, even within the machinations of massive organizations. Furthermore, creativity can strengthen self-knowledge while simultaneously enhancing one's knowledge about the world.

At this point, we need further inquiry into the ways in which knowledge innovation is pursued. Moreover, considerations of and reflections upon the question of whether all new ideas are creative must be undertaken. In the post-industrial world, creativity is no longer a natural talent or gift but instead a highly valued skill for personal development and organizational projects. We will begin, however, with the identification and clarification of the problem, as otherwise we will be, as mentioned above, blindly approaching the issue at hand.

The entire chapter will therefore focus on the problem-solving process to organize the characteristics, components, functions, and effects of different thinking skills on creativity. Design thinking makes a product fit a specific target user by aligning structure, function, and behavior. More importantly, it cultivates a new demand rather than satiating an existing, instinctive need. Creative thinking focuses on what kinds of cognition can help people improve the efficiency of their problem-solving creatively. With the rapid development and expansion of various sciences and technologies, single skills alone cannot possibly accommodate the complexity of such progress. Likewise, problems and challenges that arise as a consequence of scientific and technological advancement cannot be resolved through single-minded approaches but instead require flexible, creative modes of thinking. Reflective thinking along several different dimensions is also imperative, as it can culminate in the generation of new insights.

7.2. Thinking Skills for Problem-solving

7.2.1. Problem-solving

The meaning of a problem must always be understood before solving it. As a case in point, when one prepares a seemingly simple breakfast of coffee and toasted bread, a whole range of items must be employed: coffee beans, a coffee maker, a toaster, water, a cup, a plate, bread, a knife, butter, milk, and sugar. So, what seems like a simple breakfast actually requires multiple items in a rather complicated arrangement and order. One could be forgiven for thinking that such an activity requires little complex thought—and yet it does, especially if improvement is the goal. First, such actions, though routine, must be practiced attentively and adjusted every time for progress to be made. This ensures not just that food is enjoyed but that it is eventually prepared to perfection. Returning to the case in point, one who is attentive and mindful will reflect upon how to prepare the ingredients not just quickly but optimally, how to match the amount of coffee made with the size of the cup, and how long to leave the bread in the toaster to ensure it does not burn.

As another example, bartenders often have to master a large number of drinks with a wide variety of ingredients, which they must combine in precise proportions. In this sense, making a good cocktail is like solving a math problem: It requires judgment, deliberation, trial and error, planning, and execution. Nevertheless, it is not *the same* as solving a math problem. Alternatively, problem-solving involves a series of actions that constitute a strategy with no standard answer. Unlike a mathematical problem, which has a definitive, single solution, practical problems can have any number of solutions depending on which assumptions are made, which strategies are employed, and who is employing them.

Therefore, the purpose of developing thinking skills is not to yield a definitive outcome but instead to generate a potential solution, one that links one set of information to another in various articulations and incorporates an array of diverse experiences. When previous experiences are applied to present problems, a wide range of resources (texts, pictures, videos, audio, etc.) become available to arrive at *a*—not *the*—solution. Once realized, this solution can be extended to address other problems in the same or related fields.

Therefore, when one determines how to translate their current situation into a forward-looking condition—that is, when a problem state is transformed into a goal state—the problem has essentially been solved. Between these two states is the process of transformation itself, i.e., the intermediate state. Thus, most problems are not a single state but three: the problem state, the intermediate state, and the goal state. For instance, sending a letter involves first writing the letter, after which it is sealed in an envelope and mailed. So long as the sealed letter remains unsent, it exists in an intermediate state. According to Newell et al. (1962) and Newell and Simon (1972), all problems emerge from within what they called the "task context." This context contains all of the stimuli to which one can respond, including instructions for addressing the problem and any objects pertaining to the problem (Newell & Simon, 1972).

7.2.2. Understanding design thinking

As design has evolved into an independent discipline in recent years, design thinking has permeated different domains to support new creations. Similarly, and naturally, these domains have contributed to design thinking as well. However, we usually take the product of design for granted and view the designer's contribution as a duty. Scholars devoted to generalizing design thinking have qualified demand and the human-centered design concept based on design research.

According to Cross (2004), everyone is a designer, and design is part of human intelligence. Humans have a long history of design capabilities, as evidenced by the persistence of artefacts, indigenous designs, and traditional crafts of past civilizations (Cross, 2006). In recent years, the training of artificial intelligence to carry out design work has gradually become more popular. However, implementing artificial intelligence in design and even replacing designers is still a long way off. As human beings, designers think and work in ways that no machine has thus far been able to emulate. This is because human cognition is inscrutably complex and endlessly faceted, and as such much of what constitutes human intelligence remains unknown. Because artificial intelligence is based on the idea that the brain is a computer, it is limited in scope and function to computational aspects of the human mind—rational, analytical, linear, and propositional thinking. These aspects can in turn facilitate increased understanding of creative cognitive components, such as analogies, metaphors, concepts and conceptual spaces, sequential stages, and transformational rules. Nevertheless, artificial intelligence creators cannot mimic emotions, motivations, or even irrational thinking (Sawyer, 2017).

As a particular domain, design is a dynamic and complex process involving often confusing and subtle perceptions. To lay the foundation for a clear description of the specific components of the design process, several general definitions of design thinking should be stated:

- A process leading to an action plan to improve a situation and calling for situational awareness and empathy.
- Analysis and creative thinking directed at solving a problem while considering the relevant environment, stakeholders' needs and preferences, logistics problems, and costs.
- A series of psychological stages in which ideas are generated and sources are combined to provide better solutions.
- A series of actions involving research, analysis, idea proposal, feedback, and subsequent modifications undertaken to refine the idea.

To sum up, design thinking is a fundamentally creative process driven by specific problems and transcending traditional or obvious solutions. While not a magic formula, design thinking can produce an effective and innovative solution by systematic research, description, and rational combinations of ideas. More specific components of design thinking are outlined in Table 7-1 (Ling, 2015).

TABLE 7-1 Components of Design Thinking

Component	Description
Information collection	Study the environment and stakeholders to understand all relevant issues, conflicts, and constraints. Understand the historical perspectives and range of precedents that might apply to the problem. Conduct effective interviews and small-scale ethnographic research, and consult key knowledgeable people to accelerate understanding. The resulting data can substantially inform subsequent design investigations and help generate ideas.

Problem analysis and definition	Rigorous analysis undertaken to ensure that the most salient problems are identified, which may otherwise be overlooked. Question the initial assumptions and redefine the problem. This analysis is also a prerequisite for meaningful brainstorming carried out to provide a clear, ordered, and fine-grained view of an issue from multiple perspectives.
Ideation	Generate as many ideas as possible, without judgment or criticism, through brainstorming and imagination. Combine various influences to create innovative graphical concepts or outlines of ideas.
Compose by modeling	Develop the best ideas to a higher resolution and in greater detail. Use these ideas to create prototypes, models, or draft solutions. The goal here is twofold: propose initial solutions and facilitate their execution.
Critical assessment	Critically assess the solution or project for the purpose of improvement. Validate (or invalidate) concepts and solutions related to the problem definition by critical stakeholders, customers, and peer reviews. All feedback is valuable for making meaningful revisions. Accept constructive criticism but make changes without diluting or rejecting the strongest ideas. Then, repeat the process.

Design thinking begins with immersion in the unique context of the problem. It is a process of discovery in which clues to the solution may become apparent as the problem is fully and deeply explored from multiple perspectives.

Many observational studies of how designers work have differentiated the design process from activities typical of scientists and academics. In particular, observational studies have compared the problem-solving strategies of designers and scientists. In one study, researchers designed questions that needed to be arranged in 3D colored blocks to meet certain rules (some of which were not initially disclosed) and presented them to graduate students in architecture and science (Purcell, 1981). The two groups performed differently in terms of their problem-solving strategies. The science students usually adopted a strategy of systematically exploring possible combinations of blocks to discover the basic rules that allowed such combinations. The architecture students, on the other hand, were more likely to propose a series of solutions and then eliminate them, one by one, until they arrived at an acceptable solution. Simply put, the science students solved problems through analysis, whereas the architecture students solved problems by synthesis.

The scientific method is a mode of action for solving a problem by scrutinizing its essential nature and characteristics, while the design method is a process of inventing something of value that does not yet exist. In short, science is analytical, whereas design is constructive (Gregory & Paidoussis, 1966). To deal with poorly defined problems, designers must learn to confidently define, redefine, and change problems according to the solutions that emerge from their heads and hands. About this, Jones and Connolly (1970) commented that changing a problem to find a solution is the most challenging part of the design. In this regard, those who seek the certainty of an externally structured, clearly defined problem would likely not appreciate the work of a designer.

Professional knowledge applied during the design process is largely tacit—that is, designers' way of knowing is similar to the skilled people's "knowing" for how to execute that skill. However, it is difficult to externalize the specific knowledge that explains why design education is forced to rely so tightly on the apprenticeship learning system.

After decades of development, research on design thinking has become increasingly abundant. Professional designers' views on design provide us with insights into what design thinking means. Design thinking allows us to accept the perspectives, criticisms, and feedback of users. Cross (2006) performed landmark research in this area, conducting interviews with top designers in various fields to explore the nature of good design thinking and connect it to broader perceptions.

According to Cross (2006), a design can appear as rhetoric. The designer constructs a rhetorical argument as he/she constructs a design solution. The solution is eventually developed and evaluated against known goals and previously unsuspected meanings. Like the eminent architect Denys Lasdun explained in a critique of design's rhetorical nature (Lasdun, 1965):

> Our job is to give our clients... Not what he wanted, but what he never thought he wanted; When he gets it, he realizes that this is what he has always wanted.

This is the confidence and even arrogance of a good designer, but what lies behind this statement is that clients expect designers to go beyond the obvious, to transcend the mundane, and to develop exciting solutions, but only as practically as possible. In other words, designers want to solve problems related not only to basic needs but also, through ingenious design, to needs that might otherwise be ignored.

Furthermore, the creative designer does not propose normative solutions but instead explores a partial map of an unknown territory (Howard-Jones et al., 2005). The creative designer must explore, must discover something new, rather than returning time and again to established and familiar examples. The relationship between problems and solutions is a slippery slope, as expressed by furniture designer Geoffrey Harcourt (Franzoi et al., 1985):

> A particular design is not a completely orderly conclusion, but after the synthesis of many conditions, from a completely new perspective to find that the scheme has been implemented.

This seems to imply the irrational side of design thinking. An ambiguous design problem is one that cannot be solved simply by gathering and synthesizing information. Not all relevant information can be predicted and established in advance during the design activity. Only by trial and error can the real problems be discovered (MacCormac, 1976).

Therefore, when designers talk about design thinking, it is not uncommon to mention the role of "intuition" in their reasoning process. The concept of "intuition" in design is a convenient heuristic that can be used to make creative leaps and to interpret what happens in design thinking. Conceptual reasoning is promoted as a more useful way to guide designers to work effectively. However, design involves not only the deductive reasoning of different concepts. Certainly, logic is necessary, but the thinking process of designers revolves more around the relationship between internal and external performance. "

> You see the things in your mind that are not there on paper, and then you start making simple sketches, organizing things, and then you start peeling away layer by layer to explore deeper things... It is like a conversation. (Jacobs-Lawson & Hershey, 2005)

The recognition of the dialogue that occurs between internal and external representations foregrounds design as a partly reflexive act. The designer must have a medium through which half-formed ideas can be expressed, can be reflected, because early solutions are tentative and options should be kept open for as long as possible.

Finally, we must mention that design thinking is risky since it entails the expression of personal views and opinions. Not all designers are willing to take this risk, but many of the best designers have. Balancing risks with the right solution is no easy task. Although we believe that everyone possesses an innate ability for design, substantial training is nonetheless required to flexibly converse about design. In this regard, numerous interdisciplinary recent research are supporting design thinking for enhancing creativity in diverse contexts.

A preliminary look at some of the essential characteristics of design activities revealed that design involves identifying the appropriate problems and solving them with a substantive problem structure and development plan rather than just accepting the problem as is. And designers' cognitive strategies may be based on the universal desire to solve ambiguous problems.

In the first recorded study of design protocols (on architectural design), Thomas and Carroll (1979) found that the behavioral characteristics of designers tolerated undefined problems in that design is concerned with solving problems. Thomas and Carroll also found that one consistently expressed approach to solving problems in all protocols is to permit a topic to generate a design element and determine its quality rather than generating abstract relationships and attributes and then deriving appropriate objects to consider. The designer thus has a solution (or part of a solution) in mind before the problem is fully articulated, meaning the designer is solution-driven, not problem-driven. What matters to designers is evaluating the solution, not analyzing the problem (Eastman, 1970).

In the latest research, Gero and Milovanovic (2020) proposed a new framework for understanding and studying design cognition. Their research methods were paradigmatically divided to measure the activities of design thinking into design cognition (the designer's mind when designing), design physiology (the designer's body when designing), and design neurocognition (the designer's brain when designing) (Gero & Milovanovic, 2020). As we will see, each approach provides different tools to measure different characteristics of design thinking. The basic purpose of design physiology and design neurocognition is to convey design cognition by measuring certain aspects of the designer's representation at the time of the design. Utilizing the tools developed by advanced technology, diverse evidence has been generated that has revealed the design process. Direct (protocol analysis) and indirect (surveys, interviews, and black-box experiments) methods have been used to measure the cognitive behavior of designers. Design physiology and design neurocognition studies have provided valuable empirical information about designers' physiological behavior (by measuring eye movement, electrodermal activity, and Heart rate variability) and neurological behavior (by non-invasive brain measurement techniques).

Design thinking research began 50 years ago (Eastman, 1970). Design physiology and design neurocognition research has proliferated as more sophisticated tools have become available, such as advanced software for analyzing physiological and neurological data. Discovering the correlation between design cognition, design physiology, and design neurocognition will likely provide a strong foundation for developing new models, toolkits, and new research questions, all of which will in turn contribute to understanding design thinking in a promising way. New tools in research design will be combined with technologies from other research areas, such as brain imaging techniques, artificial intelligence, or machine learning. Potentially, future research will pursue a more integrated approach to studying design thinking, exploring underlying patterns of neurological and physiological activity as related to the design process and new tools to facilitate design activity.

7.2.3. Understanding creative thinking

Unlike design thinking, creative thinking is a broader concept, covering all fields of research. Over the past 50 years, cognitive perspectives on creative thinking have been spurred in part by the development of computers (Newell & Simon, 1972). On a practical level, computer scientists and engineers are focused on the idea that a new "machine" could relieve the burden of performing repetitive tasks. Not surprisingly, computers have become ubiquitous in recent decades for, among other applications, building cars, controlling railway trains, and launching spacecraft. With the rapid development of cognitive science, the application of cognitive perspectives to the exploration of creativity and creative thinking with respect to problem-solving has become commonplace. Many researchers have proposed that problem-solving should be defined as analyzing and transforming information into a specific goal (e.g., McCulloch et al., 2002).

FIGURE 7-1A

Bottom-up versus top-down processing (Weisberg, 2006).

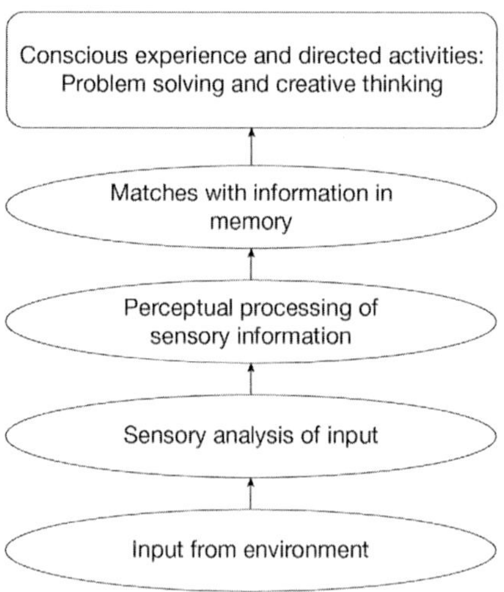

Problem-solving involves deciding what to do next. In this sense, all decision situations are equivalent (Reder & Anderson, 1982). However, as a certain amount of intelligence is required to perform simple repetitive tasks, AI programs are designed from a practical perspective for the purpose of performing target tasks in an error-free and efficient manner. Moreover, several researchers have argued that human thought can be described in similar terms (Newell et al., 1962). This association has profoundly affected the trajectory of modern psychology. Many researchers believe that machines might tell us something about the human mind via systematic training. Therefore, training a machine to think first requires understanding how humans think.

Furthermore, Finke et al. (1992) presented a creative cognitive model based on the assumption of the critical importance of bottom-up processes in problem-solving. In this context, it would be informative to study cognition-based creative thinking models, which rely more on bottom-up processes, as shown in Figure 7-1. However, the identification is not going through the system as one way direction. The primary action or event is possibly influenced by existing information in memory, i.e., top-down processing.

FIGURE 7-1B

Bottom-up versus top-down processing (Weisberg, 2006).

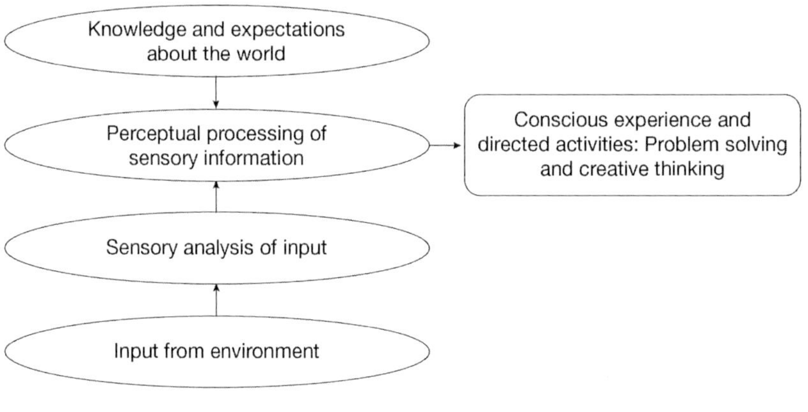

Finke, et al. (1992) emphasized that all human cognition is essentially creative. As we know, this view forms the core of the cognitive perspective and also suggests that creative thinking can be seen as the result of the application of ordinary cognitive processes, which is a hypothesis consistent with the views taken by Newell et al. (1962), Burger et al. (1981), and Weisberg (1986).

Besides, Newell and Simon (1972) suggested that it is unnecessary to limit problem-solving to creative thinking or the production of novelty. It can produce novelty without rejecting traditional ideas, and the problems involved are usually unclear. High-level motivation and perseverance may be required, but this may be a trivial aspect of these situations. If the problem involved can be resolved quickly, it will not have any broad significance, and its solution will not be noted in history. In other words, people remember that successful problem-solving involves difficult problems, but solving a difficult problem itself does not mean that any extraordinary thought process is involved. Based on the problem's internal representation, people can construct the problem space with a series of actions. In Chapter 4, we discussed the creative process in detail. In this section, we discuss creative thinking with professional knowledge and experience in problem-solving.

As we now know, a significant development in the cognitive research on problem-solving is the critical role played by knowledge and expertise, sometimes generated through conscious practice. If at least some creative progress is the result of problem-solving, then knowledge, expertise, and practice should be relevant in these cases. It becomes interesting to determine how important a role expertise plays in creative thinking, even in areas that may seem irrelevant to problem-solving.

Many researchers reject the conclusion that expertise gained through practice is a key element of high-level performance. Instead, these researchers argue that it is talent, not acquired expertise, that ultimately determines performance (Dews et al., 1996; Sternberg & Lubart, 1996). Conceptually speaking, talent and aptitude refer to the notion that the greatest achievements in any field are made by relatively few people—those whose talents make them particularly well suited to excel in their field. In contrast, findings from the literature on expertise have raised the possibility that the performance of average individuals may have few innate limitations (Ericsson, 2006)

In the study of creativity, talent versus practice is a question of immediate importance because creativity is generally considered to depend on talent. However, many studies have directly addressed some of the objections raised by talent theorists to expert opinion. Several studies have conducted experiments on children. Sloboda et al. (1996) investigated the role of talent and practice in musical performance among 257 children in the UK who were tasked with learning a variety of instruments. Five achievement levels were ultimately discerned. Students at the highest achievement level were enrolled in specialized music schools, attended competitive examinations, and continued to professionally perform music after graduation. The next highest achievement level were composed of students who failed their school entrance exams. The students at the lowest achievement level attempted to learn an instrument but gave up after six months. Sloboda et al. sought to identify at which age group talent was most prominent. Surprisingly, despite the wide range of reported talent in the sample, there was little difference between the five groups in possible markers of musical talent. Moreover, the researchers noted that parents in the highest achievement level group were more involved in initiating musical activities for their children. Thus, parental involvement was implicated in high musical achievement levels. It should be noted that the sample in Sloboda et al.'s (1996) study included students who had stopped musical training; these students comprised the control group.

Other researchers have estimated the average amount of time it takes students at different proficiency levels to pass exams (Marković, 2012) appraisal of the symbolic reality of an object (high cognitive engagement. The talent hypothesis predicts that more talented students will need less practice to advance from one level to the next. A key—and perhaps surprising—finding is that the best students need to spend just as much time studying as other students to advance from one level to the next. This suggests that those talented students who improve more quickly than others do so because they are more motivated and engaged, not because they need less practice. Thus, in the creative field, how talent is produced may not matter as much as how expertise and practice shape achievement in the context of creative achievement.

7.2.4. Understanding analogical thinking for creative problem-solving

A considerable number of studies have been conducted on problem solving or hypothesis formation via analogical thinking. People solve problems better if they have experienced associated or similar problems (K. J. Holyoak & Koh, 1987; Novick, 1988; Ross, 1987). In this context, analogical thinking has been suggested as a basic mechanism for inspiring creative tasks in which people incorporate information from well-known, existing categories, i.e., base or source domains, into the construction of a new idea, i.e., the target domain (Finke et al., 1992; Gentner et al., 1997; Perkins, 1997), as shown in Figure 7-2. Weisberg (1995) identified numerous situations in which earlier creative ideas and solutions are transferred to new situations that are analogous to the older situations. The use of analogical thinking is important for theory formation, design, and construction (Sarlemijn & Kroes, 1988). Moreover, Bingham and Kahl (2013) noted that analogical thinking is a highly effective tool for companies and organizations to cope with significant change and innovation.

FIGURE 7-2

The major component processes in analogical transfer.

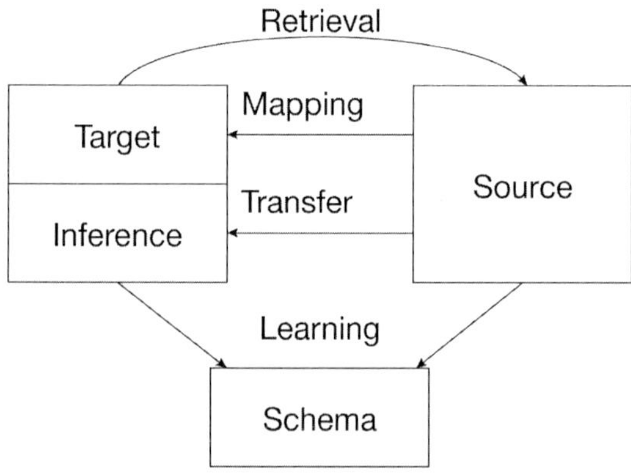

Note. Redrawn from Holyoak and Morrison (2005).

Gick and Holyoak (1980) conducted an experiment on problem-solving among university students using Duncker's (1945) radiation problem (See Chapter 4.4.2) The participants were given instructions to read and remember a target story along with two other irrelevant stories. The target story was about a general who was trying to capture a fortress controlled by a dictator and needed to get his army to the fortress at full strength. Because the entire army could not pass safely along any single road, the general sent his men in small groups down several roads simultaneously. Arriving at the same time, the groups combined and captured the fortress. A few minutes after reading this story, the participants were asked to solve Duncker's radiation problem. Without a source analog, only about 10% of the participants found the solution. When the target story had been studied, but no hint on how to use it was given, only about 20% of the participants produced the solution. Conversely, when the same participants were given the simple hint that "you may find one of the stories you read earlier to be helpful in solving the problem," about 75% succeeded in generating the analogous solution. In other words, people often fail to notice superficially dissimilar source analogs that they could readily use.

Analogical thinking also appears to play a key role in creative design: Analogical design involves reminding and transferring elements of a solution for one design problem to the solution for another design problem (Goel, 1997). Cross (2011) conducted research to understand how designers think and work, allowing people to identify what is meant by design thinking. After several interviews with professional designers and observations of their working process, Cross discovered that their inspiration arose prosaically by applying an analogy, and that this analogy encouraged creative thinking.

Casakin and Goldschmidt (2000) empirically investigated whether the use of analogy enabled subjects to perform better in solving problems. In their experimental research, three groups of subjects with varying design experience participated: experienced architects, advanced architecture students, and novice architecture students. Each subject solved a number of well-defined problems, each of which had one correct solution, and ill-defined problems, which had any number of acceptable solutions. Design problems were presented under three conditions: (a) the design problem was administered with no additional material or commentary; (b) the design problem was administered while the subjects were shown a panel with visual displays (approximately two dozen images), some of which could be used as source analogs for the problem, and some which could not; (c) same as (b) except the subjects were also explicitly encouraged to identify relevant images among the displays and use them as source analogs in their designs. All subjects were asked to present the solutions to the design problems in sketch form, on one or more sheets of paper. These sketch designs were assessed by three experienced architects: the quality and creativity of the solutions for the ill-defined problems were evaluated on a 5-point scale. The assessment results were reliable because the degree of agreement among the judges was very high. It was concluded that, for ill-defined problem-solving, all of the subjects, regardless of their level of experience, obtained significantly higher scores when using cues and being given instructions to use analogies.

7.3. Enhancing Thinking Skills

7.3.1. Expertise, experience, and creativity

When a world-class chess player makes a move that surprises his or her opponent, there is no doubt that it is a creative act. The basic motor skills of chess are trivial—pushing small pieces across the board—but the game concept is so complex that the intellectual skills involved in deciding a move can take years to acquire. Ericsson (2006) proposed that chess grandmasters acquire complex mental representations of their domain, and that these representations are the basis for their high-level performance.

A substantial body of literature has replicated and analyzed famous chess games from tournaments and world championships. Chess experts study these games in an effort to predict the moves of chess champions. If they did not correctly anticipate the move, future masters would analyze the situation more deeply and determine why the champion was doing it.

Chase and Simon (1973), in their analysis of the development of chess players' skills, concluded that no one could become a chess master without at least 10 years of study and practice, thus giving rise to the 10-year rule.

A similar rule applies to doctors with diagnostic skills in certain areas (Chase & Simon, 1973; Ericsson, 1993). According to Ericsson (1993), a similar process occurs when a radiologist reads an X-ray. This kind of knowledge is related to the understanding of creative thinking: the chess grandmaster is performing a creative act when he or she decides to move, and the oncologist and radiologist make a diagnosis when the situation presents a specific complex symptom that they have not seen.

Just as an athlete enhances a skill, a chess player can use their expertise in two ways. One way is to maintain existing playing methods and then improve them as much as possible. In this case, the player develops his or her style within the framework of an existing playing style, developing new strategies beyond those used in the past. At this point, we think these technologies are more innovative than working within the bounds of accepted wisdom.

Many psychologist (e.g., Frensch & Sternberg, 1989; Simonton, 1999) has believed that creative thinking needs to be separated from experience. There is a tension between experience and creativity, and the tension also applies to expertise. Creativity should be the result of being divorced from expertise. We have no idea about concrete things, and we have no patience to follow the usual advice. We usually pay more attention to the most profound abstractions with sharp discernment and to the freshest combinations of elements, and the subtle association of analogy habit is always ignored. To sum up, we seem to have been suddenly ushered into a cauldron of boiling ideas, where everything boils and wobbles in a dizzying state of activity where the unexpected seems to be the first law.

This description of the highest level of mental function focuses on its positive aspects: the ability to put together ideas beyond the lower level as needed. There is also a dark side to this view: If higher-order minds do not follow the normal trajectory of habitual hints, then the lower-order minds that follow this trajectory are doomed to mediocrity (Hennessey, 2015). Therefore, it is considered unable to deal with situations requiring innovation (Wertheimer, 1985).

The research on creativity that has concerned the most influential researchers shows that the problem's solution becomes closer to a random process (Boden, 1994). Thus, a free association program must play a role.

The creator can obtain insights only by relying on the resources of this lack of discipline. This view echoes James (1890)' belief that great innovations in our society must be brought about by thinkers who can cast aside habits and banal channels of association to bring together previously unformed ideas. Similarly, this view also points out that bridge experts have a limited ability to adapt to changes in the game rules (Fan, 2016). As part of their experiment, Frensch and Sternberg (1989) made two changes to the rules of the bridge. Surface changes include changes in the name and order of suits and colors. These changes are not the core of the game. By contrast, a change in depth or concept can result in a fundamental restructuring of gameplay. For example, one change is for the player who loses the last move to lead the next move, rather than the winner. Relatively broad changes require perception updates. Novices and experts participate in both types of changes. Experts' performance is more affected by these profound changes than that of novices because knowledge makes the mindless flexible but unable to adapt to changes in the world.

As for the relationship between experience and creativity, Guilford (1959), in his seminal and influential Presidential Address to the American Psychological Association (Frick et al., 1959), proposed a similarly negative concept, that of psychometrics or psychometric methods of creativity. As we mentioned in Chapter 3, Guilford (1950) proposed that the core of creative thinking is divergent thinking skills. These skills enable a person to have different ideas from the past, from the ordinary, making the thinker respond creatively to the situation he or she is facing. Although Guilford did not cite James or gestalt psychologists in his lectures, he had the same philosophical undertones as they did. The whole creativity test movement, and much of the research that has grown out of Guilford's ideas, is based on the idea that measuring and cultivating creative thinking depends on measuring and promoting divergent thinking skills.

Further evidence to support this tension was provided by Simonton (1984), who examined the relationship between education and creative achievement. Although education may be necessary to let people deal with well-defined areas in the first place, too much education may have a negative effect. This is because becoming entrenched too deeply in the beliefs and methods of a particular field could lead to a situation in which one becomes resistant to new ideas and practices (see figure 4-3). Therefore, one might expect to find a divergence between education and creativity, with those who produce the most innovations also being those who have less education.

Contrary to creative ideas that focus on breaking away from the past and thinking outside of the box, there is evidence that creative thinking can occur through references to the past. In other words, the generation of new ideas may be premised on a foundation of old ideas (Weisberg, 1986; Weisberg & Alba, 1981). It can thus be argued that a productive relationship exists between prior experiences and established knowledge and present creativity (Weisberg et al., 2003). Thus, creative thinking that relies on the past is not necessarily counterproductive, which is consistent with the suggestion that expertise may play a role in creative thinking. Moreover, specialized knowledge or even deliberate practice could play a key role in creative performance.

7.3.2. Reflection in creative practices

Reflection generally occurs when a person is feeling confused or challenged in some way, which motivates the search for a solution to the problem. The ancient Chinese philosopher Confucius (551–479 BCE) believed that reflection is the examination of the self. His view especially emphasizes the necessity of criticizing one's inner self in order to continuously improve human morality. Confucius used daily meditation to strengthen the power of reflection and thereby infuse one's life with greater meaning (Wang & King, 2006). Silent reflection is a kind of introspective template that allows people to judge whether they treat others fairly, courteously, and morally. It permits the examination, understanding, and confirmation of the quality of one's presence in society (Wang & King, 2006).

Dewey (1933) proposed that a reflective practitioner is one who is open in heart and responsible in practice. Following Dewey, Schon (1983) claimed that reflective thinking is an important factor in the capacity to solve problems (Ben-Jacob et al., 1983; Greenwood, 1993). By reflecting on the situation at hand, the practitioner can more accurately assess all possible courses of action based on previous experience to establish the most effective solution.

Therefore, reflection can be considered an interactive dialogue between the problem solver and the problem situation.

Other scholars have described reflection as what happens when one revisits prior experiences (e.g., Burkus, 2015), pays close attention to the emotions associated with these experiences, reflects upon them, and ultimately uses these reflections on the past to evaluate and respond to present circumstances, challenges, and tasks. A key factor that drives individuals in the reflective process is intention (Dorta et al., 2016). In addition to using reflections to correct erroneous actions and make more appropriate decisions during the completion of tasks, they can also be employed to examine one's assumptions about the world and the meanings they derive from them (Mezirow, 1981, 1990). Mezirow stressed the importance of critical reflection in guiding individuals to recognize how the beliefs they take for granted and the personal values they have internalized from their culture affect their interpretations of the world. Issues such as social justice, equality, and emancipation are considered in their practical decisions.

For professional practitioners in diverse fields ranging from education to management to health to art research, environment and circumstance affect both practice and reflection (Ben-Jacob et al., 1983). It was argued that complexity, uncertainty, instability, uniqueness, and value conflict are all increasing in professional practice (Greenwood, 1993). Schon (1983) pointed out that the peak of enthusiasm for professionalism occurred after the Second World War, after which there was a loss of confidence in professional skills. This is because professionals could not resolve the complex systemic problems emerging in the Western world. The harsh criticism of professionalism that occurred during this era was attributable to a misconception of expertise, which Schon called technical rationality.

Schon claimed that ignorance of practitioners' knowledge in practice has led to a crisis of confidence in the effectiveness of the profession. To address this crisis, Schon proposed a new model of professional knowledge based on reflective practice. In such reflective practice, thoughts and actions are integrated with the situation at hand (Greenwood, 1993). Reflective practitioners are those who make reflection a part of their daily practice. They will thus act and make judgments based on their knowledge and wisdom of a particular area of expertise. This practice is widely recognized in the contemporary professional and educational world, where skillful knowledge is required.

Dewey (1933) additionally pointed out the difference between ordinary and reflective thinking. He believed that randomness may be true of continuous thinking, but it is not characteristic of reflection. The way of a sequential thiking is sorted to determine the next correct result, which, in turn, refers to the previous result. This concept relies on identifying subtle clues between events and experiences in a "meaningful" way. It also implies the balanced judgment or evaluation of these subtle clues, which seems to involve a process of rationality and self-criticism. However, in contrast, reflection is a fundamental element of strategic thinking. According to Schon (1983), "reflection" and "action" are inextricably linked. These concepts of reflection and action (or inaction) are key to understanding the practice of reflection and the nature of its knowledge (Helyer, 2015)it is also increasingly associated with reflecting on action (Schon, 1983.

Simultaneously, the idea that thinking interferes with action and illustrates how practitioners describe their intuitive understanding through reflection in action has been refuted. This view represents a misunderstanding of the complementary relationship between thought and action. In actual reflection on action, as we have seen, action and thought complement each other. "Doing" extends the act of thinking, moving, and exploring experiments during testing, while reflection is the feedback to "doing" and its results. It takes a surprising outcome to trigger reflection. The production of satisfying behavior stops reflection. In other words, reflective thinking enables the practitioner to understand what they are trying to do.

Another prominent scholar, Jack Mezirow, incorporated reflective thinking and reflection in his transformative adult learning model. We noted an earlier work by Mezirow (1981), which divides rethinking into at least seven levels, including:

- Non-reflective action (relative to the reflection action)
- Habitual action (habitual behavior is that undertaken by individuals

based on earlier experience and automatically reinforced by frequent use or activity). It is seldom conscious.

- Thoughtful action (deliberate action using existing knowledge rather than the assessment of that knowledge, such that the significance of learning is still present in existing plans and ideas).
- Introspection. Unlike thoughtful action, which is related to cognition, introspection pertains to emotional reflection. It refers to how we feel or think about ourselves. This feeling can be personal and can include our awareness of the feelings of others. However, it does not involve the determination of how or why those feelings develop; it only involves awareness of those feelings).
- Reflective action (effective testing, including assumptions about the problem-solving process of content or criticism).
- Content reflection (content and processes are equivalent in level. The two are distinguishable in terms of their subject matter. Content resets what to focus on, and how to review the process.

Empirical research on reflective thinking has recently made some progress, but it is still far from sufficient. Under the influence of Mezirow, a study from Hong and Choi (2011) constructed three dimensions of reflection to discuss designers' reflective activities when solving design problems. The three dimensions of reflection include time, object, and reflection. This framework further developed and validated a novel self-report questionnaire, Reflective Assessment for Design Problem Solving (ARTID), as an effective tool for exploring reflection. The overall results confirmed that the ARTID questionnaire had an acceptable level of validity and reliability. The participants' reflection on the model also demonstrates the practical value of using educational practice and research tools. Simultaneously, the ARTID questionnaire is considered an effective diagnostic tool for exploring when and how designers reflect during the design process. Some limitations need to be considered for the purpose of research and educational practice.

Although 294 subjects participated in four data-collection phases to validate and further develop the ARTID questionnaire, it is recommended that a larger group of subjects be assessed to further improve the quality and validity of the questionnaire. Another limitation of the ARTID questionnaire is that due to the complexity of solving design problems, not every aspect of the designer's reflection may be detected. Moreover, participants may interpret items on the questionnaire differently due to variations in word choice. To improve the ARTID questionnaire, it may be combined with other research methods, such as the thinking aloud protocol (Adams & Pandey, 2003) or videotaping the design process (McDonnell & Holbrook, 2004), to observe the reflective behavior of designers. Findings from various data sources can be further triangulated to provide stronger evidence.

So far, we have not fully understood many aspects of practitioners' knowledge, including the role of reflection in practice. By understanding how practitioners reflect on their work and by observing how they expand their expertise through experience, we can begin to ask the right questions about the nature of knowing. This can be achieved through the oral and written narratives of professional practitioners.

7.3.3. Superficial and structural similarity in analogical thinking

Dunbar (1995) focused on scientific analogies, identifying three different kinds: (1) local analogies, i.e., one part of one experiment is related to a second experiment; (2) regional analogies, i.e., involving systems of relationships applied in one domain but used in a similar domain; (3) long-distance analogies, i.e., a system is found and applied in a different domain. In addition, Nathalie Bonnardel and Marmèche (2004) described how analogy-making allows two kinds of analogies: intra-domain analogies, in which the target (e.g., the situation or problem at hand) and the source (a previous similar situation) belong to the same conceptual domain; and inter-domain analogies, in which the target and the source belong to different conceptual domains.

Gentner et al. (1997) claimed that creativity is best realized with deeply structured representations that are relatively firm, structurally guided alterations. Dunbar and Blanchette (2001) found that the generation task motivated people to use more structural similarity. In the generation task, subjects were asked to generate sources for a given target; while in the reminding task, subjects were given various sources to read and then given new stories and asked which old stories they were reminded of by the new stories. This study revealed that in the generation task, people can and do use analogical sources that do not have superficial features in common with the target. Most of the analogies were generated (80%) dependent from superficial features of a given target. However, when the task was changed to a reminding task, the results mirrored those of research on analogical reminding—people used predominantly superficial features.

Many studies have suggested that structural similarity could be represented by matching the relation of each element in one idea to the other idea by introducing the structure-mapping framework (Falkenhainer et al., 1989; Forbus et al., 1994; Forbus & Oblinger, 1990). Intra-domain analogies would be based on both superficial similarities and structural similarities between the target and the sources, whereas inter-domain analogies would be based only on structural similarities (or underlying principles) between the target and the sources.

For creative idea generation, it needs to adopt not superficial similarity but structural similarity in using analogical thinking, which is, a long-distance analogy, i.e., a cross-domain analogy enables us to generate more novel ideas than a local analogy, i.e., within-domain analogy, or regional analogy, i.e., similar-domain analogy. The process of structural comparison acts as a bridge by which similarity-based processes can give rise to abstract rules (Gentner & Medina, 1998). Carrying out an analogy can lead to a schematic structure in which the domain objects are replaced by variables while retaining the common relations (Winston, 1982)

Especially for creative designers, cross-domain analogy plays an important role in creative idea generation. For instance, Le Corbusier, who made frequent use of analogical reasoning, transferred the structural principle of the double-membrane shell to the roof for designing the Ronchamp chapel. Afterward, adjustments were made to guarantee the proper functioning of this concrete shell to its role as a roof, including insulation, drainage, as well as aesthetic and structural properties concerning the large overhangs that shape the building with its special silhouette (Goldschmidt, 2001).

Many authors have argued that structural similarity is the crucial defining feature of analogical thinking. The power of analogical thinking is to reveal the common structure and to import structure from a well-articulated domain into a less coherent domain, making it the foremost instrument of major theory change (Gentner et al., 1997). Goldschmidt (1995) affirmed that the carrying over of surface features only, without a structural similarity to underpin them, may lead to a false analogy and consequently to a wrong solution to a problem.

7.4. Discussion and Assignment

7.4.1. Group task

Group size: 3–5 (depending on the class size and its diversity)

Task 1) Categorize the following business cases based on their structural similarity, i.e., how they create value, but not by surface similarity, such as foods, travel, and language. (For 20 min.)

TABLE 7-2 Business cases of collective intelligence

	Case	Description
1	Conveyer belt Sushi restaurant	Various kinds of sushi are provided in appropriate quantities on a conveyer belt. A QR code with an IC chip is placed on the back of the sushi plate for forecasting the customer demand.
2	Amazon.com recommendation	Recommending books to customers base on the purchasing or browsing history of similar type of customers.
3	Tabelog	Users can search restaurants based on a variety of specifications, such as their location and customer reviews.
4	POS system	The point of sale is usually placed in the cash register in the form of a smartphone, tablet, laptop, PC, or mobile POS device. This builds a database of relevant information, such as purchasing date and time and other information about the buyer, about each good and service so that managers can decide which products to recommend to consumers.

5	Match.com	An online dating service that matches users for dating.
6	InnoCentive	A crowdsourcing platform for matching people who need business solutions or are facing social, policy, scientific, and technical challenges, or who are competing to provide innovative ideas. Its global network of millions of problem-solvers and cloud-based technology helps clients to transform their economics of innovation through rapid solution delivery and the development of sustainable open-innovation networks.
7	Live weather info for everyone, Yahoo Weather	Users can vote for the current weather of their region, and how many people voted for the current weather is recorded, such as "xx people feels sunny, xx feels rain, xx feels cloudy," with the official weather forecasting information. Users can check sudden changes in weather through real-time voting of other users.
8	Wedding Park	Detailed information of around 4,000 wedding venues in Japan with user reviews of those who visited or were married in the venues. Users can search and select the best wedding venue and plan for them.
9	Hotel reviews in Rakuten Travel	A hotel reservation service with customer reviews. The reviews are on a 5-point scale and evaluate services, locations, rooms, meals, bathroom amenities, and other facilities.
10	Uber taxi	A platform matching customers in need of transportation with nearby drivers.
11	Lang-8	A social networking service for those who want to learn or teach their mother tongue with others. Users can receive lessons on the writing or pronunciation of recorded sentences by the native speakers. Users comprise an online community to find friends and participate in community interaction.
12	@cosme	Comprehensive information about cosmetics to help users determine which products would be good for them. Users can check information from reviews and rankings for each item based on the evaluations of other users of similar age, skin condition, or skin type.

13	Cookpad	Users can post recipes or photos of food. Users can search various recipes for similar type of foods and share their experiences.
14	Bike lovers' map	It provides map information for the bicyclers. Users can draw a route or add itineraries of GPS log data using the icons of useful information on the map, and write tips of riding. Users can post additional information regarding search the route without hills, safe road, public toilet, good view, etc. for bike lovers.
15	Reddit	An open social forum permitting users to post their opinions or comment on those of others regarding any number of topics.
16	Kiva.org	A crowdfunding service for the small-sized entrepreneurs in developing countries

Task 2) Give a title to each category and describe the value creation mechanism of the category. (For 10 min)

Task 3) Presentation: All group members should contribute to the group discussion and preparation for the presentation. The presenter will be randomly selected by the instructor. (For 3 min)

7.4.2. Assignment

Review the academic literature on the topic of thinking skills, and use this knowledge to make recommendations for enhancing thinking skills in your field of interest.

REFERENCE

Adams, R. P., & Pandey, R. N. (2003). Analysis of Juniperus communis and its varieties based on DNA fingerprinting. *Biochemical Systematics and Ecology, 31*(11), 1271–1278.

Ben-Jacob, E., Goldenfeld, N., Langer, J. S., & Schön, G. (1983). Dynamics of interfacial pattern formation. *Physical Review Letters, 51*(21), 1930.

Bingham, C. B., & Kahl, S. J. (2013). How to use analogies to introduce new ideas. *MIT Sloan Management Review, 54*(2), 10-12.

Boden, M. A. (1994). Dimensions of Creativity (Chapter 4). *Dimensions of Creativity*, 75–117.

Bonnardel, N., & Marmèche, E. (2004). Evocation processes by novice and expert designers: Towards stimulating analogical thinking. *Creativity and Innovation Management, 13*(3), 176-186.

Burger, E. D., Perkins, T. K., & Striegler, J. H. (1981). Studies of wax deposition in the trans Alaska pipeline. *Journal of Petroleum Technology, 33*(06), 1–75.

Casakin, H. P., & Goldschmidt, G. (2000). Reasoning by visual analogy in design problem-solving: the role of guidance. *Environment and Planning B, 27*(1), 105-120.

Chase, W. G., & Simon, H. A. (1973). Perception in chess. *Cognitive Psychology, 4*(1), 55–81.

Cropley, A. J., & Cropley, D. (2009). *Fostering creativity: A diagnostic approach for higher education and organizations*. Hampton Press Cresskill, NJ.

Cross, N. (2004). Creative Thinking by Expert Designers. *J. of Design Research, 4*(2), 0. https://doi.org/10.1504/jdr.2004.009839

Cross, N. (2006). Designerly Ways of Knowing. In *Design: Critical and Primary Sources*. https://doi.org/10.5040/9781474282932.0018

Cross, N. (2011). *Design Thinking: Understanding How Designers Think and Work:* Berg.

David Burkus. (2015). *The Myths of Creativity* (Vol. 53). https://doi.org/10.1016/j.gr.2017.08.001%0Ahttp://dx.doi.org/10.1016/j.precamres.2014.12.0

Davidson, J. E., Sternberg, R. J., & Sternberg, R. J. (2003). *The psychology of problem solving*. Cambridge university press.

Dewey, J. (1933). How we think: A restatement of the relation of reflective thinking to the educative process. DC Heath.

Dews, S., Winner, E., Kaplan, J., Rosenblatt, E., Hunt, M., Lim, K., ... Smarsh, B. (1996). Children's understanding of the meaning and functions of verbal irony. *Child Development, 67*(6), 3071–3085.

Dorta, T., Kinayoglu, G., & Boudhraâ, S. (2016). A new representational ecosystem for design teaching in the studio. *Design Studies, 47*, 164–186. https://doi.org/10.1016/j.destud.2016.09.003

Dunbar, K. (1995). How scientists really reason: Scientific reasoning in real-world laboratories. *The nature of insight, 396*, 73.

Dunbar, K., & Blanchette, I. (2001). The in vivo/in vitro approach to cognition: the case of analogy. *Trends in Cognitive Sciences, 5*(8), 334-339. doi: http://dx.doi.org/10.1016/S1364-6613(00)01698-3

Eastman, C. M. (1970). Representations for space planning. *Communications of the ACM, 13*(4), 242–250.

Ericsson, K. A. (2006). The influence of experience and deliberate practice on the development of superior expert performance. *The Cambridge Handbook of Expertise and Expert Performance, 38*(685–705), 2.

Ericsson, K. A., Krampe, R. T., & Tesch-Römer, C. (1993). The role of deliberate practice in the acquisition of expert performance. *Psychological Review, 100*(3), 363.

Falkenhainer, B., Forbus, K. D., & Gentner, D. (1989). The structure-mapping engine: Algorithm and examples. *Artificial Intelligence, 41*(1), 1-63.

Fan, J. (2016). The role of thinking styles in career decision-making self-efficacy among university students. *Thinking Skills and Creativity, 20*, 63–73. https://doi.org/10.1016/j.tsc.2016.03.001

Finke, R. A., Ward, T. B., & Smith, S. M. (1992). *Creative cognition: Theory, research, and applications*.

Forbus, K. D., Ferguson, R. W., & Gentner, D. (1994). *Incremental structure-mapping*. Paper presented at the Proceedings of the sixteenth annual conference of the Cognitive Science Society.

Forbus, K. D., & Oblinger, D. (1990). *Making SME greedy and pragmatic.* Paper presented at the Program of the Twelfth Annual Conference of the Cognitive Science Society, Cambridge, Massachusetts.

Franzoi, S. L., Davis, M. H., & Young, R. D. (1985). The effects of private self-consciousness and perspective taking on satisfaction in close relationships. *Journal of Personality and Social Psychology, 48*(6), 1584.

Frensch, P. A., & Sternberg, R. J. (1989). Expertise and intelligent thinking: When is it worse to know better?. *Advances in the psychology of human intelligence, 5*, 157-88.

Frick, J. W., Guilford, J. P., Christensen, P. R., & Merrifield, P. R. (1959). A factor-analytic study of flexibility in thinking. *Educational and Psychological Measurement, 19*(4), 469–496.

Gentner, D., Brem, S., Ferguson, R. W., Markman, A. B., Levidow, B. B., Wolff, P., & Forbus, K. D. (1997). Analogical reasoning and conceptual change: A case study of Johannes Kepler. *The journal of the learning sciences, 6*(1), 3-40.

Gentner, D., & Medina, J. (1998). Similarity and the development of rules. *Cognition, 65*(2–3), 263-297. doi: http://dx.doi.org/10.1016/S0010-0277(98)00002-X

Gero, J., & Milovanovic, J. (2020). A framework for studying design thinking through measuring designers' minds, bodies and brains. *Design Science, 6*, 1–40. https://doi.org/10.1017/dsj.2020.15

Gick, M. L., & Holyoak, K. J. (1980). Analogical problem solving. *Cognitive psychology, 12*(3), 306-355.

Goel, A. K. (1997). Design, Analogy, and Creativity. *IEEE Expert: Intelligent Systems and Their Applications, 12*(3), 62-70. doi: 10.1109/64.590078

Goldschmidt, G. (1995). Visual displays for design: Imagery, analogy and databases of visual images. *Visual databases in architecture*, 53-74.

Goldschmidt, G. (2001). Visual analogy: A strategy for design reasoning and learning. *Design knowing and learning: Cognition in design education*, 199-220.

Greenwood, J. (1993). Reflective practice: a critique of the work of Argyris and

Schön. *Journal of Advanced Nursing, 18*(8), 1183–1187.

Gregory, R. W., & Paidoussis, M. P. (1966). Unstable oscillation of tubular cantilevers conveying fluid II. Experiments. *Proceedings of the Royal Society of London. Series A. Mathematical and Physical Sciences, 293*(1435), 528–542.

Guilford, J. P. (1950). *Fundamental statistics in psychology and education.*

Han, J.-I., Choi, H.-K., Lee, S.-W., Orwin, P. M., Kim, J., LaRoe, S. L., ... Lee, S. Y. (2011). Complete genome sequence of the metabolically versatile plant growth-promoting endophyte Variovorax paradoxus S110. *Journal of Bacteriology, 193*(5), 1183–1190.

Helyer, R. (2015). Learning through reflection: the critical role of reflection in work-based learning (WBL). *Journal of Work-Applied Management, 7*(1), 15–27. https://doi.org/10.1108/jwam-10-2015-003

Hennessey, B. A. (2015). Creative Behavior, Motivation, Environment and Culture: The Building of a Systems Model. *Journal of Creative Behavior, 49*(3), 194–210. https://doi.org/10.1002/jocb.97

Holyoak, K. J., & Koh, K. (1987). Surface and structural similarity in analogical transfer. *Memory & Cognition, 15*(4), 332-340.

Holyoak, K. J., & Morrison, R. G. (Eds.). (2005). *The Cambridge handbook of thinking and reasoning* (Vol. 137). Cambridge: Cambridge University Press.

Hong, Y. C., & Choi, I. (2011). Three dimensions of reflective thinking in solving design problems: A conceptual model. *Educational Technology Research and Development, 59*(5), 687–710. https://doi.org/10.1007/s11423-011-9202-9

Howard-Jones, P. A., Blakemore, S.-J., Samuel, E. A., Summers, I. R., & Claxton, G. (2005). Semantic divergence and creative story generation: An fMRI investigation. *Cognitive Brain Research, 25*(1), 240–250.

Jacobs-Lawson, J., & Hershey, D. (2005). Influence of Future Time Perspective, Financial Knowledge, and Financial Risk Tolerance on Retirement Saving Behaviors. *Financial Services Review, 14*(4), 331.

James, W. (1890). The Principles of Psychology.

Jones, B., & Connolly, K. (1970). Memory effects in cross-modal matching. *British Journal of Psychology, 61*(2), 267–270.

Kaufman, J. C., Cole, J. C., & Baer, J. (2009). The Construct of Creativity: Structural

Model for Self-Reported Creativity Ratings. *The Journal of Creative Behavior, 43*(2), 119–134. https://doi.org/10.1002/j.2162-6057.2009.tb01310.x

Kaufman, J. C., & Sternberg, R. J. (2010). *The Cambridge handbook of creativity.* Cambridge University Press.

Lasdun, D. (1965). An architect's approach to architecture.'. RIBA Journal, 72(4), 184–195.

Ling, D. (2015). Complete DesignThinking Guide for Professionals. In *Kemampuan Koneksi Matematis (Tinjauan Terhadap Pendekatan Pembelajaran Savi)* (Vol. 53).

MacCormac, R. (1976). Redefining densities. *Built Environment Quarterly, 2*(4), 320–326.

Marković, S. (2012). Components of aesthetic experience: Aesthetic fascination, aesthetic appraisal, and aesthetic emotion. *I-Perception, 3*(1), 1–17. https://doi.org/10.1068/i0450aap

McCulloch, P., Taylor, I., Sasako, M., Lovett, B., & Griffin, D. (2002). Randomised trials in surgery: problems and possible solutions. *Bmj, 324*(7351), 1448–1451.

McDonnell, K. A., & Holbrook, N. J. (2004). A Poisson regression model approach to predicting tropical cyclogenesis in the Australian/southwest Pacific Ocean region using the SOI and saturated equivalent potential temperature gradient as predictors. *Geophysical Research Letters, 31*(20).

Mezirow, J. (1981). A critical theory of adult learning and education. *Adult Education, 32*(1), 3–24.

Mezirow, J. (1990). *Fostering critical reflection in adulthood.* Jossey-Bass Publishers San Francisco.

Newell, A., Shaw, J. C., & Simon, H. A. (1962). The processes of creative thinking. *Contemporary Approaches to Creative Thinking, 1958, University of Colorado, CO, US; This Paper Was Presented at the Aforementioned Symposium.* Atherton Press.

Newell, A., & Simon, H. A. (1972). *Human problem solving* (Vol. 104). Prentice-hall Englewood Cliffs, NJ.

Novick, L. R. (1988). Analogical transfer, problem similarity, and expertise. *Journal of Experimental Psychology: Learning, Memory, and Cognition, 14*(3), 510.

Perkins, D. N. (1997). Creativity's camel: The role of analogy in invention. *Creative thought: An investigation of conceptual structures and processes*, 523-538.

Purcell, P. (1981). How designers think. In *Design Studies* (Vol. 2). https://doi.org/10.1016/0142-694x(81)90033-8

Reder, L. M., & Anderson, J. R. (1982). Effects of spacing and embellishment on memory for the main points of a text. *Memory & Cognition, 10*(2), 97–102.

Ross, B. H. (1987). This is like that: The use of earlier problems and the separation of similarity effects. *Journal of Experimental Psychology: Learning, Memory, and Cognition, 13*(4), 629.

Sarlemijn, A., & Kroes, P. A. (1988). Technological analogies and their logical nature *Technology and Contemporary Life* (pp. 237-255): Springer.

Sawyer, R. K. (2017). Teaching creativity in art and design studio classes: A systematic literature review. *Educational Research Review, 22*, 99–113. https://doi.org/10.1016/j.edurev.2017.07.002

Schön, D. (1983). The reflective practitioner basic books. *New York*.

Simon, H. A. (1990). Invariants of human behavior. Annual Review of Psychology, 41(1), 1–20.

Simonton, D. K. (1984). *Genius, creativity and leadership*.

Simonton, D. K. (1999). *Origins of genius: Darwinian perspectives on creativity*. Oxford University Press.

Sloboda, J. A., Davidson, J. W., Howe, M. J. A., & Moore, D. G. (1996). The role of practice in the development of performing musicians. *British Journal of Psychology, 87*(2), 287–309.

Sternberg, R. J., & Lubart, T. I. (1996). Investing in creativity. *American Psychologist, 51*(7), 677.

Thomas, J. C., & Carroll, J. M. (1979). The psychological study of design. *Design Studies, 1*(1), 5–11.

Wang, V. C. X., & King, K. P. (2006). Understanding Mezirow's theory of reflectivity from Confucian perspectives: A model and perspective. *Radical Pedagogy, 8*(1), 1–17.

Weisberg, R. (1986). *Creativity: Genius and other myths*. WH Freeman/Times Books/Henry Holt & Co.

Weisberg, R. W.. (2006). *Creativity Understanding Innovation in Problem Solving, Science, Invention, and the Arts.*

Weisberg, R. W., & Alba, J. W. (1981). *Gestalt theory, insight, and past experience: Reply to Dominowski.*

Weisberg, S. P., McCann, D., Desai, M., Rosenbaum, M., Leibel, R. L., & Ferrante, A. W. (2003). Obesity is associated with macrophage accumulation in adipose tissue. *The Journal of Clinical Investigation, 112*(12), 1796–1808.

Weisberg, R. W. (1995). Case studies of creative thinking: Reproduction versus restructuring in the real world.

Wertheimer, M. (1985). A Gestalt perspective on computer simulations of cognitive processes. *Computers in Human Behavior, 1*(1), 19–33.

Winston, P. H. (1982). Learning new principles from precedents and exercises. *Artificial Intelligence, 19*(3), 321-350. doi: http://dx.doi.org/10.1016/0004-3702(82)90004-2

Yanagisawa, H., & Takatsuji, K. (2015). Effects of visual expectation on perceived tactile perception: An evaluation method of surface texture with expectation effect. *International Journal of Design, 9*(1), 39–51.

Bio

Editor and co-author

Eunyoung Kim is an associate professor in the School of Knowledge Science, Japan Advanced Institute of Science and Technology, Japan. She has a PhD in Engineering from the University of Tokyo, Japan (transferred from the PhD program of Department of Digital Information Convergence Stuey, at the Graduate School of Convergence Science and Technology, Seoul National University, Korea) and a master's degree in international commerce from Seoul National University, Korea. She also studied in RWTH Aachen University, Germany with fellowship, and Georgia Institute of Technology, GA, USA during her graduate study. Her research interests include learning process design for creating innovations, social creativity and innovation, utilizing information technology for international development, business and management.

Before starting her career in academia, she worked as a business consultant in both global and local consulting firms, a researcher in a national research institute, a manager in an energy sales company and non-profit foundation for corporate social responsibility and lead numbers of projects.

Co-author 1

Thao Thanh Luong holds a master's degree in human resources management from Griffith University, Australia, and a bachelor's degree in business administration from the University of Economics Ho Chi Minh City, Vietnam. She is currently pursuing her doctoral degree under KIM Laboratory in Graduate School of Knowledge Science at Japan Advanced Institute of Science and Technology, Japan. Her research interests are in the areas of innovations in hospitality and tourism education.

She is also a hospitality trainer (CHT) and educator (CHE) certified by the Educational Institute of the American Hotel and Lodging Association (AHLEI), USA. In more than ten years working in the service industry, Thao held different positions in the Human Resources Department at Saigontourist Group, one of the largest hospitality and tourism enterprises in Vietnam, before being appointed as the Vice-Principal at Saigontourist Hospitality College (STHC) in 2016. At Saigontourist Group, Thao was in charge of devising and implementing strategies to ensure professional development for over 200 middle managers and supervisors within the company's properties across Vietnam. During her tenure at STHC, she was in charge of managing various vocational college core activities, including curriculum design, teacher education, international relations, and student recruitment.

Co-author 2

SUN Qianang holds a Master's degree in Fine art and a Bachelor of Art Design from the School of Art Design, Jingdezheng Ceramic Institute, China. Currently, she is a PhD candidate in KIM Laboratory in Graduate School of Knowledge Science at Japan Advanced Institute of Science and Technology. Her research interest involved creative craft design, design reflection and Material experience in design.

Before starting her career in academia, she is a practitioner of ceramic design with running an independent ceramic studio and also in charge of assisting the creative course in the ceramic institute. In more than seven years working in ceramic creation, SUN has invited to participate in the network project in Gudagergaard Ceramic Centre, Denmark, as an only Chinese ceramic artist and display her creation <Ask and Answer>, in 2016. And her work <The Secret> has displayed in Shiri Oni Studio, Japan, in 2018. The creative experience and valuable communication with artists from different backgrounds inspired her to pursue more knowledge of craft design and design reflection from an academic perspective to enrich her capacity as a professional in her future career.

Co-author 3

Nilima Haque Ruma is currently a PhD student at Eunyoung KIM laboratory in the school of Advanced Science and Technology at Japan Advanced Institute of Science and Technology (JAIST). She did her second master's degree in the field of Knowledge Management, School of Knowledge Science, JAIST. She did a master's degree and bachelor's degree in Sociology from Shahjalal University of Science and Technology (SUST), Sylhet, Bangladesh. Her research focuses on innovation in business models, SMEs, women empowerment, and rural development.

Before starting her higher studies in Japan, she worked as a Project Facilitator in a non-government organization where the project aims to empower rural women in Bangladesh. Besides research, she used to do voluntary activities at institutions and the communities. She received the 'JAIST President Award' as recognition both in research and voluntary activities.

Topics on Creating Innovations for Graduate Students

初版発行 2021年9月3日

編　著 Eunyoung Kim

著　者 Thao Thanh Luong, Qianang Sun,
Nilima Haque Ruma, and Eunyoung Kim

発行所 博英社

〒 370-0006 群馬県 高崎市 問屋4-5-9 SKYMAX-WEST
TEL 027-381-8453(営業、企画)/FAX 027-381-8457
E-MAIL hakueisha@hakueishabook.com

ISBN 978-4-910132-12-9

定　価 3,190円（本体2,900円＋税10%)